HAPPY   BIRTHDAY RALPH

FROM

MOM & DAD

July 2003

OSCAR PETERSON

Alex Barris

OSCAR PETERSON

A Musical Biography

HarperCollins*PublishersLtd*

Canadian Cataloguing in Publication Data

Barris, Alex, 1922–
Oscar Peterson : a musical biography

ISBN 0-00-200082-2

1. Peterson, Oscar, 1925–
2. Jazz musicians – Canada – Biography.
3. Pianists – Canada – Biography.
I. Title.

ML417.P48B27 2002   786.2'165'092
C2002-900559-0

HC 9 8 7 6 5 4 3 2 1

Printed and bound in the United States
Set in Stempel Garamond

Two men, each in his own way, have a great deal to do with turning jazz, America's sole original contribution to the art of music, into a world-famous art form.

One is the late Norman Granz, who died at his home in Switzerland in November 2001. The founder of Jazz At The Philharmonic, Granz built a public passion for jazz in North America, and then took JATP on the road, entertaining audiences around the world. He worked tirelessly to create and enlarge a market for this music.

The other is John Hammond, who died in 1987 at the age of 77. A lifelong devotee of jazz, he helped steer into the spotlight the varied and impressive talents of (among others) Count Basie, Billie Holiday, Teddy Wilson, Charlie Christian, Benny Carter, Lionel Hampton, Fletcher Henderson, Chu Berry, Gene Krupa, Lena Horne and, most assuredly not least, the man who later became his brother-in-law, Benny Goodman.

There have been, of course, many other jazz supporters, impresarios, producers and promoters, from Eddie Condon to George Wein, from George Simon to Whitney Balliett. I salute them all.

But it is my belief that nobody did more to further the cause of jazz than Norman Granz and John Hammond. So it is to their memory that I dedicate this book.

Author's Note

Let me try to explain why I have called this book a "Musical Biography." The intention was to trace Oscar Peterson's life and career as a musician—not just any musician, but Canada's greatest gift to the world of jazz.

To the extent that that is possible, I believe that anybody's private life is his own business, and not ours. Consequently, references to Oscar's personal life are included in this book only where they have some bearing on his musical or professional activities.

Contents

1

THE JOE LOUIS
OF THE PIANO

It was in the liner notes for Oscar Peterson's 1967 album *My Favorite Instrument* that music critic and author Gene Lees wrote: "I have believed for many years that Oscar Peterson is not only the greatest pianist in jazz today, but the greatest it has ever known."

Some eight years later, writing in *Maclean's*, Lees continued his ode: "Peterson has astounding speed. Only Phineas Newborn and the late Art Tatum, one of his idols and mentors, have equaled him. And he has a power of direct swing that Tatum never equaled. . . .

"Oscar's awareness of his predecessors, his knowledge of jazz history, is so great that I doubt that there's anything in the tradition of jazz piano that he hasn't encompassed in his work. Oscar is the great eclectic of jazz piano. Bach was a great eclectic. History cares less who did something first than who did it best. Oscar does all the things his predecessors did, but better."

Give or take the odd disgruntled Art Tatum devotee, you aren't likely to find too many jazz lovers who would disagree with that appraisal. Significantly, the enthusiasm for Peterson comes not only from jazz fans and critics, but from other musicians and singers. Phil Nimmons on Peterson: "The piano is like an extension of his own physical being. I'm amazed at the speed of his creativity."

The late Carmen McRae: "Oscar Peterson happens to be my

favorite all-around pianist. There are pianists I like because of one thing and pianists I like because of another. But overall I like Oscar best."

Shirley Horn, when she was asked about her most significant influence as a jazz pianist, replied: "It has always been Oscar Peterson. He is my Rachmaninoff."

Murray Ginsberg: "Oscar Peterson is to jazz what Glenn Gould [was] to classical music."

The incomparable Charlie Parker once said of Oscar: "I wish I could play like his right hand."

Count Basie added: "That Oscar Peterson plays the best ivory box I've ever heard."

And Marian McPartland reported hearing another musician say "One should leave the piano when Oscar comes in. This man is dangerous."

Peterson has been at the head of the class since he first burst onto the jazz scene more than half a century ago. The Montreal-born pianist was well-known in Canada before he gained recognition in the United States and abroad. But once he stepped into the international spotlight, the awards kept coming. *Down Beat*, the pre-eminent American jazz periodical, chose him as Best Jazz Pianist of the Year fourteen times, beginning in 1950—only a year after he was first introduced at New York's Carnegie Hall. He also won the annual *Playboy* poll as Best Jazz Pianist fourteen times.

At last count, his records have won eight Grammy awards. In 1990, his CD *Live at the Blue Note*, with his veteran sidemen—guitarist Herb Ellis and bassist Ray Brown, plus drummer Bobby Durham—was nominated in two categories: Best Jazz Performance, Solo, and Best Jazz Performance, Group. Peterson and company won in both categories.

His standing within the jazz community began to grow in the 1950s and never stopped. As evidence of this, consider the considerable list of jazz artists (apart from his own trios and quartets) with whom he has recorded. It reads like a Who's Who of Jazz. Here are some, in no particular order:

Louis Armstrong, Dizzy Gillespie, Count Basie, Ella Fitzgerald, Roy Eldridge, Phil Nimmons, Buddy Rich, Milt Jackson, Coleman Hawkins, Stephane Grappelli, Harry "Sweets" Edison, Clark Terry (as well as Terry Clark), Gerry Mulligan, Marian McPartland, Jon Faddis, Toots Thielemans, Zoot Sims, Benny Carter, Joe Pass, Buddy DeFranco, Ed Bickert, Freddie Hubbard, Stan Getz, Flip Phillips, Ben Webster, Lester Young, Willie Smith, Louis Bellson, Eddie "Lockjaw" Davis, Dave Young, Charlie Shavers, Lionel Hampton, Bill Harris, Sonny Stitt, Jake Hanna and the Modern Jazz Quartet.

For many years Peterson has coped with arthritic pain in his hands. He suffered a more serious setback in 1993, when he suffered a stroke that damaged his left side and might well have ended the music career of a lesser man.

But not Oscar Peterson. Two years later, he was playing again, and while his left hand was doing relatively little, the right was so dazzling and his creativity so impressive that the limitation of the left was hardly noticed.

On July 1, 1995, Ray Conlogue wrote of Peterson's return to public performance in *The Globe and Mail*: "Necks craned as longtime fans tried to glimpse whether or not the upstaged left hand was doing any work at all. It was, but only as an occasional dab at a rhythm line. In up-tempo numbers his right hand flew like a hawk over the keyboard, hesitating only once or twice in the evening. And as he eased into 'Love Ballade' . . . it was more than moving to see the old lyric expressiveness return."

In October 1997, Clive Davis wrote in *The Sunday Times* in London of Peterson: "That he is playing in public at all is no mean achievement. At one point, he says, he was convinced that he would never perform again; it took long bouts of physio-therapy before he was able to fight his way back. As he observes with characteristic understatement, 'I've learned something about patience.' "

Earlier that same year, bass player Dave Young was chosen Musician of the Year by *The Jazz Report*, the Toronto-based jazz quarterly published by Bill King and Greg Sutherland. Oscar Peterson was there, in a wheelchair, to make the presentation. Peterson spoke glowingly of Young and acknowledged his debt to the bass player; it was Dave Young who gave him back his confidence, got him to play again, Peterson publicly acknowledged.

In 1998, when speaking to *The Toronto Star*'s Geoff Chapman, Oscar Peterson said: "The stroke meant an adjustment, that's all. It was not so much an encumbrance. I just play and the only long-term effect is fatigue. But that's also part of growing old." He was seventy-three at the time.

Guitarist Herb Ellis, who worked in the Peterson trio for many years, may have said it best when he observed "He is the world's definitive pianist . . . Oscar is the Joe Louis of the piano."

Incidentally, I have a favorite personal memory of an unexpected encounter with Peterson, which I still treasure, some fifty years later. On one of the numerous tours of Norman Granz's Jazz At The Philharmonic—sometime in the early 1950s, as I recall it—the group arrived in Toronto to play a concert at Massey Hall, which I was to cover for *The Globe and Mail*. I arrived early and wandered backstage to see who else might be around. Just by luck, I encountered Oscar Peterson with Ella Fitzgerald, both of whom would later be performing on stage that night.

Peterson had just discovered an ancient celeste, a sort of miniature upright piano, just collecting dust somewhere in the wings. He simply couldn't resist trying it out and, as I got there, he began to play—and Ella joined in vocally—the lovely 1940 Hoagy Carmichael–Ned Washington song "The Nearness of You." For me, those few magic, informal minutes became the indelible highlight of that evening.

Oscar Peterson has enthralled millions of people with his music. Here are some of the stories behind the man and his music.

2

PLACE ST. HENRI, MONTREAL

Kathleen Olivia John was born in St. Kitts, in the Leeward Islands, in 1890. She emigrated to Canada and settled in Montreal, working as a domestic. In 1917 she met Daniel Peterson, who was born in the Virgin Islands. They married that same year and lived in Place St. Henri, a neighborhood which Oscar Peterson was later to celebrate in his *Canadiana Suite*.

He remembers it as a bustling area, with French, Italian and Irish families and a small but tightly knit black community— "much tighter than I think it is even now," he commented many years later.

In an interview with Gene Lees, Oscar Peterson spoke of his family: "The interesting thing about my dad is that he became a musician through being a sailor. From what I understand, he was a boatswain on a ship and he bought himself some kind of little organ—I never did find out exactly what kind—and taught himself to play. And when he decided to settle in Canada—he sailed here—he met my mum."

Daniel Peterson worked on the railroad as a sleeping car porter. "If you were black in Montreal and you were lucky enough to have a job, then you were working for the railroad," Oscar explained.

Daniel and Kathleen Peterson had five children, of whom Oscar was the fourth. First came Fred, who died of tuberculosis at the age of fifteen. Next came Daisy, who was to become Oscar's first music teacher; then Charlie, Oscar and May. All of the children were exposed to music, thanks largely to the insistence of their parents. Oscar recalls that his father "felt that we could do other things and he felt definitely that music could be part of it—an escape from the railroad."

Kathleen, Oscar's mother, would always say "God knows best." One result of this was that Oscar became "reasonably religious—to this day—Sunday was a busy day for me. Go to church, then Sunday school."

Oscar remembers that "my dad's philosophy was that in order to overcome all the barriers, we had to do something special—I would come home with good grades. I think I had 99.9. He'd say, 'Weren't they handing out any hundreds?' "

Oscar first learned to play the trumpet at the age of five. But two years later, he contracted tuberculosis and was confined for thirteen months at Children's Memorial Hospital. When he was released, he was pronounced cured, but his lungs had been weakened and his father wanted no further strain on Oscar's lungs. He decided that Oscar should forget about the trumpet and study piano. In fact, Oscar was not heart-broken—he had already been fiddling with the piano, so the switch from horn to keyboard was not, in his view, any large sacrifice. (Later, when Oscar tried to join the RCAF, the history of his tuberculosis caused him to be turned down. He was also rejected by the army.)

Both of Oscar's brothers, Charlie and Fred, played piano. In fact, Oscar was fond of saying that Fred was the best pianist in the family.

Charlie (who was sometimes called Chuck) began studying piano, but then switched to brass instruments—especially the trumpet, which he called "my baby." Although he preferred the piano, he had a three-year stint in the army where a piano wasn't a very practical instrument for a marching band. When he came out of the forces he fully intended to go back to his piano playing. But no music opportunity was readily available, so he took a job in an aluminum plant, where he suffered a terrible accident that destroyed his left arm. That was the end of his musical aspirations.

Daniel Peterson's influence on his children was to be a lasting legacy, most notably, of course, through Oscar, who said: "There's a good way and a bad way to expose children to music. If they're exposed in the wrong way, it can turn them against it. Fortunately we were introduced to it in a good way, and we all learned to play."

He got so he couldn't keep away from the piano. He told musicologist Len Lyons: "I'd start out in the morning with scales, exercises and whatever classical pieces I was working on. After a break I'd come back and do voicings; I'd challenge the voicings I'd been using and try to move them around in tempo without losing the harmonic content.

"I also practised time by playing against myself and letting the left hand take a loose, undulating time shape while making the right hand stay completely in time. Then I'd reverse the process, keeping the left hand rigid and making the right hand stretch and contract. You know, practising that way takes the urgency out of getting from Point A to Point B in a solo. It gives you the confidence to renegotiate a line while you're playing it. It gives you a respect for different shapes."

He devoted hours every day to the piano. "I practised from 9 a.m. to noon," he said in 1959, "took an hour off for lunch, practised from one to six in the afternoon, then went to dinner, and went back to the piano about 7:30. I'd keep practising until my mother would come in and drag me away from the piano so the family could get some sleep.

"I think at ten I was playing the usual things that kids play at ten—the 'Minute Waltz' and some things I wouldn't even attempt to play now. And I would hear my older brother, Fred, fooling around with things like 'Oh Dem Golden Slippers' and 'Tiger Rag,' and I'd say, 'What is that?' And I finally found out that it was jazz, and it kind of intrigued me."

Daniel Peterson did not approve of his sons' new-found interest in jazz. But he was forced to give in after a family conference in which Kathleen sided with her sons, arguing that "There might be a field for it."

When Oscar was eleven, he studied with Lou Hooper, a pianist, composer and teacher of African, Cree and Irish descent born near Windsor, Ontario. Hooper had lived in Harlem for several years, where, among other things, he backed such early jazz icons as Ethel Waters, Ma Rainey and Mamie Smith.

But another important early influence on the young Peterson was Paul de Marky, the Hungarian-born pianist/teacher/composer who emigrated to Canada in 1924—the year before Oscar was born. Recalled Peterson to biographer Gene Lees: "Paul de Marky came into my life at a very important time. I was fourteen. I went to this man. He totally awed me with his beautiful sound on the instrument, his beautiful touch and his command of the instrument, and I was so inspired by him I can remember unbeknownst to him going early to my lessons because I found he would practise and I'd just sit and listen to him. He'd be sitting there playing and playing, with this beautiful sound that he'd get out of the instrument."

After a lesson, de Marky would ask young Oscar what he was working on "in the jazz field." Oscar remembered playing "The Man I Love" for de Marky, and de Marky commenting: "The melody is choppy. Make it sing."

Oscar told me: "I had a certain amount of confidence, but Paul de Marky really sort of made a believer out of me, from a musical and artistic standpoint. It's one thing to know you can play, to know you can skate up and down the rink, but as to how well you look doing it, how much finesse you have, how much confidence, how much interest you can create in your audience, I guess that all has to do with it. He made me believe that I did have something to offer the music world."

Oscar remembers his time as a music student: "What I went through as a student was probably what everyone else grooming themselves for the classical field goes through—Czerny, Hanon, Dohnanyi. All of these things just serve to broaden digital control. It was something I wanted to get behind me as quickly as possible.

"Probably I started feeling comfortable around the age of sixteen or seventeen. That's when I started feeling that I could transmit to the keyboard most of what I conjured up mentally. Prior to that it was a scuffle. I'd be thinking something and then run into a snag on executing it. That used to bug me."

Peterson's classical music training and continuing interest in classical music gave him a bit of an edge over other jazz pianists of his time. For example, throughout the 1940s his concert programs usually included Chopin's "Prelude in A Minor" as a basis for improvisation.

Peterson learned another lesson during his formative years: "My classical teacher used to tell me, 'If you make a mistake, don't stop. Make it part of what you're playing as much as possible. Don't chop up your playing by correcting things, even when you're playing for yourself. It's a bad habit, it will make you a sporadic player.'"

Gene Lees, writing for *Down Beat* magazine in 1959, told about Oscar's time at Montreal High School: "A schoolmate, Martin Siegerman, recalled that Peterson was already showing signs of the phenomenal skill he would later possess. Boogie-woogie was the fad and, Siegerman said, 'Oscar always had a gang of kids around him, asking him to play.' When he did play, they heard boogie at faster tempos than most of them knew were possible."

In 1982, Paul de Marky (then eighty-five) remembered teaching Peterson: "I taught him technique, speedy fingers, because that's what you need in modern jazz. Tatum had the speediest fingers. I gave Oscar Chopin studies. And then mostly, as I found that he was so good at melodic ballad style, I gave him the idea of big chords, like Debussy had them. Big rich soft chords. And his ballad playing is remarkable, when he plays those old-timers like

'Laura' and 'Tenderly.' If you have a natural talent for your fingers and harmony, they can't go wrong if they wanted to."

It could be argued that Lou Hooper and Paul de Marky were equally important—each in his own way—to the evolution of Oscar Peterson into the super-musician he was to become. Hooper was Peterson's link to early Harlem jazz—to Willie "The Lion" Smith and James P. Johnson and even Fats Waller. And de Marky was his link to Franz Liszt and the tradition of nineteenth-century bravura piano playing.

In 1980, during an interview with *Contemporary Keyboard*, Oscar was asked whether he still liked playing classical music.

He responded: "I enjoy some of the Liszt things and Ravel and of course Bach. It's hard to find a pianist who doesn't play Bach."

In that same 1980 interview, Peterson gave another indication of his reverence for Franz Liszt. "I was most honored," he said, "when I played at the Montreal Olympics in 1976 because Paul de Marky came down to hear me play. I'm not nervous about playing in front of anybody, but that night I was like water backstage when I was told that he was seated with my sister down in front. My knees started to shake. It was obviously a throwback. . . . But I finally got into the set, finished it and went down to see him. I remember his first words to me. He grabbed my hands, looked at me, and said, 'You know, Franz Liszt would have loved to play with you.'"

3

"EVERYONE WENT TO MRS. SWEENEY"

"Long ago, in the dark ages of sexual politics, people used to say: Behind every successful man there's a woman.

"Well, behind recreational piano players and professional musicians alike, there's a music teacher. And for thousands of Montrealers, that music teacher is Daisy Sweeney."

That was how Lucinda Chodan began a profile of Mrs. Sweeney that ran in *The Montreal Gazette* in 1987.

The sister who sat with Paul de Marky was Daisy Peterson (later Sweeney), not only Oscar's first teacher but the one who also taught such other future jazz piano artists as Oliver Jones and Joe Sealy. Oscar has never been reluctant to give his sister—only five years his senior—credit for helping him in his formative years. "Daisy is certainly gifted in teaching other people," Oscar has said. "She has a way about her. She can imbue them with the belief that they can play. I know—I was one of her students."

On another occasion, Oscar spoke again about Daisy's early influence on her siblings: "Daisy would come home with her lessons and she in turn passed on to us what she had learned. She was responsible for my learning an awful lot of things that I might not have otherwise learned."

For her part, Daisy commented: "I was overpowered by the freedom with which Oscar could play."

It was Daisy who asked Oscar to go for a walk with her, when he was fourteen years old, to the CBC studio in Montreal. She knew that Ken Soble, who oversaw a nationwide amateur contest on the CBC, was auditioning Montreal musicians. Oscar was so shy she had to push him onto the stool and make him play. Soble promptly scheduled him for the program and put him on the air. Oscar went on to Toronto and won the finals— including a cash prize of $250.

Eventually regarded as one of Montreal's great classical piano teachers, Daisy Peterson started at the bottom. She worked as a domestic when she was a girl, for $4.50 a week, and took formal piano lessons from Paul de Marky, which cost her $3 a week. But she persevered until she earned a bachelor's degree from McGill University in 1947.

"There were very few jobs for women anyhow, and I was told there was no job at the children's hospital except cleaning toilets. I said, 'When do I start?' And of course, they didn't want me at all." Daisy reflected: "They weren't the worst of times, but these were attitudes you had to rise above. I remember my mother saying, 'Every kick is a boost.'"

Racism, Daisy remembered, extended into the black community. At community dances, she found that girls with darker skin (like hers) were passed over by boys in favor of those with lighter skin. "If we had plays, you had to look white. How does it make a child feel? If I go into your home, I don't expect to be able to walk all over and have the feeling that I have in my home. But when I *am* home, if I feel the same discrimination, where do I go? Because this is the end of the line."

The Peterson parents loved music. When the Depression hit, they decided to buy a piano, Daisy remembered, "because they realized we wouldn't be able to afford to do anything else." The piano soon became an integral part of the household.

"I remember one day my dad went to get his pay," said Daisy, "and it had been garnisheed because he missed a payment [on the piano]." As a result, the Petersons didn't eat for a few days. "My mother kept us in bed so we wouldn't use up our energy," Daisy recalled. "Then my dad came in and said, 'Daisy, you can get up and wash Oscar and come down to breakfast.' I remember getting out of bed and having no feet because I was so weak. That always stayed in my mind—and yet the piano has served us well."

Having been a charter member of the Montreal Black Community Youth Choir and later the Montreal Jubilation Gospel Choir, Daisy remembered her church background. "I remember the music," she recalled. "I remember the lights of the church. Even Oscar, as a baby—it must have had an effect on him."

Oscar concurs: "I remember Sunday was a busy day for me. Making sure everything was in the right place and then off to church we'd go. And we'd come out of church and then go right back to Sunday school."

Daisy, Oscar told me, was "sort of the mainstay of the younger set in the family. We used to call her strait-laced. But she was that way. She was directional. Daisy set out to do something, she'd do it, whatever it took. And she approached her music that way. But she had one quirk I never did understand. Daisy was the classical pianist in the family. But she had the worst nerves going. I mean, she'd practise all day, day in and day out. And if I walked into the room, my mother, May, anyone in the family, it was great. But if you, Alex, walked in the room, or someone she had not met, she couldn't play. She'd freeze."

To help Daisy overcome her nervousness, Oscar said, "I got her into the Alberta Lounge with me, to do intermissions. She didn't do very many of them, but she did a few. I tried to break her of the habit that way."

I asked Oscar if Daisy was like their mother.

"Well," he said, "it depends on what way you look at it. My mother was very matriarchal, and Daisy tended to have some of those qualities. And yet, she and my mum would disagree on many points. But Daisy's a very determined person, that's one thing I can say about her. She sort of takes after my mum. She would decide to do certain things, and we'd have to do them."

Years later, Daisy recalls teaching brother Oscar: "He had the range and the depth that I've never seen as yet in [other] pupils. He had a good ear, and any note that was played, he knew. That was when I realized he had something special.

"If he made a mistake, I'd stop him and say, 'Play it again.' He'd say, 'Let's take it from the beginning.' I'd say, 'Why the beginning?' Then I realized he had memorized it. He was just playing it by ear. I was overpowered by the freedom with which he played."

A modest, sedate woman, Daisy Sweeney is reluctant to take credit for the achievements of her students.

"No one can force you to hear if you can't hear," she once said. "They say Oscar is great because of me. You can't make a rose a rose. You can nurture it, but should you be credited for the rose? A rose is a rose, and it's the same thing with great men."

Says Oscar of his sister: "Daisy is a great tutor. Daisy has great patience. She understands human weaknesses and she can relate to someone having difficulties. And Daisy is a great pianist."

Peterson was to become the most successful (and famous) of Daisy's students, but there were others, too, who became acclaimed musicians—Oliver Jones, for instance, nine years younger than Oscar, who lived just down the street from the Petersons. He later said he used to sit on the Petersons' porch and listen to Oscar play. Later, he, too, studied with Daisy for eight years.

"Everyone went to Mrs. Sweeney's," he said. Among her other piano students were Billy Horne, Milton Sealey, Joe Sealy and Reg Wilson.

According to Lucinda Chodan, thousands of other Montreal youngsters "trooped to the Negro Community Centre every Saturday morning for forty years to study music with the modest, soft-spoken woman who is still universally and respectfully addressed as 'Mrs. Sweeney.'

"They paid twenty-five cents a lesson if they could afford it; deserving students who didn't have the money were given scholarships. And Mrs. Sweeney made sure that everyone got a chance to play. Those who didn't have a piano were given a recorder or a cardboard keyboard to practise on."

Emily Clyke, a longtime colleague at the Negro Community Centre, said of Daisy: "When times were tough, she'd even see that the students had clothes to wear. She was a tremendous influence on people in the community, but it was always behind the scenes. . . . She even managed to wangle pianos for their homes. She would get someone to loan them a piano, or she'd persuade a service club to donate a piano to the centre and then she'd have it installed in their home. . . . I don't even know if people knew how much she helped."

To Oliver Jones, "She was the strongest musical influence I had. She was always a strict teacher, but if the kids had any problems, they could always talk to her. She's one of the finest teachers we have."

In March 1987, some two hundred Montrealers—friends, family and former students—gathered to thank Daisy Sweeney with a dinner and a presentation to the guest of honor. And, of course, there was music, too.

"She is just so loved in the community," said Terry McGimpsey, one of the organizers of the tribute and another former student. "When we began telling people about the tribute, they would say, '*Anything* for Mrs. Sweeney.'"

The only person who was hesitant about the tribute to Mrs. Sweeney was . . . Mrs. Sweeney. "Why me?" she said. "I don't see it, to be honest. There are so many people who work behind the scenes and do more than I do. I have taught simply because I think music plays such an important part in a child's life."

She told the organizers she might not be able to attend the tribute. "I told them, I teach that night. They told me, 'You'd better not teach.'"

As ever, that evening Daisy was self-effacing about the influence she had on such accomplished former students as Oliver Jones and her brother Oscar. "I hate to say I taught Oliver," she said, "because whatever you gave him to do, he came back with it accomplished—he was such a gifted person. It was the same with Oscar."

Her favorite memory in all her years of teaching had nothing to do with the acclaimed musicians she schooled, but with a young girl who came to one of those Saturday morning classes at the Negro Community Centre years ago.

While Daisy was registering the forty or so pupils who had signed up for music lessons, she invited the children to come up to try the piano. One fifteen-year-old girl kept hitting the same note on the piano with one finger. Noticing Sweeney's bemused look, someone piped up: "She's in the dumb class at school, Miss."

"I realized she was a slow child, and I didn't have a clue how I was going to teach her," remembered Daisy. But they worked through the music, first note by note, then bar by bar. At the year-end Negro Community Centre recital, the girl was able to play a duet with Daisy Sweeney.

"That, I think," said Sweeney, "was my greatest achievement."

4

OSCAR'S EARLY INFLUENCES

Oscar was soon featured on a weekly broadcast on Montreal radio station CKAC, titled "Fifteen Minutes Piano Rambling." During the war years, Oscar performed on CBM, the CBC's English-language outlet in Montreal, and also on "The Happy Gang," at that time a CBC national network radio program (created by Bert Pearl) whose alumni included the renowned Robert Farnon, plus violinist Blaine Mathé, organist Kathleen Stokes and vocalist/accordionist Eddie Allen.

It was about this time that Oscar met pianist/saxophonist Harold "Steep" Wade, also of West Indian parentage. During his brief life—he died at thirty-five—Wade was an influence on or mentor to a number of Montreal's jazz pianists, including Oscar Peterson. Peterson recalled that Steep used to call him "kid."

In a 1980 interview with jazz historian Mark Miller, pianist Wray Downes paid lavish tribute to Steep Wade: "He just petrified me, because in my book, had he lived I don't think there would have been an Oscar. . . . He was a demon on the piano."

Oscar himself said: "Steep Wade was my favorite pianist. He had one thing—I know because I was very close to him—he had the same sense of time as Nat Cole: impeccable. He could not sit down at the piano unless it swung. If I learned nothing else from anyone, that's one thing I learned from Steep. . . . Technically, he was not a great pianist, but he had a way of playing things, of making them work musically, of making them his statement. You could always recognize Steep."

Mark "Wilkie" Wilkinson, drummer with the Louis Metcalf band, recalled that "Oscar practically lived at the St. Michel. Oscar and Steep were very tight."

Sometimes Herb Johnson, an alto saxophonist in Metcalf's band, would seek young Peterson's help with an arrangement he was working on. Peterson in turn recorded with Wilkinson and bassist Al King on some of his 1947 trio recordings.

Interestingly, that remark—about a musician's recognizability—identifies a quality that has long been one of Peterson's advantages. For any performing artist, the audience's ability to identify—by his or her sound—the work of an individual performer is a great plus.

The most obvious example was bassist Slam Stewart, whose "sound" consisted of bowing his bass fiddle and humming in unison with that sound, although an octave higher.

Clarinetist Irving Fazola had an identifiable sound with his warm, mellow tone. Count Basie, despite many imitators, could swing better than any of them. A serious jazz listener could tell the difference between Benny Goodman and Artie Shaw, between Red Nichols, say, and Muggsy Spanier.

Peterson's greatest challenge was, of course, the estimable Art Tatum, in whose shadow he dwelled glumly for some years. But there were differences—Tatum liked to indulge his changes of mood by changing the tempo, a personality trait that made it difficult—if not all but impossible—for his own trio sidemen to keep up with his mood (and tempo) shifts.

Oscar, on the other hand, was always a more dependable small group leader: his "will to swing," as Gene Lees put it, was relentlessly reliable.

(It's interesting to note that at the time when Peterson was a dazzling young player, the word "swing" was much in use—but not the word "jazz." For some reason, "jazz" was regarded as an old hat expression, whereas "swing" was considered modern. This was probably because the big band era, when Oscar was still a teenager, popularized "swing," perhaps because the young audience of the time preferred it to the older word "jazz." In fact, Duke Ellington may well have been the first person to use the word "swing" in connection with music. In 1932, he wrote a tune called "It Don't Mean a Thing If It Ain't Got That Swing," which became quite popular and remains so to this day. Only with time—and some education—did the public accept the notion that "swing" was, indeed, a type of "jazz." Before he was twenty years old, Oscar and the record companies disagreed over what he played. The record makers referred to it as "hot jazz." In 1945, at age twenty, Oscar was quoted as saying, perhaps a bit defensively: "Swing is sophisticated, grown-up jazz. I play swing.")

During his years at Montreal High School, Oscar played with the school band known as "The Victory Serenaders" and also professionally with a band known as "The Jump Crew." Eventually he went to his father and said he was no longer interested in high school and wanted to quit. Oscar recalled his father's words: "He said, 'You gonna be a jazz pianist? There are a lot of jazz pianists out there.' I didn't know what he meant. 'I'm not going to let you quit school to become a jazz pianist. If you want to be the BEST, then I'll let you go. But you have to be the best. There is no second best.' "

But this was not so much a dressing-down as a pep talk. Daniel Peterson set high standards for his children (perhaps especially Oscar) because he wanted them to excel, and both by example and sternness made it clear he expected the best—not only *for* them but *from* them.

Incidentally, Oscar's father, Daniel, eventually got over his rejection of Oscar's choice of musical genre—he became an enthusiastic convert. "I love swing," he was quoted as saying in 1945. "Fellows like Oscar and Duke Ellington play wonderful music."

There was a point when Oscar's musical future hung in the balance. In his teens, he recalled, "I had a block. I was suddenly bored with music. I just felt I'd reached a saturation point. I seemed to have done everything I could do and I was dissatisfied with my progress. So I went to an aircraft factory. A riveter."

That fallow period, when the music in his head was blocked out by the pervasive noise of the machines, was good for him. He soon snapped out of his funk and turned his attention back to music.

The whole issue of Oscar's wish to leave high school soon became academic, mostly as a result of Oscar's winning the Ken Soble amateur contest. He was soon playing military camps with shows sent out by radio stations CKAC and CBM, the CBC station in Montreal. Then he became a guest artist for "The Merchant Navy Show" on the CBC's Trans-Canada Network. That was when his friend Art Morrow persuaded Oscar to perform as a featured soloist in "Recipe Time," then broadcast from CBM. That was how his playing came to the attention of Johnny Holmes, then one of Montreal's top band leaders.

The Holmes background is worth some exploration. John Gilmore did this admirably in his book *Swinging in Paradise: The Story of Jazz in Montreal.*

> Johnny Holmes was born into a white, working-class family in central Montreal. He quit school at twelve to start bringing in some money as an office boy. He also taught himself to play the cornet and read music. With a few tips from his father and older brother, labourers who played cornet and trombone respectively, the young Holmes advanced quickly; he took only a handful of private lessons. By fourteen he had switched to trumpet, and his musicianship had matured to the point of attracting an offer of employment from one of the fledgling symphony orchestras that were struggling to fill the void left by the dissolution of the Montreal Symphony Orchestra at the onslaught of the Depression. The orchestra, however, could only offer Holmes six dollars a week, a dollar less than his office job paid. The family could not afford the loss of income, and he declined the offer. . . .
>
> Like others of his generation, Holmes was captivated by

the sound of swing. In 1940 he helped form a part-time swing band called the Esquires. The ten-piece band thought of itself as a cooperative outfit, but the members soon assigned Holmes—at twenty-four the oldest member—the task of managing their business affairs. . . . As the war siphoned off the band's original members one by one, Holmes shouldered more and more of the responsibilities. Eventually the band began appearing under the name the Johnny Holmes Orchestra. . . .

Oscar Peterson was seventeen years old when he joined the Johnny Holmes Orchestra in 1942. The war was swallowing up young men, and Holmes had lost two pianists in quick succession to the army. . . . Holmes was still casting around for a new pianist when saxophonist Art Morrow showed up at rehearsal one evening with a nervous black teenager in tow. Young Peterson didn't have any experience working in a big band. . . . Eager to impress Holmes, he unloaded every musical idea and cliché he knew into the first tune the band asked him to play. . . .

Holmes took Peterson aside during a break in the rehearsal and tried to explain to him what was required of a big-band pianist. He asked Peterson if he had ever listened to Tommy Dorsey's band. When the teenager said he had, Holmes advised him to try playing like Dorsey's pianist, Joe Bushkin—filling in behind the saxophones, but not trying to dominate the band. "He got it right the first time," said Holmes. "He played just like Bushkin."

Gilmore put the band's influence into context with this observation: "Long after the music of the Johnny Holmes Orchestra has been forgotten, the band will be remembered for the role it played in the development of Montreal's first international jazz star, Oscar Peterson."

* * *

When he was still in his mid-teens, Oscar was sitting at home, thoughtful.

"What's up?" asked his perceptive mother.

"I'd like to make a record," said Oscar.

"The way to do that," said Mrs. Peterson, "is to call up the man who makes them and tell him about it."

"As very phoney as this sounds," Oscar remembers, "out of frustration and desperation I called up RCA and asked to speak with whoever was in charge of artists or whatever."

He was put through to a man named A. H. Joseph at RCA Victor, who invited Oscar to come in for an audition. Joseph listened carefully, and before long Peterson had cut his first recordings: "The Sheik of Araby" and "I Got Rhythm." That record was soon a best-seller, as was his next 78 rpm disk, featuring "Louise" and "My Blue Heaven."

Two years later, in 1947, Oscar recorded a tune titled "Oscar's Boogie," which resulted, perhaps inevitably, in his being referred to, for a while, as "The Brown Bomber of Boogie Woogie."

The first major article to appear about Oscar Peterson was written by Harold Dingman for *Liberty* magazine in the January 1946 issue. The article proclaims: "Oscar Peterson, who is the most commercially successful pianist of his age in Canada— and perhaps the most commercially successful pianist of his age anywhere—is big and broad and a shade darker than most Negroes. When Oscar smiles, his huge face is suddenly alight with white and his shy eyes smile too, so that strangers get a feeling of personal warmth and eager friendliness. There isn't anything peculiar about this, because he is a genuine person, who has not been spoiled. Oscar accepts every job he can get in Canada, but has rejected three major offers from south of the border."

In that article, Dingman mentioned that Peterson was making a "comfortable income" from his earliest records but continued to live "on Montreal's shabby St. James Street West, down by the railway tracks and the canal. Canadians know St. James Street as the workshop of high finance, but not many persons who live outside of Montreal know that it is also a narrow, straggling dirty street of factories and tenements. That's Oscar's street, although his home is well furnished. Oscar was born in a rented parsonage on Deslisle Street in St. Henri Ward."

Dingman goes on to offer this sketch of Montreal: "Montreal, like its sister cities everywhere, is not consistent about racial prejudice. Johnny Holmes's band, with Oscar at the piano, has played in the homes of rich young debutantes at coming-out parties, and Victoria Hall, the band's regular stand, is in one of Montreal's better areas. . . . In Montreal there is no Sugar Hill, New York's residential area for the well-to-do Negroes. Almost the entire Montreal Negro colony lives in an ill-defined section down by the railway tracks."

In 1988, Peterson himself talked about the Montreal of his youth, in an interview with Greg Quill of *The Toronto Star*: "Back in the 1940s and early '50s, Montreal was a little like New York. It was a lot easier to break out from there than it is now. There were tremendously good local players as well as some of the best from the United States, who'd come up for a weekend and just sit around and play. I'd hobnob with them, and there was a certain amount of competitiveness, which also produced some wonderful music. Montreal was a very active jazz center until club owners started putting in strippers instead of music. Before long, there was nothing to hear."

* * *

Although Prohibition was repealed in the United States in 1933 (soon after Franklin Delano Roosevelt became president of the country), the laws prohibiting the sale of liquor or beer in restaurants or "saloons" remained in force in Ontario for another fourteen years.

Not until 1947 did cocktail lounges or restaurants licensed to sell mixed drinks become legal in Ontario. For the record, the first two licenses granted in Ontario were both in Toronto—the Silver Rail, on Yonge Street, and the hitherto sedate King Edward Hotel.

And, inevitably, as many of these places recognized the advantage of offering entertainment along with food and beverages, the press began giving more and more space to them. Instead of a daily newspaper's entertainment pages covering only theater and movies, they now felt obliged to give more and more ink to these new entertainment venues—the licensed premises that offered singers and/or instrumental trios, quartets or other such musical attractions.

Once the floodgates were opened, liquor licenses in restaurants or cocktail lounges proliferated. In the next few years, Toronto (as well as other Ontario cities such as Windsor, London and even Ottawa) boasted numerous places where mixed drinks were served, usually with food, depending on the kind of license granted and, in order to lure customers inside, some sort of entertainment was offered.

In Toronto, for example, after the King Edward Hotel got its license, the Royal York Hotel soon followed suit—as did the Prince George, the less elegant Barclay Hotel, the Walker House, the Spadina and, in due time, many more, including the Park Plaza, where Calvin Jackson, a talented transplanted American pianist, held forth for a number of years.

As an "entertainment columnist" for my newspaper, and as a lifelong jazz devotee, I was naturally drawn to such places.

The earliest clipping concerning Oscar Peterson of my own that I've been able to dig up (in my far-from-complete files) dates from sometime in 1949—before I had ever seen Peterson—in a weekly column I was writing for *The Globe and Mail*, titled "The Record Album." I had started at the *Globe* early in 1948, as a general assignment reporter, which meant covering everything from fires, burglary and labor disputes to murders and deadly dull service-club luncheon speeches.

Eddie Phelan, a lovely man who was the paper's telegraph

editor (and for whom I worked in my spare time while I was a copy boy at the syndicate department of *The New York Times*), shared my interest in jazz. So, early in 1949, I was allowed to begin my weekly record column—in addition, of course, to my other regular duties, and for little or no extra cash. But the money didn't matter nearly as much as the chance to write about my favorite kind of music.

In the course of reviewing that week's batch of records—some, but not all of them, jazz—I mentioned that my favorite side was "Oscar Peterson's cover of the old Ellington tune, 'Rockin' In Rhythm.' This guy Peterson continues to play such brilliant piano as is seldom heard these days, and gives us a knockout number like this; he accomplishes wonders . . ."

It is interesting to note that in the mid-1990s RCA Victor issued a double CD of Oscar's recordings, titled *Beginnings*, which includes some thirty-one Peterson recordings from this period, 1945–1949, in Montreal. Of special note are "Sweet Georgia Brown" and Ellington's "Rockin' in Rhythm," both recorded in 1949 and both featuring an early Peterson trio that included guitarist Ben Johnson and bassist Austin Roberts. Right on its heels came a second album, simply titled *Oscar Peterson 1951*. This one has twenty tunes, most of them standards, featuring Oscar and bassist Austin Roberts—no drummer. But there's one out-of-the-ordinary tune on the CD, listed as "Hungarian Dance" by Brahms. And Oscar even manages to sneak a bit of "Three Blind Mice" into it.

But it was to be another two years before I would see Oscar in person. I first saw him in Hamilton, Ontario, in the Hunting Room of the Fischer Hotel, where he was supported by bass player Ray Brown. Only a year earlier, Oscar had heard Brown play and said, "Some day, I want him as my bass player." That relationship has endured for half a century.

5

"A DETERMINED MAN"

"I owe a good deal to my mother," Oscar said to journalist Harold Dingman early in 1946. "In the write-ups about me, my father always gets the credit for teaching me to play, but my mother should get some credit, too. When I wanted to swing, she backed me up and said she thought there might be some future in it."

Oscar's gallantry aside, Daniel Peterson was indeed a strong influence on his young son's budding musical orientation.

Speaking about his father, Oscar recalled: "He didn't see the same obstacles that I saw. I'd say, 'Gee, you know, this can't be done.' And he'd say, 'Why not? If it got there, you can remove it. Or if it isn't there you can put it in there.' It was that simple to him. And I think he instilled a great determination in me. Because he was a determined man."

Yes, indeed, Daniel Peterson was "a determined man." It was, after all, Oscar's father who fell passionately in love with music and spread his gospel throughout his family—first to his wife, then to his children. All five of Daniel Peterson's children were steered toward music.

He would lay down the law regarding musical studies while he was away on the railroad. Oscar remembered: "My dad would leave and he would give us each a task, pianistically. You had to know this, you had to know that, and when I come back from Vancouver or Saint John, have it together. There were no ifs, ands or buts. Have it together. It was that simple. He would come back and then he would call each of us in turn into the room where the piano was, and he would say, 'Okay, fine, may I have the scale? What did you have?' 'I had the G scale.' And he'd go through the scales, the arpeggios, all the things we were supposed to have learned."

"I guess my Dad's philosophy," Oscar recalled, "was that in order to overcome all the barriers, we had to do something special. He seemed to apply that to everything—including the piano."

In another, later interview, Oscar remembers the trains: "Sometimes, I used to go down and help him with his [sleeping] cars. I think that was when he made up his mind that he didn't want us to end up working for the railroad. I think that's when Dad, in his own mind, decided this was *not* a profession he wanted us to follow."

A chief difference between father and son was that Daniel was devoted to classical music—which accounted for Oscar's early studies of Chopin, Liszt and Bach, among other composers.

"After I made the decision to go into music," Oscar said about decisions facing him as a teenager, "I remember thinking about it and saying, 'How do you manage to put all this together, how do you string this together to make it financially and artistically feasible?' I'd say, 'It's okay to play, but what do I do? Do I play a concert this week? You have to be good to play a concert. How do I get to that stage? How do I make money until I get to that stage? Do I play in an orchestra?

"'And if I get into an orchestra, does it mean that I'm going to be stuck there for the rest of my life? Or do I do some studio work? And does it mean I'm going to be stationed there for the rest of my life? And how do I get to make recordings, and what if the recordings don't work?'

"I can remember sitting up one night thinking that there really was no way for me to make a decent living being a jazz artist. And happily, of course, I've proven myself wrong."

By 1945, when Oscar was twenty years old, word of his

prowess on the piano had spread below the Canada–US border. He had—and turned down—offers to join Count Basie and Jimmie Lunceford, both then leaders of top-grade, jazz-flavored bands.

"I prefer to stay in Canada," he said in an interview. "Bands here in Canada easily measure up to some of the name bands in the States. I know I could make twice as much money right now, but I believe I'll make just as much right here in Montreal. This is my home, anyway. With Johnny we play along about the same style as any top band in the United States. And I get more kicks and bangs out of playing with his band."

At the time, trumpeter and arranger Holmes led one of Montreal's most popular swing bands. The Holmes band boasted a healthy jazz quotient and, in the words of jazz historian Mark Miller, "benefited from Holmes's ability to identify talented younger musicians," who included Maynard Ferguson, Art Morrow and Oscar Peterson.

Initially, Holmes wasn't impressed when Peterson auditioned for a place in the band. John Gilmore picks up the story in *Swinging in Paradise*:

> But as the rehearsal ground on, the bandleader began to see a glimmer of hope in the teenager's hyper-exuberant playing. "He was a diamond in the rough," Holmes recalled some thirty years later from retirement. "He already had amazing technique, but he shot everything in the first chorus. . . .
>
> At the end of the rehearsal, Holmes hired Peterson, then went one step further. He fixed a date with the pianist for a private get-together, to go over the band's music. The meetings became more regular as a friendship developed. Over the next two years Holmes and Peterson met several times a week, for up to two hours at a time. Holmes played only rudimentary piano, and there was nothing he could

show Peterson about keyboard technique. He did, however, coach the young pianist on jazz conception and delivery, playing records to illustrate fine points of phrasing and performance. The influence on Peterson's playing was profound.

"I was overdoing boogie-woogie and was completely lost for slow tunes," Peterson told a magazine [*Liberty*] in 1946, after making his first recordings. "Holmes was responsible for changing this; he built up my technique and was responsible for the style I put on records."

It's interesting to note that despite Oscar's feeling that he was "lost for slow tunes," his virtuosity and range amply showed in his recordings of *My Fair Lady*, *West Side Story*, *Fiorello!* and *Porgy and Bess*, as well as a collection of Cole Porter songs.

Harking back to the time he joined the Holmes orchestra, Oscar later said: "The problem with that regimentation was getting used to it. Up to this time I'd been playing anything I wanted to play any way at all. I went up and sat in with the band and I enjoyed it. And I suddenly thought that this is another facet of music that I hadn't really been exposed to—a big dance orchestra. And I wanted to get some experience in that way, and I remained in that band I can't really recall how many years."

As for A. H. Joseph, who first recorded Oscar Peterson (for RCA Victor), he was happy that the first four Peterson records had "sold thousands."

"I had the boy in mind for some time because his popularity was growing and the young crowd in Montreal were talking about Holmes' band and the boy at the piano. I guess we would have got after him soon if he hadn't approached us. He is under contract to us now and we are happy about it. We are pleasantly surprised that he is selling everywhere and the future looks long and promising."

But Oscar himself was not too thrilled. "My first two boogie records seem to have typecast me," he told *The Vancouver Sun.* "But even if it's good commercially I can't play boogie all my life. We had a big argument about it at Victor. They said—Peterson, do you want to be a good commercial musician or do you want to be a collector's item? I said, 'A collector's item!' "

Despite his own misgivings about being considered a boogie-woogie specialist, the success of those early records helped make his name known outside Montreal. He made his first forays outside Quebec—to the Winnipeg Auditorium—which drew some 4,000 fans, and Massey Hall in Toronto in 1946—and by the end of that year he had placed twenty-eighth among pianists in the *Down Beat* readers' poll. *Metronome*, the other leading swing/jazz periodical, tossed a somewhat backhanded compliment his way. Jim Butler wrote: "For a country reputedly as unhip as Canada in the creation of musicians, a miracle has occurred. His name is Oscar Peterson."

Even so, Butler made a remarkable prediction for that time, which was 1947: "If Oscar Peterson continues to improve as steadily as he has in the past year, there is no reason why he can't be in the same class as Teddy Wilson, Errol Garner and, yes, even Art Tatum." (With hindsight, one is tempted to wonder how Garner got into such distinguished company.)

*   *   *

When Oscar joined the Johnny Holmes band he was its only non-white member. At the time, black musicians were usually referred to as "colored" or "Negro." (I have actually seen more than one use of the word "negro"—without so much as the grudging dignity of a capital "N.")

Numerous earlier black musicians had played in otherwise white bands in various parts of Canada, among them Shirley Oliver, Tommy Thompson, Frankie Nelson, Ollie Wagner, Charlie Adams, Alf Coward and Jimmy Jones.

Many years later, Oscar himself expressed some discomfort

about his stint with the Holmes orchestra. "I was the only black musician in the band," he said. "If there had been several it might have been different, but when you're the only black man in an otherwise white band, you sort of stand out."

Even so, his prominent role in the Johnny Holmes Orchestra was not universally accepted. The Holmes band suddenly found itself unwelcome at the Ritz-Carlton Hotel.

The Montreal Herald reported the story: "The Johnny Holmes Orchestra, booked for several gigs at The Ritz, among them a deb dance and the IODE [Imperial Order Daughters of the Empire] Blue Orchid Ball, may not carry through with their chores. Seems the Ritz is objecting to their colored pianist, that brilliant virtuoso Oscar Peterson, and Johnny and the boys consider the issue more important than a few bookings."

According to Gene Lees, Holmes threatened "to take out newspaper ads in the *Herald*, *Star* and *Gazette* announcing that the band would never again play the Ritz-Carlton because of its apparent policy of racial discrimination. In the event, the IODE intervened on the band's behalf and the evening went ahead as planned, Holmes exacting a measure of satisfaction by featuring Peterson even more than usual."

According to John Gilmore's book *Swinging in Paradise*:

> Peterson blossomed with the band. As time passed, Holmes recognized that his pianist was a major contributor to the band's success and popularity. He acknowledged Peterson's drawing power by paying him more than any other band member; eventually, Peterson was earning a living from the band, the only member besides Holmes to do so. Holmes also began including Peterson's name on the band's publicity flyers and newspaper ads, billing the band as 'the Johnny Holmes Orchestra with Oscar Peterson.' He gave Peterson liberal solo space in his arrangements. . . . Finally, Holmes began turning the last fifteen

minutes of every dance over to Peterson and the band's bassist and drummer, giving the pianist the first taste of the trio format that was to become the staple of his career.

According to Johnny Holmes, as quoted in John Gilmore's book:

"The last fifteen minutes we played all the slow and dreamy music so the kids could dance very close together. We just let Oscar play. He'd call the tunes. . . . But he'd be playing, say, 'Body and Soul,' and someone in the band would call out another tune, say, 'I Surrender Dear.' And he'd have to incorporate that right away into 'Body and Soul,' whether it was on the third beat of the bar or whatever. He never got hung up once. And they were calling out ridiculous things, classicals, everything. He would never get hung up at all. . . . The band idolized him. The greatest audience he had was the band."

Oscar, reflecting on his time with the Holmes orchestra, said: "We had a few encounters and, strange as it seems, they probably could have been avoided if there had been a few more black men in the band. But if you're the only man of that race in a band, you're noticed. . . . A lot of musicians were trying to break down the color barrier, but it was a promoter, Norman Granz, who did more than anyone to break it down. He just refused to accept it."

Oscar remained with the Johnny Holmes Orchestra for four years, during which Holmes and he became more than good friends. Holmes was first his employer, then his manager and eventually his mentor, which Peterson readily acknowledges.

During that period, Oscar made a favorable impression on numerous visiting American musicians—not only Basie and Lunceford, but also Coleman Hawkins, Frankie Newton, Wilbur DeParis, Mezz Mezzrow and others—all of whom, after hearing him play, urged him to leave Montreal for the United States.

Oscar's presence posed no real problem for Johnny Holmes, who took his young featured pianist with him to a summer assignment in the Laurentian Mountains, at Ste. Agathe. Harold Dingman wrote, "Johnny Holmes' band, with Oscar at the piano, has played in the homes of rich young debutantes at coming-out parties, and Victoria Hall, the band's regular stand, is in one of Montreal's better areas."

But, by the fall of 1947, Oscar was feeling the urge to try out his wings, to run his own show, lead his own group, albeit a small one. This is how Mark Miller described the situation in his book: "Peterson had outstripped the Johnny Holmes Orchestra long before he finally put it behind him. But as a jazz musician on the rise, he was breaking new ground in Canada; the opportunities available to him would be severely limited as long as he remained in the country. Typically, his recording activities continued apace in 1947 . . . but his concert work that year was restricted to a return appearance at Massey Hall, where he was accompanied in May by three Toronto musicians, among them Stan Wilson, the guitarist."

Oscar himself voiced his ambition to move to the United States as early as the summer of 1944. But he sensed it wasn't time yet. First, he had to become more clearly established in Canada—and not just as the "featured pianist" with Johnny Holmes.

6

OSCAR AND NAT

Long after Peterson had become the world's most acclaimed jazz pianist it was still a label he didn't like. "I am not a jazz pianist," he once argued. "I'm a pianist who plays jazz."

On another occasion, Peterson expanded on that theme: "Too many jazz pianists limit themselves to a personal style, a trademark, so to speak. They confine themselves to one type of playing. I believe in using the entire piano as a single instrument capable of expressing every possible musical idea. I have no one style. I play as I feel. To play as you feel means that you master the piano and not let it master you. It also means that you must make use of everything that has been done before, in the classics as well as in jazz, adding your own creative ideas."

Countless millions of careful listeners can listen to Peterson for a few moments and react, "That's Oscar."

But it's abundantly clear by now that from the time he first drew the public's attention, at this café or that club around Montreal, Peterson's remarkable speed, dazzling technique, sheer mastery of the instrument and total grasp of harmonics set him far ahead of virtually all his competitors—save one.

As early as February 1946, Oscar gave a concert of both jazz and classics at His Majesty's Theatre in Montreal. *The Montreal Herald*'s review began: "It isn't every 20-year-old Negro pianist who can fill a house the size of His Majesty's Theatre and send his audience into ecstasies of appreciation on the occasion of his concert debut. . . . Young Peterson, who made his local concert debut with an established reputation as a result of his radio programs and recordings, gained in musical stature and public acceptance last night to a degree seldom encountered in the field of popular music."

As early as March of 1950, Peterson was attracting serious attention not only outside Montreal but outside Canada. That was when *Down Beat* carried a piece by the Montreal CBC producer Henry F. Whiston, which concluded with this comment: "Oscar's popularity has increased considerably during the last couple of years and fans are springing up in this country. He has had several major bids from U.S. bands, plus an offer from [Norman] Granz, but he prefers to stay in Canada until the time is ripe.

"Visiting American musicians, including Coleman Hawkins, Nat Cole, Woody Herman, Buddy Rich, Ella Fitzgerald, Duke Ellington, the Delta Rhythm Boys and many more all reach the unanimous decision that he's one of the greatest—a man to watch in '50."

Peterson himself has wavered in the degree of self-confidence he has felt or expressed about his own capabilities at the keyboard: "You walk over to a piano and say, 'Well, let's have a conversation for the next couple of hours,' and either it's going to accept what you have to say and give you some feedback, or it's going to lie to you and say something else, or it isn't there. And if you get the feeling it isn't there, it's pretty hard to have that conversation, and it can be a helpless feeling. You know what you're trying to do, and if you can't make it happen and the people react well anyway, that's really infuriating. It may sound stupid, but it's true."

In 1955 he told *Down Beat*: "Playing the piano, you feel like the greyhounds trying to catch up with the mechanical rabbit. The rabbit—and the piano—always wins."

The very first Oscar Peterson Trio—with Austin "Ozzie" Roberts on bass and Clarence Jones on drums—opened at the Alberta Lounge in Montreal on October 8, 1947. Roberts was a veteran of the Cy McLean band, originally from Sydney, Nova

Scotia. Clarence Jones was a Montreal-based musician.

After more than five years with Johnny Holmes, Peterson was on his own. As John Gilmore related it in *Swinging in Paradise*:

> Radio Station CFCF broadcast the trio live from the club. During his two-year residency at the Alberta Lounge, Peterson spent most nights after work sitting in and socializing with the Louis Metcalf band at the nearby Cafe St. Michel, where he immersed himself in bebop. Visiting American musicians were invariably stunned on first hearing Peterson, whether at the Cafe St. Michel or elsewhere. . . .
>
> Lou Hooper, Jr., was at the Chez Maurice Danceland one night in late 1948 when the pioneer bebop trumpeter Dizzy Gillespie brought his big band in from New York City for a two-night stand.
>
> "On the first night," [Hooper recalled], "Oscar was there, and pretty soon people were shouting out, 'Get Oscar to play! Let Oscar play!' So finally Diz says, 'Okay, Oscar, come on, where are you?' They pulled out the most difficult piano chart they had. It was one of those things where the band wails, then stops dead, and the piano's supposed to play. So they built up to this break, and we're all saying to ourselves, 'Watch this!' And when the break comes, Oscar leans back and . . ."
>
> Momentarily lost for words, Hooper, Jr., resorted to sweeping hand gestures and boiling vocalizations to convey an image of the tidal wave of notes that poured from the piano as Peterson laid into in with all fingers flailing.
>
> "The whole brass section stood up and looked at him and said, 'Who in the hell is *that*!' Diz just stared at him for a minute, then started shouting, 'Blow! Blow! Go ahead and blow, man!' Then Oscar *really* got going. Well, from that point on the band just kept putting numbers in front of him so they could listen to him play. We didn't go with

them afterwards, but Oscar told us that Diz kept him up till about six o'clock in the morning at some after-hours club, keeping him playing, and he kept asking him, 'Do you really *hear* them chords?' "

Not only did he hear them and play them, but he was soon dazzling every musician who heard him. No less a jazz icon than Duke Ellington said to Oscar: "You're somebody that they just can't ignore. Not only jazz players pay you tribute, but classical players, too."

Given his early training, it should be no surprise that Peterson sees a link between jazz and classical music. "Both," as Roy Shields wrote in an article for *The Toronto Star* in May 1982, "are more sophisticated forms of the musical spectrum that endure despite ever-changing pop-music fashions."

Shields then added Oscar's own observation: "I don't believe that a lot of the things I hear on the air today are going to be played for as long a time as Coleman Hawkins records or Brahms concertos."

Jazz critic for *The Toronto Star* Geoff Chapman wrote of Peterson: "In the 1970s it was clear that his skills were such that a full range of orchestral effects was possible without benefit of accompanying musicians."

Another journalist referred to Oscar as "the baronial jazz pianist with the Rolls-Royce of techniques."

One admiring musician summed it up this way: "Oscar plays piano *both* hands."

Looking back, many years after he had achieved his fame, Oscar talked about what his own hopes had been: "Before, the piano was very conciliatory, like 'We'll have an eight-bar solo here' or whatever. I think I helped bring the piano to the level of being accepted as a fully complementary star of its own. In doing so, people realized the piano was a much broader instrument.

"You could sit down alone at a piano and hold people's attention for two hours. A piano could be more than just heard at intervals. Depending on how it was played, it could be a high-impact instrument like drums or horns. That's all I ever wanted to do with the piano."

It is a matter of musical history that Oscar Peterson's idol—and model—was the great Art Tatum. He was also influenced, at least in his youth, by the work of such jazz pioneers as James P. Johnson, Willie "The Lion" Smith, Fats Waller and Teddy Wilson.

But despite his admiration for the early Tatum trio (with guitarist Tiny Grimes and bassist Slam Stewart), it was another instrumental trio that captured Oscar's attention—the Nat "King" Cole Trio. That was the sound that Peterson hoped to match or better when he formed his own first small group.

Nathaniel Adams Cole (originally Coles) had had an interesting musical history. Born in Montgomery, Alabama, in 1919, the son of a Baptist preacher, he grew up in Chicago. He was to become an outstanding jazz pianist—out of Earl "Fatha" Hines, leaning toward Bud Powell. By the mid-1930s Nat Cole was in Los Angeles, which was not then a swinging town, musically speaking.

He worked at various clubs and bars around Los Angeles. "I played every beer joint from San Diego to Bakersfield," he often said. It was a bad time for Cole. At one point, he was so desperate for money that he rummaged through the few songs he had written and then made the rounds of music publishers around Hollywood Boulevard and Vine Street—the Los Angeles version of Tin Pan Alley. "At the end of the afternoon, footsore and weary, I sold 'Straighten Up and Fly Right' to a publisher for fifty dollars, outright no royalties."

Finally, things began to change for Nat. The owner of a club called the Swanee Inn heard him play and offered to book Nat, if Cole could put together a quartet. The club operator would pay them twenty-five dollars each a week.

Cole rounded up guitarist Oscar Moore, bass player Wesley Prince and drummer Lee Young (brother of the more famous Lester). But Lee was not enthusiastic about all this—he wanted to play with a big band. In fact, he failed to show up at the

Swanee Inn on opening night, so the Nat "King" Cole Quartet suddenly became the Nat "King" Cole Trio.

Things were going nicely for Nat Cole. The more attentive music fans appreciated his crisp, swinging piano style. What was supposed to be a one-month booking stretched to six months.

In her biography of Cole, Maria, Nat's second wife, recalled a radio interview in which Nat said: "When I organized the King Cole Trio back in 1937, we were strictly what you would call an instrumental group. To break the monotony, I would sing a few songs here and there between the playing. I sang things I had known over the years. I wasn't trying to give it any special treatment, just singing. I noticed thereafter people started requesting more singing, and it was just one of those things."

But it turned out to be more than "just one of those things." One night at the Swanee Inn, a drunk demanded that Nat sing "Sweet Lorraine" (which had been Jimmy Noone's theme song back in Nat's Chicago days).

Ever the gentleman (and the professional), Cole obliged. That night had two important results:

1. It marked the beginning of Nat Cole's rise to stardom as a singer.

2. It began to deprive the jazz world of one of its most gifted pianists.

From then on, the public wanted to hear Nat sing. He went on to make hit record after hit record. Among them, in no particular order, were songs such as "Route 66," "Nature Boy," "Mona Lisa," "Ramblin' Rose," "Lush Life," "Unforgettable," "Too Young," "Walkin' My Baby Back Home," "Smile," "Those Lazy, Hazy, Crazy Days of Summer" and "Portrait of Jennie."

Cole's excursion into vocalizing made him a singing star and pretty well ended his career as a pianist. Oscar also went through a singing phase—although this was well after he had become established as *the* jazz pianist. His brief career as a singing pianist was not something Peterson remembered as any sort of peak in his musical career.

"To be honest," Oscar confessed to me in a 1991 interview, "I only sang because the audience badgered me to. And the only way I knew how to sing, for some reason, came out sounding much like Nat. I wasn't ashamed because I really loved what Nat did.

"He set many good examples for myself and other trio players. By seeing him work, he taught me how to control a group and also a great deal about the importance of having good time. I learned that by playing certain phrases in certain places a group could be steered.

"Of course, there was no need for two Nat Coles on the scene. One night, Nat came backstage after one of our shows and jokingly said, 'I'll make a deal with you, Oscar. I won't play the piano if you promise not to sing.'

"I stopped soon after that."

*   *   *

Another jazz legend, the inimitable Count Basie, recorded two albums with Peterson. Basie was the ultimate minimalist in jazz piano, who could produce exactly the right keyboard punctuation to top off his band's swinging style. He was the exact opposite of Peterson, who, in the words of another reviewer, could "play better with one hand than most pianists do with two."

Said Basie of Peterson: "Oh, he's a lovely fellow, but you never know when he's going to sneak up on you and destroy you with his playing. He can be a monster."

Basie liked to magnify his feelings of inadequacy whenever he was pitted against "that wonderful monster"—as happened in various Norman Granz concerts and recordings. "We'd play a few bars each," Basie recalled, "and he'd play a chorus, and I would stumble through one, and he'd catch me stumbling along and pick me up and help me. He was wonderful.

"But some nights he'd forget, and I'd have to hit the piano real hard to let him know I was still there, so cut it out and don't get carried away. He was wonderful but he was also terrible. Sometimes I'd just think about how I was going to be with that monster that evening, and my whole day was ruined."

The first album Basie and Peterson recorded was *Satch and Josh* (1975), followed two years later by *Satch and Josh Again*. Basie later recalled: "The last day we were in the studio, I made my first two tracks with a fantastic young piano player named Oscar Peterson. . . . Oscar sat in with the band on 'Be My Guest,' and naturally he tore it up. He always tears it up. Hell, he can't help it."

In his album notes for *Satch and Josh*, British jazz critic Benny Green wrote: "In the mutual admiration society which Basie and Oscar Peterson formed between them, we get the juxtaposition of the two styles which could hardly be more contrasted even if contrast had been the sole aim of the exercise. Peterson's technique is prolific and flawless, Basie's sparse and flawless . . . When Oscar leaps into his solo in 'Jumpin' at the Woodside,' or when Basie slips into the lower register for that simple last bridge of 'These Foolish Things,' we sense that the experiment has been an unqualified success and that both men realize it."

I recall vividly witnessing one of those Basie-Peterson concerts in Los Angeles in 1975, and it was rather the way Basie described it. They sat at two grand pianos, facing each other like duelists, and Basie peered at Peterson every time Oscar launched into one of his bravura keyboard explosions. But then Oscar would lie back and let the Count inject his clean, crisp musical footnotes.

In the mid-1970s, André Previn, himself a pianist and a composer/arranger of considerable stature, wrote about Peterson: "I suppose there are misguided actors who find fault with Olivier, boxers who deny Muhammad Ali, and Sunday painters who shrug their shoulders at Picasso, but it seems to me impossible for anyone who ever was a good boy and learned the piano up to and including 'The Merry Farmer' in Grade 2, to refrain from standing in awe of Oscar's accomplishments. Listening to him throughout an evening is like taking a refresher course in the history of piano jazz; he has a respectful sense of the past, the immediacy of the present, and an optimistic view of the future. Through all of his playing pervades a great sense of joy, of pleasure in the mastery of the instrument, and of happy communication with his audience. Despite his obvious erudition, he makes us remember what fun jazz can be, and what a sense of security it is to be in the hands of a champion.

"Simply the world's greatest jazz pianist and one of the greatest virtuosos in jazz—that's the title Oscar Peterson has won from music audiences, critics and fellow artists."

And in Benny Green's words, "Peterson stands as one of the greatest soloists of all time, a player whose technique never obscures the lucidity of his thoughts or the wonderful buoyancy of his execution. What Earl Hines began forty years ago with his discovery that the pianist's right hand was itself a solo instrument, reaches its final consummation in Peterson.

"Peterson is surely the most articulate, all-consuming pianist since the late great Art Tatum—his undisputed idol. He is an artist not to be underestimated—or missed."

Peterson himself once analyzed his own contribution and that of his trio: "My group has always retained that fire, that feeling of pressure, of playing with honesty. I could never think of giving up what I'm doing. I could never, for instance, settle down and become a studio musician. That kind of job was offered to me years ago, but it doesn't represent the way I want to live."

Norman Granz, his friend and manager for many years, said: "He is one of the few pianists who is representative of a whole symphony in texture when he performs solo."

Once, while in Rome, Peterson told an interviewer: "When you play jazz, you have this tremendous range to choose from. We're not like pop musicians who have to perform the same top ten tunes every night of a tour. When I feel like the group has something going in one mood, I pretty well stick to it. Of course, you have to take into consideration what seems to be getting to the audience."

Oscar's own celebrity didn't render him jaded. Apart from the countless jazz greats with whom he has played, he has met, over the years, numerous other celebrated figures—in and out of the music business. From Fred Astaire and Gene Kelly to Frank Sinatra and Marlon Brando and Vladimir Horowitz.

One of his more amusing encounters was with the famed actor Charles Laughton, whom Oscar met in London. As author Gene Lees tells it in his book on Peterson, *The Will to Swing*, Oscar and Laughton were both waiting for a taxi outside a London hotel. Oscar couldn't resist the opportunity to tell the noted actor how much he, Oscar, admired his work.

After listening to Oscar's praise, Laughton asked: "And what do you do, young man?"

"I'm a jazz musician," said Oscar.

"Hmm," said Laughton, "a jazz musician. Do you have any pot?"

7

ENTER NORMAN GRANZ

Norman Granz was for half a century Oscar Peterson's close friend and manager. His own remarkable career, however, might never have started had he not been weaned off the then-fashionable big bands by a famous 1939 recording made by Coleman Hawkins.

Hawkins had just returned to the United States after living in Europe for several years. His recording (with a small group) of Johnny Green's "Body and Soul" was a simple, straightforward, two-chorus version of the tune, which remains, perhaps, the definitive version of that tune. The comprehensive *Penguin Guide to Jazz on CD* describes it as "the most spontaneously perfect of all jazz records." What evidently appealed to Granz were the possibilities offered by a small, informal jazz group, as opposed to the rigidities of big swing-era bands.

Considering that Granz has been the Sol Hurok of jazz—that is, the world's premier provider of jazz concerts, tours and recordings—jazz was secondary to his lifelong fight against racial segregation and discrimination. Born in Los Angeles on August 6, 1918, Granz many times stated that his chief motivation for promoting and producing jazz concerts was to fight racial discrimination. "My main reason," Granz said about his formation of Jazz At The Philharmonic, "was to try to improve race relations. Wherever we go, we go together. Never do we go to the Deep South where we have to be segregated." (But later, he even took on that challenge, as a means of fighting segregation.)

"Black musicians were playing all over Los Angeles in the early Forties," he told *Down Beat* magazine, "but almost entirely to white audiences. This was because there were very few places that welcomed blacks as patrons. . . . One day Billie Holiday came to me and complained that Billy Berg, who owned the club [where she was appearing], wouldn't admit some of her black friends."

Granz went to Berg with a proposal: "Give me Sunday nights when the club is dark and the house band is off, and I'll give you a jam session and a crowd of paying customers."

Berg was interested, but Granz added some conditions: one, integrate the audience; two, pay the musicians; three, put tables on the dance floor so people would listen instead of dance; four, allow integrated crowds the other six nights of the week.

Granz got his way and, pretty soon, Sunday nights quickly became Berg's most lucrative sessions—and other club owners began contacting Granz to make similar deals. It didn't take long for Granz and his band of traveling players (which included a then-unknown pianist named Nat Cole) to build a little weekly circuit for themselves.

The next step was the concert stage, first at Music Town in south Los Angeles. Then came the birth of the legendary Jazz At The Philharmonic (JATP), so named because the first large-scale concert Granz put on was a benefit held at the huge Los Angeles Philharmonic Auditorium. JATP began touring in 1944 and continued for more than three decades, in addition to holding periodic reunions, first in the United States and Canada, and then in Europe. Granz himself took up residence in Switzerland at the end of the 1950s, returning to North America only when his business required it.

All things considered, 1944 was a banner year for young Granz. That was also the year he put together *Jammin' the Blues*, still regarded as the best—possibly the only—really important short film ever made about jazz. (Jean Bach's *A Great Day in Harlem*, produced in 1995, is probably the best feature-length documentary yet made about jazz.) Technically, a Warner

Brothers employee was credited as "producer" of *Jammin' the Blues*, but it was a Granz production all the way.

Perhaps inevitably, there was some controversy about *Jammin' the Blues*. Among the fine jazz musicians featured in the Granz short were Lester Young, Harry "Sweets" Edison, Dickie Wells, Jo Jones, Illinois Jacquet and Barney Kessel. Guitarist Barney Kessel was the only white musician in the group.

In the mid-1970s, I met Leonard Feather in Los Angeles. The English-born Feather was a musician, composer, writer, critic and producer. Among his achievements was the massive *Encyclopedia of Jazz*, first published in 1955, then updated in 1976. In the course of our conversation, Feather told me that when Granz made *Jammin' the Blues*, he had purposely arranged to have Barney Kessel shown in a kind of shadow, to disguise the fact that Kessel was a white musician among black musicians. The reason for this, presumably, was that "mixed" bands were frowned upon at the time—certainly in films.

Later, Granz vehemently denied this charge. "No, no, no, that's not true," said Granz. "Mili wouldn't have allowed it."

The whole idea, he insisted, had been to take Gjon Mili, a renowned stills photographer, and turn him into a cinematographer. But nobody would have dared tell Mili how to light his shots—he was too highly respected.

But in Bill Crow's 1990 book, *Jazz Anecdotes*, Kessel is quoted as saying the story, about his being filmed in poor lighting to disguise the fact that he was a white musician in an otherwise black band, is accurate.

"Well, that's absolutely true," said Kessel. "They wouldn't be able to sell it below the Mason-Dixon line. Jack Warner really didn't want to go through with the project when he saw that everyone was black but me. He spoke to Norman Granz about it and asked why he didn't just get a black guitarist. . . . Norman said no, because the people that were here are not here because they are black or white, they're here because they are the people he [Granz] wanted. They kicked it around for a while and finally the solution was that I was in the shadows. It kind of inferred, pictorially, that I might be black."

Granz told me during an interview that from the outset he was having difficulties with Warner Brothers. "They had no concept of what jazz was all about," he said.

First of all, the producer wanted the music to be pre-recorded, which was standard procedure for all musical movies at that time. Granz insisted that jazz must be played live, that to pre-record it would rob it of one of its basic appeals: spontaneity. He more or less won that round, but lost another. The Warner brothers insisted on using a singer named Marie Bryant in the short, and when they discovered she could also dance, they insisted on including a dance number in the show. In any case, *Jammin' the Blues* went on to win an Academy Award nomination for best one-reel film of 1944.

Granz believed the film would have won the Oscar but for the fact that Warner Brothers had another film (*I Won't Play*) nominated in the same category and threw the company's support behind that film, rather than *Jammin' the Blues*.

During the run of Jazz At The Philharmonic, many of the most talented musicians in jazz worked for Granz: Louis Armstrong, Coleman Hawkins, Flip Phillips, Bill Harris, Illinois Jacquet, Hank Jones, Howard McGhee, Jo Jones, J. J. Johnson, Roy Eldridge, Charlie Parker, Lester Young, Dizzy Gillespie, Milt Jackson, Thelonious Monk, Willie Smith, Ray Brown, the incomparable Ella Fitzgerald and many more—including one "Shorty Nadine," who in fact was Nat Cole. (He couldn't use his real name because he was under contract to Capitol Records and technically couldn't record on another label.)

Similarly, in 1945, JATP recorded "How High the Moon," which was to become, along with "Perdido," a jazz anthem. The drummer on the record is Gene Krupa, but because he, like Nat Cole, had a contract with a different recording company, he was billed only as "Chicago Flash."

People in the music business scoffed at Granz's idea of releasing albums of these concerts—complete with audience response (which was often somewhat raucous) and the very occasional clunker. But Jazz At The Philharmonic was only one aspect of Granz's producing-recording career. There were also such magnificent once-in-a-lifetime projects as *The Jazz Scene*, a magnificent package recorded in 1949 (on six 12-inch 78-rpm discs) that presented, in various combinations, such diverse artists as Duke Ellington, Neal Hefti, Coleman Hawkins, Charlie Parker, Buddy Rich and Bud Powell.

The Jazz Scene was issued on the Mercury label in a limited and numbered edition. Only 5,000 copies were made (mine is number 4396). It was later reissued on LP, but it's hard to find. My own favorite on this album is the combination of Lester Young, Buddy Rich and Aye Guy (code name of Nat Cole) playing "I Want To Be Happy." The package also had some marvelous photos by Gjon Mili and some equally exquisite David Stone Martin drawings. The gifted Martin was to do numerous album covers for Granz, some abstract, some featuring vaguely identifiable musicians (Dizzy Gillespie, Flip Phillips), but eventually all the JATP records featured a silhouette of a trumpet player, taken from a photo of Charlie Shavers.

Of course, the stubborn but dedicated Granz proved the doubters wrong. By the mid-1950s the annual gross of the JATP tours was hovering around the $5 million mark. But much later, Granz recalled that while he made money on the tours, the records brought him virtually no profits—at least in the early days.

Bill Coss, then editor of *Metronome*, wrote in that publication in October 1955: "There is no doubt that his presence in jazz has done an enormous amount of good for all concerned."

The New Yorker's jazz critic, Whitney Balliett, referred to Norman Granz as "the first person who has ever been able successfully to mass produce jazz."

But Granz and the new mass media of television never did get along together very well. On one occasion, he worked with

Timex for one of their television specials. Granz provided the services of Ella Fitzgerald; also on the show were Benny Goodman, Duke Ellington and Count Basie. Granz later referred to it as "shabby, a lousy show." He also pointed out that there had never been biographical television programs on Louis Armstrong, Duke Ellington or Ella Fitzgerald.

Referring to Hollywood television producers, Granz said: "They just don't have the aesthetic judgment or the courage to go with an art form. They don't let you do what you do."

As suggested by *Jammin' the Blues*, Granz suffered no shortage of nerve. In 1952, he put together an LP package (six sides) called *The Astaire Story*, in which the legendary star tap danced to and sang some forty standard popular songs composed by the likes of Berlin, the Gershwins, Porter, Kern and the team of Arthur Schwartz and Howard Dietz.

In his album notes, Granz refers to the dancer, rather reverentially, as Mr. Astaire. He wrote, "For years, I've had a great admiration for Mr. Astaire, and so I feel, have a few million other people. I'm not so sure that it was only his dancing and singing; perhaps it was his clothes, or the way he wore them; or maybe it was the way he walked. (As a matter of fact, I don't even like to call him a dancer; I really believe that he is a graceful walker. And his grace is that God-given kind that transcends ordinary hoofing.) But whatever it is, there was something about Mr. Astaire that made him everybody's boy.

"Particularly, he was the favorite boy of the great song writers. I did some research on the subject of Mr. Astaire and his songs and curiously . . . he has had written for him and introduced more songs that have become all-time hits than almost any other living artist on the current musical scene. For one thing, Mr. Berlin, Mr. Porter, Mr. Gershwin and Mr. Kern, among others, liked what they wrote, both musically and lyrically, and Mr. Astaire is a great respecter of their melody and of the phrasing and content of lyrics."

Granz being the jazz fan he always was, he made certain that

Mr. Astaire's accompaniment was the best available. And Granz being Granz, he couldn't resist tossing an extra bouquet to the only musician on the date who was one of his two clients (the other being Ella Fitzgerald): "Though Mr. Astaire in his own comments mentions them [the other musicians], I should like to pay special tribute to Oscar Peterson, the great Canadian pianist. His backing of Mr. Astaire was always in perfect taste and his solos were a delight."

Astaire himself said, "Luckily for the spirit and design of this venture, I had the perfect group of fellows to work with. They are Flip Phillips on tenor saxophone, Charlie Shavers, trumpet, Oscar Peterson on piano, Barney Kessel, guitar, Ray Brown, bass and Alvin Stoller on drums."

Indeed, among the highlights of *The Astaire Story* are three ad lib dances—two medium and one slow—that feature Astaire simply dancing and talking, accompanied only by the rhythm section, with Oscar featured heavily.

Commented Whitney Balliett, "The notion of recording Astaire with jazz musicians was a good one, and it is a pleasure to hear him unfettered by visual images and a large orchestra."

The musicians were, of course, perfectly suited to this kind of session. (Brown and Kessel became Peterson's bass player and guitarist, respectively, in an early Oscar Peterson Trio.)

Granz, in an inspired move, had Astaire "sit out" a few numbers, so that the aforementioned musicians could play three instrumentals written by Oscar: "The Astaire Blues," "Jam Session for a Dancer" and "The Second Astaire Blues." And they did indeed swing mightily.

Granz arranged to have the recording session photographed by Gjon Mili, the same photographer he had boldly turned into a cinematographer for *Jammin' the Blues*.

*   *   *

Granz's deep commitment to ending discrimination was never questioned. "Jazz is America's own," he said. "It is played and listened to by all peoples—in harmony together. Pigmentation differences have no place . . . as in genuine democracy, only performance counts."

This statement is quoted in the Geoffrey C. Ward book *Jazz: A History of America's Music*, which accompanied the mammoth Ken Burns TV series of the same name.

Wherever Granz's people were booked to appear, if airlines, hotels or restaurants dared to try any sort of discrimination, Granz would immediately cancel. Drummer Stan Levey recalled: "He would just check everybody into the Hilton Hotel. We'd all show up in the lobby and [there would be] a lot of, you know, throat clearing, and he'd say, 'This is our group. Let's have our rooms.' He was terrific. Norman really broke a lot of barriers. We just showed up: 'Here we are.' "

Jazz critic Nat Hentoff once referred to Granz as "the most influential non-musician on the jazz scene."

Another writer mentioned his "patrician manners and a card-shark's savvy." The same writer said of Granz: "His tolerance for the unintelligent, the half-baked, the incomplete, or the second-rate seems to be next to zero. He is, at least when it comes to jazz, a snob."

Inevitably, Granz formed his own record companies—one after another. There was (briefly) a "Norgran" label, then "Clef," which became "Verve" and eventually "Pablo," which he admitted choosing because of his admiration for artist Pablo Picasso. (Referring to his stewardship of Pablo Records, he told me, in 1975, "Of course, I do what I want. What the hell—it's my money.")

In time, Granz became a close friend of Picasso. "I ran my film [*Jammin' the Blues*] for Pablo and he really dug it," Granz told Leonard Feather. Asked how many Picasso paintings he owned, he said: "A lot. My entire collection of paintings is worth better than two million. Some are in London, some in Geneva, and many of them I have loaned out to musicians."

The Granz social conscience never dimmed. Many years later,

John McDonough wrote a series about him for *Down Beat*, in which he included the following tribute:

> Granz may or may not have helped civilize the American jazz audience. But he certainly helped integrate it. When JATP became a big earner, he threw its weight around freely in the cause of social justice, which remained his first after-profit goal. Promoters who wanted Granz and the money he could bring had to accept his iron-clad clauses against discrimination at the door. JATP played the first mixed dance in Kansas City and the first mixed concert in Charleston, South Carolina. A sold-out performance in New Orleans was canceled over Jim Crow seating policies. Granz hit a restaurant in Jackson, Michigan, with a lawsuit when it refused to seat him, (singer) Helen Humes and a party of his musicians. No institution was too far removed to get a scolding. In 1947, Spencer's Department Store in Dayton, Ohio, invited Granz to an autographing party in its record department. When he showed up accompanied by several black musicians from the tour the store disapproved. Granz not only refused to do the autographing by himself, he yanked his entire record inventory from the store and ordered his distributor to quit selling his albums to its buyers.

Granz was never shy about revealing his successes. In 1960, he sold Verve Records to MGM for $2,750,000. He also freely admitted that he made a lot of money out of JATP. And why not? He was, after all, an entrepreneur, a businessman. But he had the distinct advantage of being able to make big money by doing something he loved to do. "After thirty-five years in the business," he told John McDonough, "I'm still happiest in the studio."

But it should also be said in his defense that he provided a lot of work—work that paid well—for a lot of musicians, who might well otherwise have starved. It was, after all, in the mid-Fifties when Granz was touring JATP and making records that rock and roll emerged to attract a new generation of young people who had not yet experienced the pleasures of jazz. Granz went doggedly on with his jazz programs.

In his book *The Pleasures of Jazz*, Leonard Feather quoted Norman Granz: "Whenever there's any writing about jazz nowadays, people dismiss me as though I were a retired man. Hell, right now, I'm promoting more jazz concerts than anyone else in the world, including George Wein."

The musicians in the Granz stable, those he employed again and again in concerts, tours and recordings, had a healthy respect for the impresario. Trumpeter Roy Eldridge, a veteran of numerous Granz events, said: "They should make a statue to that cat, and there's no one else in the business end of this business I would say that about."

Eldridge and Granz seemed to have formed a mutual admiration society. Once, during a European tour, a reporter asked Granz which musician most typified jazz for him. Oscar Peterson, who was present, urged Granz to name Art Tatum, his own idol. But Granz disagreed. "No," he said, "it's Roy Eldridge who embodies what jazz is all about. He's a musician for whom it's far more important to dare, to try to achieve a particular peak—even if he falls on his ass in the attempt—than it is to play it safe. That's what jazz is all about."

There's a good example of that in a 1974 album that Roy made with Oscar Peterson in Los Angeles—just the two of them: Roy playing both open and muted trumpet, Oscar playing piano and organ. Roy plays open horn on "She's Funny That Way," with Oscar on organ. It's done in slow, ballad fashion. Roy is excellent throughout, but at the finish, he goes for a high note—higher than he had to—and overshoots it by a bit. It's just a minor mistake in an otherwise flawless performance, but you can't help but admire his fearlessness, his refusal to play it safe.

Despite the amazing success of his Jazz At The Philharmonic

tours, in 1957 Granz abruptly abandoned the North American concert scene. Two years later, he took up residence in Switzerland, and was rarely seen on this continent after that for more than a few days, usually on business involving Oscar Peterson and Ella Fitzgerald, the only two artists he ever managed. ("I can usually do that by phone," he added.)

Working from his home in Geneva or from his apartments in London and Paris, he continued to tour JATP in Europe, but later moved beyond that to promoting appearances in England and Europe by Duke Ellington, Count Basie, Ray Charles and Dave Brubeck. He returned to the United States in 1967 for a short tour with Benny Carter, Coleman Hawkins and some of his old standbys, including Peterson and Fitzgerald. When the tour ended, Granz told Leonard Feather: "Never again. I made a profit but it's too much aggravation. It's no fun any more, at least not in the States."

By way of further explanation, he added: "The success of our concerts was due to the inter-mixing of musicians with contrasting ideas and styles, but the younger cats coming up don't like to jam informally. They all want to be leaders. That's all right for them, but it's contrary to the spirit of Jazz At The Philharmonic. They talk about playing 'free jazz,' but what they play actually has a lot less freedom than the music of Jazz At The Philharmonic."

As late as 1980, Granz still felt jazz was not getting the attention it deserved: "I really dispute the idea that North America, the birthplace of jazz, is so supportive of this music. How many radio stations are there around and how many play jazz? Very few."

Oscar has his own story to tell about starting out with JATP, as he recounted to Don Freeman of *Down Beat*: "I was a rookie, a kid of twenty-three. I was like Mickey Mantle starting with the Yankees. I had heard about these big names for years and now I was playing with them. In the first place, I didn't know how they'd take me—a kid from Canada with the big buildup. I knew I could play a little but this was the big leagues.

"To tell the truth, I wasn't relaxed very much. I couldn't, not being sure of myself, or of how the musicians and the public would accept my work. The first tour was pretty rough for just that reason.

"And now it's altogether different. I have confidence in myself because everybody else has confidence in me. What's more, I'm playing a lot better, too. I know where I stand."

It was in that same period, the Fifties, that Granz recorded Art Tatum on his Pablo label. Granz felt that Tatum was woefully unappreciated. He featured Tatum both as a solo pianist (recording 121 numbers that were subsequently issued) and in eight different group settings with other top artists like Benny Carter, Roy Eldridge, Ben Webster, Harry "Sweets" Edison, Lionel Hampton, Buddy DeFranco and Buddy Rich. This was in 1953. Tatum died in 1956, at the age of forty-six. It wasn't until 1974 that Granz managed to re-acquire (after years of legal wrangling) and reissue the Tatum sessions—all seventeen of the albums.

Over the years, Norman Granz hired, recorded and featured far more jazz musicians than any other jazz impresario. "Sometimes I'd read a critic who'd say I over-recorded artists," Granz commented some years later. "But if you took away all the albums I did with Billie, Parker, Lester, Art Tatum, Ben Webster and even Ella in the Fifties, many artists would have gone totally unrecorded and most wouldn't have had more than a couple of records. For all the people who say I over-recorded artists, my most profound regret is that I may not have recorded them enough. Now it's too late in many cases."

But in all his years in the music business, he managed personally only two artists: Ella Fitzgerald and Oscar Peterson.

Granz was Ella's manager from 1954, although it took protracted negotiations with Decca (to whom she was under an exclusive recording contract) to get her for his JATP label. Early in 1956, Decca wanted to issue the soundtrack of *The Benny Goodman Story*, but Benny's band then included several musicians who were under contract to Norman Granz.

"Now I had Decca over a barrel," Granz recalled. "They asked me what I wanted. I said I wanted Ella's contract, and they said okay."

Ella stayed with Granz until her death in 1996.

He was Oscar's manager from 1949 to 1988. But they were more than manager and client. They became (and remained) close friends. It was for him that one of Oscar's sons was named Norman.

With his usual candor, Granz once admitted: "None of those artists needed me. I needed them. But that relationship with Oscar was kind of special. It blossomed when we played Europe, because that was a totally foreign area to Oscar."

Peterson willingly expresses his admiration for Granz: "Perhaps the real star of Jazz At The Philharmonic was Norman. He took jazz to heights that weren't imagined a few years before. We traveled around the world and what Norman wanted—in fact, all of us wanted—was some respectability for jazz. We wanted to take it out of the back alleys and give it some dignity as an art form."

(This was somewhat reminiscent of Artie Shaw's comment, years before, when he wanted to take his band into concert halls to "make a lady of jazz.")

Oscar further comments: "It was almost impossible to play in the South because of the pressure, the threats. Norman Granz decided to use Jazz At The Philharmonic as a wedge into segregation in hotels, restaurants, concert halls."

When I last spoke to Oscar, he still had nothing but praise for Granz. The impresario was after Oscar to quit smoking for years. He kept nagging Peterson, emphasizing that he should quit if he wanted to have some "pleasant years" in the future. Said Oscar: "He finally had it written into our contract: no smoking."

Norman Granz spent the last years of his life living in Geneva, Switzerland, and occasionally visiting London. He was more than comfortable financially, but not in health. After suffering from cancer for some years, he died in November 2001.

How Norman Granz met Oscar Peterson is a story full of twists and turns and even a touch of movie melodrama—certainly worth another whole chapter. Coming right up.

8

THE "DISCOVERY" OF OSCAR

Leonard Feather almost officially discovered Oscar Peterson. One night, early in 1949, he received a phone call from an excited Dizzy Gillespie, who was then appearing in Montreal. "Leonard," said Dizzy, "there's a pianist up here who's just too much. You've never heard anything like it. We gotta put him in the concert."

To his regret, Feather has acknowledged, he failed to follow Dizzy's tip.

It's a little startling to realize that more than half a century has slipped by since Oscar Peterson landed smack in the middle of the jazz world's spotlight. It is equally remarkable to reflect that during those fifty-plus years, he has rarely been out of that spotlight. There is no Canadian performing artist whose name is more widely known—around the world—than Oscar's.

The story of how Peterson landed in that spotlight is certainly worth recalling—even though there is some doubt as to its absolute authenticity. Norman Granz is actually credited with "discovering" Oscar. In the summer of 1949, Granz was taking a taxi to Montreal's Dorval airport. The taxi's radio was on and Granz was attracted to the music being played by a pianist. He thought it was a recording, but the taxi driver told him the music was a live broadcast coming from the Alberta Lounge in Montreal. Granz told the cab driver to forget the airport and head to the lounge.

Oscar's version is that Granz, after listening to him play at the Alberta Lounge, asked him, "Why do you make those terrible boogie-woogie records? That's not you. You don't play like that." Oscar replied that he played what he was asked to play. (Peterson soon thereafter dropped boogie-woogie.)

Another bit of advice that Granz gave Peterson was this: "Don't prostitute yourself." And Peterson never has. He never, for example, crossed over into such trends as disco or pop. Indeed, he has said that the jazz guitarist George Benson "prostituted his original talent." It's not that Peterson hates disco as a musical form, but he feels some musicians stray too far from their roots.

"I don't mind someone being successful in that way," he said of Benson, "but don't take yourself too seriously. If you want to hear me, come and hear me. But you won't see me going through the act with the white suit and the bare chest. I'm there to play."

However, this famous night at the Alberta Lounge was not, in fact, the first time the two had met, as I learned from Oscar later. They had met the year before, at the Café St. Michel in Montreal, the night of a JATP concert. When Oscar arrived at the café, Granz was having an unpleasant conversation with the doorman, who insisted Granz had to pay to get in. Granz felt he shouldn't pay, because all his JATP musicians were in there jamming. Recognizing Granz, Oscar told the doorman to let Granz in and, if necessary, he, Oscar, would pay the cover. Oscar finally persuaded the doorman to let Granz in. He then introduced himself to Granz, who was still angry over his encounter with the doorman. But Oscar didn't play that night.

Granz invited Oscar to come to New York to play at the Carnegie Hall concert on September 18, 1949, that would launch that season's concert schedule. Oscar had some misgivings about this bold leap. He was doing well in his native Montreal, where he had built up a considerable reputation. But Granz convinced him to take a shot at a wider audience and larger venue.

When Oscar got to New York that September, there was a glitch: he didn't belong to New York Local 802 of the American Federation of Musicians, so he could not legally be advertised or presented at a union concert. Granz hit on a solution: he arranged for Peterson to be in the audience, as if by coincidence, for the first half of the concert. Then he would go backstage and, after the intermission, Granz would announce that he had "spotted" Oscar in the audience and invited him to play in the second half.

"His performance caused a sensation that signaled the start of a major career," enthused Helen McNamara, who profiled Oscar in the *Encyclopedia of Music in Canada*. "Few jazz musicians would be recorded more extensively; few if any Canadian musicians would enjoy as comparably high an international profile."

It's a lovely overnight-stardom story and essentially a true one. But more fascinating still is Oscar's own recollection of that important night at Carnegie Hall, which he related to me in a conversation we had a few years later.

During the first half of that concert, Oscar, even then a hefty young man, was seated in a front-row seat, next to an equally large young black woman, who was enjoying the concert tremendously. In those days, JATP fans were often as demonstrative as rock fans are now; they shouted and applauded the sometimes showy playing of such soloists as Flip Phillips and Illinois Jacquet, who loved to get the crowd worked up.

The young woman's pleasure was apparently marred somewhat by the presence of the placid young man seated next to her. She clapped and shouted her approval of every solo, then turned to her neighbor, who showed no outward indication of excitement.

"Aren't you enjoying this?" she demanded of him at one point.

"It's fine," said Peterson. Like most musicians, he wasn't given to noisy expressions of approval, the way some fans were, but he didn't go to the trouble to explain this to her.

At the intermission, Peterson drifted backstage, as planned, and waited in the wings—a little nervous, he later recalled—to be introduced in the second half of the show. When Granz made his announcement about the exciting young Canadian pianist who happened to be in the audience and had been persuaded to play, Peterson walked out, bowed in response to the polite applause, and sat down at the keyboard.

Without his willing it, his eyes went to the front row, where the excitable large young woman was executing a series of double-takes. She looked at the young man seated at the piano, looked at the empty seat next to her and realized the man on the stage was the "square" who had been sitting next to her during the first half.

"Then," Oscar smiled as he recalled the moment, "she settled back, folded her arms and looked up at me, as if to say, 'Okay, smart ass, go ahead and try to make me enjoy it.'"

And he certainly did just that. In the words of Mike Levin, who reviewed that concert for *Down Beat*, Oscar Peterson "stopped the Norman Granz Jazz at the Philharmonic concert dead cold in its tracks":

> Balancing a bulky body at the piano much in the fashion of Earl Hines, Peterson displayed a flashy right hand, a load of bop and [George] Shearing-styled ideas, as well as a good sense of harmonic development. And in addition, he scared some of the local modern minions by playing bop ideas single finger in his *left* hand, which is distinctly not the common practice. Further than this, Peterson impressed musicians here by not only having good ideas and making them, but giving them a rhythmic punch and drive which has been all too lacking in too many of the younger pianists. Whereas some of the bop stars conceive good ideas but sweat to make them, Peterson rips them off with an excess of power which leaves no doubt about his technical excess [sic] in reserve.

He never did learn the identity of the young woman, but he still remembers her amazement at seeing him on stage, let alone hearing him play.

Remarkably, Oscar still remembers what tunes he played that first night in Carnegie Hall: "I Only Have Eyes for You" and "Tenderly." The latter tune, especially, was such a hit that for many years thereafter, Oscar's fans always requested it.

Not long after the Carnegie Hall concert, I wrote a piece for *The Globe and Mail*, where I was working. The headline (which I didn't write, because reporters never write their own headlines) read "Oscar Peterson Expert at Piano":

> Down in New York, they still remember Oscar Peterson as the Canadian pianist who stole the show from all the big-timers at a Carnegie Hall session a few months ago.
>
> Oscar, the big, beefy lad with such a tremendous following in Montreal, is currently making the Casino [Theatre] customers do nip-ups every time he runs his large hands over the keyboard. . . .
>
> Peterson's New York excursion last September made history, at least in jazz circles. The concert was one of Norman Granz's Jazz At The Philharmonic affairs. Among the all-stars on the program were Lester Young, Roy Eldridge and Coleman Hawkins.
>
> Granz, the master of ceremonies, then announced that Oscar was in the audience and might be prevailed upon to play. He did and the rafters shook from the cheers and applause. . . .
>
> Now Peterson is making the rounds again, playing night clubs and theatres, making a few records and still trying— as he has been for some time—to make enough of a success of his talent in Canada so that he won't have to move to the United States.
>
> Some day he may become part of Canada's biggest

export to the U.S., but, for the time being at least, he is a Canadian jazz musician playing in Canada.

There's another small fact about Oscar's debut at Carnegie Hall that's worth mentioning. Norman Granz wanted Oscar to play solo, but Oscar was not anxious to do so. Buddy Rich, the brilliant and energetic drummer, had appeared earlier and, as usual, had played so hard he was literally exhausted by the time he left the stage. Granz asked Buddy if he would come back out to play with Oscar, but Rich was so tired he begged off. At that point Granz decided he wanted Oscar to play alone. "I don't want anything to distract from your playing," he told Oscar. But Peterson was still uneasy, so Granz finally relented, saying, "Okay, you can have Ray Brown." And that was how Oscar made his New York debut, assisted by Ray Brown, playing "Tenderly."

Many years later, Oscar looked back on his exciting debut with Jazz At The Philharmonic, when he won the crowd over with "Tenderly": "By the time it was over, you know, the tune was over, they were screaming, and it was then I got the signal, you know, I guess you can stay on stage. It was a dream come true. More than a dream, a fantasy—to be suddenly thrown in with them."

Despite that auspicious Carnegie Hall debut, Oscar did not immediately become a Big Star. Granz felt it would be better for Oscar to return to Montreal and take stock. In fact, Granz and Oscar planned the pianist's career: "the kind of sober strategy," noted English critic Richard Palmer, "that characterizes many classical virtuosi's preparation but is very rare in the jazz world."

"Let's just cool it," advised Granz, "and see what the reaction really is, and then plan it from there. I don't want you coming in and being just another saloon pianist."

Both Oscar and Ella made many tours with JATP during the Fifties and Sixties. Oscar made the annual trips to Europe and later expanded his own touring to include Japan, Australia, South America and Mexico.

Oscar always expressed tremendous respect for Norman Granz. To the charge that was leveled at JATP—namely, that it encouraged exhibitionism over musicianship—Oscar pointed out that Granz couldn't be blamed for such exhibitionism. "He does not endorse it, believe me," Oscar has said. "But Norman can't play the instrument. All he can do is advise and criticize. He has helped many jazz musicians. My travels with his group certainly have broadened me. The stability has given me a firm base, the kind that's so important for all musicians if they want to develop into worthwhile human beings.

"I think it's so important for musicians to have that firm base, a foundation. A family is the greatest thing of all. . . . You can trace all kinds of delinquency—juvenile and the kind we come across—in lack of firm foundation. I think a good home life is the greatest asset anyone can have. The trouble with most young musicians these days is that they have no real roots. They leave home for New York and they get detoured from a normal life. They're like a hanging string and they can wind up on either side of the line. But if they have faith in something in addition to their music, they'll probably turn out all right."

Oscar felt that young musicians should be encouraged and helped, he told George Simon. In that connection, at some time in the future he planned to open a hi-fi recording studio and allow young musicians to use it free of charge while they worked out new musical ideas.

On Norman Granz and JATP, Ella Fitzgerald's memories were pleasant indeed: "It was just a happy thing. There's no 'You're better than I am' or 'I'm better than you.' We all go out together to make the show and I think that's why it's been so successful with the Jazz At The Philharmonic tours, because we're all out for each other."

Peterson was equally enthusiastic about his JATP experiences: "You can't possibly play with Jazz At The Philharmonic without learning something," he said during an interview in 1992. "Roy Eldridge, Dizzy, Ella and the gang taught me many things—not only about playing music but about living life. I also learned what a privilege it was to play with Ella Fitzgerald."

It was probably inevitable that in time Oscar Peterson would become the closing act of the Jazz At The Philharmonic concerts. As Herb Ellis commented, "On Jazz At The Philharmonic, Oscar was the 'closer.' He played last, because he could generate more heat than anybody, and he was the right closer. You can't top that."

Oscar has always had his serious side. One aspect of that side is his loyalty to and affection for the musicians he has worked with over the years—Ray Brown and Herb Ellis, of course, but also Phil Nimmons, with whom Oscar (and Ray Brown and Ed Thigpen) founded the Advanced School of Contemporary Music, and other jazzmen he has recorded or worked with, including Count Basie, Dizzy Gillespie, Lester Young and Roy Eldridge—all of them now gone. "I miss them all," said Oscar. He was especially fond of Count Basie, with whom he recorded and appeared in concert many times.

If there is one possession that Oscar especially prizes it is a watch that Norman Granz had given to Count Basie sometime in the 1950s. A few months after Basie died in 1984, his possessions were auctioned off in New York. Norman Granz bought a gold bracelet that Ella Fitzgerald had given to Basie some thirty years before. He gave it to Ella. And he also bought (for $1,500) the watch he himself had given to Count Basie. Granz then gave the Basie watch to Oscar. "He's the logical one to give it to," said Granz. "Basie loved him." Oscar later told Gene Lees: "Having Basie's watch means a lot to me."

9

"AFTER ME . . ."

In the late 1930s, a talented young pianist (reportedly Hank Jones) was listening to a piano recording on the radio. "They're trying to tell me that's one man playing. But I don't buy that," he said. "There's three guys playing on that record."

He was wrong, but perhaps his mistake was understandable: he was listening to a recording by Art Tatum.

Trumpeter Rex Stewart, who was slated to succeed Louis Armstrong in the famous Fletcher Henderson orchestra in 1925, heard Art Tatum play the piano. This was such an unnerving experience for him that, as Stewart said in his book *Jazz Masters of the Thirties*, he "toyed with the idea of giving up the horn and going back to school."

Tatum was an acknowledged genius of the piano, and an altogether remarkable man. Born almost blind in one eye, he was mugged as a teenager and lost completely the use of the other eye. As often happens, the loss of sight sharpened his other senses—particularly his hearing and also his memory—for sports statistics, sounds and card playing. He played bridge, sometimes with experts. When his hand was dealt, he would hold his cards up about an inch from his "good" eye, adjust the cards into suits and memorize them; he never had to look at his hand again. He could recall every card that was played, when and by whom. Then he would play his own cards masterfully.

It was part of his impish humor that he also liked to show off his infallible hearing. When he was working in the 52nd Street jazz clubs in New York, he would go, during intermission and guided by a friend, into Hansen's drug store, a nearby musicians' hangout. When there were enough people around, seated at the bar, he would ask people around him to drop some coins on the marble top of the bar. Then he would identify them by sound: "That's a quarter, that's a nickel, that's a dime," and so on. And he was invariably right.

In time, it was Oscar Peterson's turn to be fooled—and intimidated—by Tatum. At the time when Peterson was being hailed as a young genius, his father brought home an Art Tatum recording. The two listened and then the elder Peterson asked: "What do you think?" Oscar replied: "They're great. Who are those two guys?"

Grover Sales, in his book *Jazz—America's Classical Music*, published in 1992, quoted Oscar Peterson describing his reaction to first hearing Tatum: "When I was a teenager, I was feeling very smug about my prowess at the piano, very sure of myself, when my father laid my first Art Tatum records on me. I slid into a funk and didn't touch the piano for three months—I felt it was useless to practise."

(In other interviews, the life span of that "funk" varied as Oscar told the story. But the message remained essentially the same: Oscar was seriously intimidated by Tatum's playing.)

But when Oscar told his father that he wanted to quit high school to pursue a music career, he knew that "According to Dad's expectations, Art Tatum was the man I would have to measure up to."

In the early 1980s, author/critic Len Lyons asked Oscar about his first brush with Tatum. Oscar replied, "When I was getting into the jazz thing—or thought I was—as a kid, my father thought I was a little heavy about my capabilities, so he played me Art's recording of 'Tiger Rag.' First of all, I swore it was two people playing. When I finally admitted to myself that it was one man, I gave up the piano for a month. I figured it was hopeless to practise. My mother and friends of mine persuaded me to get back to it, but I've had the greatest respect for Art from then on."

Even as far back as 1945, Oscar had nothing but praise for Tatum: "For me, Art is not only the greatest jazz pianist but he's also the greatest instrumentalist on *any* instrument. He's a creator. He knows what he's doing and he believes in himself and his music. You've seen him and I'm sure you've noticed what an air of confidence he has about him. It's warranted, every bit of it."

In the early Fifties, he was playing with the trio in Washington, DC, at a club called Louis and Alex's, Oscar recalled. "I used to kid Ray [Brown] about [bassist] Oscar Pettiford. We'd be playing and I'd say, 'Watch it now, Oscar Pettiford's out there!' He'd say, 'Hell with him. I'm going to stomp him.' He'd do the same to me about Art Tatum because we both had tremendous love and respect for these men. On the third night of the gig we were playing 'Airmail Special' and Ray said, 'Watch it, Art's out there.' 'Hell with him,' I said. 'He's got to contend with me.' See, he'd pulled that about a dozen times, and I would always go into my heavy routine. 'No, this time he's *really* out there,' Ray insisted. 'Look over at the bar.' There he was. I closed up the tune immediately and took it out. The set was over. I froze! Ray took me over to meet him, and I still remember what Art said: 'Brown, you brought me one of those sleepers, huh?' He told us to come by this after-hours joint and he'd see what he could do with me. I was totally frightened of this man and his tremendous talent. It's like a lion; you're scared to death, but it's such a beautiful animal, you want to come up close and hear it roar."

They went to the after-hours club and Tatum asked him to play, but Oscar was too intimidated.

"So Art told me this story about a guy he knew down in New Orleans. All he knew how to play was one chorus of the blues, and if you asked him to play some more, he'd repeat that same chorus over again. Art said he'd give anything to be able to play that chorus of the blues the way that old man played it. The message was clear. Everyone had something to say. Well, I got up to the piano and played what I'd call two of the neatest choruses of 'Tea For Two' you've ever heard. That was all I could do. Then Art played and it fractured me. I had nightmares of keyboards that night."

Tatum and Peterson became good friends, but Oscar remembered that he had "this phobia about him, and it lasted a long time. I simply couldn't play when he was in the room. One day, he took me aside and said, 'You can't afford this. You have too much going for you. If you have to hate me when I walk into the room, I don't care. I want you to play.'

"I don't know how it happened exactly, but one night at the Old Tiffany in Los Angeles, I was into a good set when I heard Art's voice from the audience saying, 'Lighten up, Oscar Peterson.' I knew it was Art, but it didn't bother me. I got deeper into the music instead, and I knew I was over it. Both Art and my father died within a week of each other, and I realized in one week I lost two of the best friends I had. That's been the Art Tatum thing with me."

In James Lester's biography of Tatum, *Too Marvelous For Words*, published in 1994, Red Norvo tells a lovely Tatum-Peterson story: "A bunch of guys, piano players, were playing, see, and Oscar Peterson was there, and they got him to play, too. So Art came in, very quietly, with somebody, and he was sitting at the bar drinking, see. So some of the guys saw Art, and they said, 'Art, you gotta play!' And he'd listened to these three or four piano players play, see, so he didn't want to play. So finally, he sat down and started to play, and he played, I don't know, just zooom, cut the whole thing—this was right after Oscar played—and then he went into 'Little Man, You've Had a Busy Day.'"

Bassists as accomplished as Red Callender and Ray Brown could not stay with Tatum once he started throwing in those chromatic progressions and lightning changes of key, according to Peterson biographer Richard Palmer.

Oscar and André Previn once joked about it.

Peterson: "Can you imagine being in a group with Art Tatum?"

Previn: "No. It's difficult for me to imagine being in a *room* with Art Tatum."

By 1980, of course, Peterson felt a lot more self-confident. As he told an interviewer that year, "I think my playing's a lot more mature now. I find that what I want to do with my playing is a lot more specific. Maybe, too, it's more pensive. A lot of that old heat, that I-must-do-it-all-now feeling has been replaced. Maybe it's more melancholy."

His playing, after all the adulation it brought him, was soon criticized for being too facile, too technical. It wasn't for nothing, wrote Peter Goddard in *The Toronto Star*, "he was called Art Tatum's heir. He obviously had Tatum's facility, his mind-bending virtuosity, and had swallowed it whole. But in recent years, it has taken on a more magisterial tone. It has grown grander. The tempi are slower. The rhythms strut boldly, not so sassily."

Frank Conroy, writing in *Quarter Notes* in 1981, said it was easy to see why Tatum thought of Peterson as his heir: "Alone of his generation, Peterson had a technique comparable to Tatum's. He could play very fast, with authority and in all jazz styles. He understood Fats Waller as well as he did the more modern players. His speed did not preclude, as speed almost always does, a certain percussive attack that allows for hard-swinging music. He played the whole piano, accepting the challenge of its range; he knew harmony, counterpoint, and theory, and in all respects seemed up to the task of heir apparent. If there was a certain shallowness to his improvisations, that was no more than the fault of a young player, and it could be assumed he would grow out of it. The music itself would lead him out."

Even though Tatum died almost half a century ago (in 1956), it seems impossible for journalists/critics to write of Peterson without mentioning Tatum. As recently as April 2000, Geoff Chapman, *The Toronto Star* jazz critic, covered Oscar's premiere performance of the *Trail of Dreams Suite* at Roy Thomson Hall, closing his article with this bit: "There were hints of Art Tatum in his quicksilver runs and he showed how to move from lullaby to locomotive in milliseconds when the delicate 'Evening Sun' was shunted suddenly into the meaty 'Backyard Blues.' "

It was Gene Lees who drew another comparison between Peterson and Tatum: "Consider the Tatum influence. Oscar plays the runs as fast as Tatum did. And he plays them with more power, more muscle and above all, with more swing. Oscar's dynamic sense is greater than Tatum's. I don't say these things lightly; before I sat down to write these words, I made a careful comparison. I alternated this album on my turntable with one that I consider to be among Tatum's best. Despite the musical wonder of Tatum's playing, his work, for me, lacked the emotional depth and stylistic range that Oscar displays here."

For *Quarter Notes*, Frank Conroy assessed the jazz scene and Tatum's place in it:

> Jazz was neater then, more clearly defined, and it was possible to have a king and appropriate to have a line of successors—the orb and the scepter passing in an orderly fashion while the revolutionaries of bop grumbled in the back of the cathedral, caps doffed. Tatum was indeed an aristocratic player, with virtues that were classical. Sophistication, wit, clarity and brilliance were always present in his music, as was emotion. For all of the flash, he was a particularly warm player who seemed driven to play out of emotional necessity, out of the need to share his feelings. ... In retrospect it is easy to see why Tatum thought of Peterson as his heir. Tatum must also have been flattered by the younger man's veneration of him.

Peterson himself was unstinting in his respect for Tatum. As he told Tim Perlich of *Now Magazine*, "Art Tatum made great strides . . . but unfortunately people didn't know much about what Tatum was doing then. People tried to pass him off the same way they tried to pass me off, saying he was just a technician. Art was a great player but his advancements were the harmonic sequencing and clusters he played on. The critics at the time didn't realize that, though."

Somebody once asked Norman Granz why he wanted another record company. This was in 1980, when he started the Pablo label, having already had Norgran and Verve.

"You ask me why I wanted another record company," Granz said with a shrug of disbelief. "Until Pablo came along, no one was recording Count Basie. Here was a national resource being ignored. Good Lord. When I had Verve, I had twenty-one albums by Art Tatum. The moment MGM bought Verve they deleted them all. They reasoned that no one would listen to Tatum anymore. They didn't reason that there was a new generation of twenty-year-olds out there, some of whom would want to listen to Tatum again."

Tatum was aware of Oscar Peterson's potential and evidently was not reluctant to encourage the younger pianist. At the end of his short life (he had just turned forty-six when he died), Tatum reportedly said to Peterson: "After me, it'll be you."

10

MUSIC AND FUN

A sure way to get a quick rise from Oscar Peterson is to refer to "serious music" as a handy way of distinguishing classical music from jazz. Oscar is quite "serious" about his music. "I always put that saying down; I don't know what that means," he has said.

But that he is serious about his music doesn't mean he is without a sense of humor—nor does that apply to numerous talented musicians with whom he has worked over the years.

In 1956 to 1958, when I was host and head writer of a CBC talk-variety television show called "The Barris Beat," we arranged to have Oscar Peterson as a guest on one show. As it happened, that week coincided with the annual Academy Awards presentations, also known as "Oscar night." I introduced Peterson by making reference to the upcoming awards, then said that on this night we had "our own Oscar."

Peterson made his entrance standing on a dolly that was wheeled in, his arms held across his chest in the manner of the famous Oscar statuette. He loved the gag.

Another time, we were doing a show at the time of Yom Kippur, the most sacred Jewish holy day. Oscar Peterson was again our guest. I introduced him, and he played the first of his two scheduled tunes. Then, as the script called for, I was to walk over to the grand piano where Oscar was seated and have an informal chat with him before he played again. I don't recall why, but there happened to be a trayful of sandwiches on the studio floor near where I was standing. So I picked up one of the sandwiches (which was cut in half, diagonally) and carried it with me to the piano. I offered Oscar half the sandwich, which he accepted. Then we did our chat, each munching away. It was simply a relaxed, fun way to do our exchange.

The following week I received an irate letter from a woman who said I should be ashamed of myself—a "nice Jewish boy like you"—eating a sandwich on television on Yom Kippur, when all good Jews were supposed to be fasting. I then had the ticklish job of writing to the woman and explaining to her that (a) I meant no offence to her or any other TV viewers, and (b) I was not (am not) Jewish. (Oscar, incidentally, got away without a scolding.)

Another time (some two decades later), I was hosting a CBC-TV show called "Barris and Company." This, again, was a talk/variety series with prominent guest stars—of whom Oscar Peterson was one. On this occasion, we had an excellent big band led by the brilliant trumpeter/flugelhorn player Guido Basso. Guido, like Oscar, was born and raised in Montreal, of Italian immigrant parents. "I spoke three languages," Guido once told me, "Italian at home, French in school and English on the street."

In the band, among other fine musicians, was the late trombonist Teddy Roderman, who happened to be Jewish. When I introduced Oscar as our guest star, he came out from the wings wearing a turtleneck shirt under a Nehru-type jacket. Hanging around his neck was a gaudy gold-colored chain, from which dangled a large plastic bagel. After he played his first tune, I walked over to the piano for the *de rigueur* chat with the distinguished guest.

I couldn't resist asking him about the plastic bagel hanging around his neck.

"Well," said Peterson, "this is for Teddy Roderman. He invited me to his home for dinner the other night. And he served me watermelon."

Oscar also enjoys throwing his sidemen off balance. Ray Brown, his long-time bassist recalled: "Oscar will come to work and say, 'I feel awful. I sure don't feel like working tonight.' And then, the first tune, he'll kick off a tempo so fast it'll nearly kill you."

Brown played in the Oscar Peterson Trio for some fifteen years, and for six of those years (plus periodic reunions), Herb Ellis was the guitarist. Over the years I've had opportunities to talk with Herb, and he has only fond memories of Oscar: "Looking back, it was just dynamite for me, because being with Oscar Peterson was exactly what I wanted to do, it was tremendous. Oscar Peterson and Ray Brown—I considered them then, and I consider them now, the two best on their particular instruments. It was what I always dreamed of."

Speaking of Oscar, Ellis said: "I think the depth he plays with, the emotion and energy combined—they grab you. . . . On Jazz At The Philharmonic, he was the closer. He played last, because he could generate more heat than anybody, and he was the right closer. You can't top that. When you walked on stage with Oscar, he expected the best from you, which is only fair and right."

It was at about that time that Herb Ellis dropped a line on me that I still cherish. He was appearing in Toronto, at the Royal York Hotel's Black Knight Room, and he played a lot of standards—familiar popular tunes by the likes of George and Ira Gershwin, Jerome Kern, Cole Porter and Richard Rodgers. After finishing a Kern tune, he said: "You may have noticed, I play a lot of old things by Kern and Gershwin. I don't know; to me a Burt Bacharach tune sounds like a third alto part."

Oscar periodically gave up smoking. But whether he was smoking or not, he always carried a Dunhill lighter with him, courteously lighting cigarettes for others. During one engagement at Chicago's famed London House, where the tables were crowded up close to the bandstand, Peterson was cooking with an up-tempo number when a woman at a front table, very close to the piano, took out a cigarette and put it into her mouth. In a split second, Peterson's right hand came out of his pocket with the Dunhill in it. He continued to play with his left hand and, with the right, lit the woman's cigarette. Ed Thigpen started laughing so hard that he couldn't play, Ray Brown crumbled and the music quickly became chaotic. It was right after that when Dizzy Gillespie nicknamed Oscar "The Flame."

Oscar recalls practical jokes the trio pulled on each other, especially in the early days: "We were three kids growing up together, so there would be the occasional prank pulled.

"It usually ended up as a two-on-one situation because Ray and Herbie were roommates and no one in their right mind pulls anything on their roommate. So for me, it was more like self-defence.

"Between sets at a show once, they taped the inside edges of the piano keys with transparent tape—just two keys on one end and maybe three more farther down. When we came back on Herbie called for a tune that was particularly fast and tough, like 'Airmail Special.' I got right into the thing and hit those taped keys and, Oh, no! There was nothing there. After that I began de-tuning their guitar and bass strings during our breaks."

But the fun never stopped. In bassist Bill Crow's delightful book, *Jazz Anecdotes*, he cites a couple of stories:

> Oscar would secretly loosen one of Herb's guitar strings before a concert and then engage him in conversation right up to the moment they began playing. Or he'd pretend to be de-tuning the guitar without really changing anything, then would make Herb think he was out of tune by starting the next piece in a higher key than they usually played in.
>
> On a Jazz at the Philharmonic tour of Japan in 1953, Oscar played the same trick on Brown, loosening the G string of his bass several turns and then distracting him with conversation while Norman Granz announced the trio and Ella Fitzgerald. When they took the stage and began to play, Ray's G string was so loose it didn't make any notes at all, just thwacks and buzzes. Ella gave him a

dirty look as he cranked his string taut again, while Oscar and Norman laughed with delight.

Later, Ray went to a Japanese Pachinko parlor and pocketed a handful of the little steel balls that are used to play Japan's most popular game. During the next concert, as Oscar was on his way to the piano to accompany a Bill Harris [trombone] solo, Ray reached into the grand piano and scattered the Pachinko balls across the strings. Harris announced *But Beautiful* and nodded for Oscar to begin the introduction. Every note Oscar played sizzled and twanged as the Pachinko balls danced among the strings.

Oscar picked the balls out of the piano with one hand while playing with the other. As he retrieved each ball he tossed it at Ray's bass. Bill Harris suffered through his solo, rather poorly accompanied. On his way off stage, he whispered to Oscar, "One day. One day."

That day didn't come until the next year's tour at the Rome opera house. Harris overheard Peterson agreeing to Granz's request for him to sing a number. When the trio went onstage, Bill gathered up a huge tray full of glasses and empty bottles and put it on top of a ladder behind the back curtain. Oscar started to sing *Tenderly*. Bill waited for the title word, then pushed over the ladder and ran. The crash was gratifyingly dreadful. Because the stage was steeply raked, the noise seemed to go on forever; the bottles and glasses that hadn't broken kept rolling to the footlights at the front of the stage.

Harris had run upstairs so fast that he was able to rush down again, protesting, "Norman, what's going on here? Don't you realize there's an artist performing out there?"

Granz was so furious that no one dared to identify the culprit.

In 1973, I was involved in one gag pulled on Oscar. We were in Vancouver to tape a program featuring Oscar's trio and singer

Carmen McRae. The show's designer, the very resourceful Jack McAdam, came up with a lovely idea. One set involved a stage set about a foot or two higher than the studio floor. On the stage would be a baby grand piano for Oscar to play. Jack managed to borrow four lovely marble-like statuettes, standing a couple of feet high, of young women dressed in ancient Grecian gowns. He placed these at the corners of the little stage.

But I had an idea for a gag. I sent Jack out to find one of those little statues of a black jockey, in uniform, that one used to find on the lawns of wealthy white Southerners. He actually found one and brought it back to the studio. My idea was to put it on the little stage—at the left front corner—in place of one of the Grecian ladies. This would be just to surprise Oscar and, of course, would be removed after the gag.

When Oscar came into the studio for rehearsal that afternoon, the little black jockey was in place and the whole crew—cameramen, technicians, etc.—were standing around waiting to see how Oscar would react to the gag. He walked in, exchanged a few greetings as he walked through the studio toward the little stage, and then spotted the little black jockey.

Without a moment's hesitation, without even turning around, he said: "Barris, I'll get you for this!"

I have no idea how he knew it was my doing.

There's yet another Peterson story I like, and although it just may be apocryphal, I think I'll include it anyway. Seems Oscar was playing in a club one night (in Detroit, according to my informant) and found himself competing with an excessively loud and offensive drunk. Oscar got halfway through "Sweet Georgia Brown," then stood up and announced to the club manager, "It's either him or me." The drunk was hastily ejected from the club, whereupon Oscar sat down at the piano and continued to play "Sweet Georgia Brown"—exactly where he had left off.

Bill Harris was a great one for practical jokes. On one tour, he managed—without being spotted—to switch Dizzy Gillespie's and Roy Eldridge's trumpet mouthpieces. Any brass or wind mouthpiece is as much a part of the musician as his breath. His embouchure is, in a sense, married to that particular mouthpiece. What Harris did was roughly the equivalent (probably worse) of switching the scripts of two radio actors—both of them are lost. In the case of the switched mouthpieces, first Dizzy and then Roy tried to play with the switched mouthpiece and the results were anything but funny—except, of course, to Bill Harris. Dizzy couldn't get any kind of sound with Roy's mouthpiece. Totally baffled, he looked at the bell of his trumpet, but that supplied no answers.

Roy decided to come to the rescue. "I've got it, Birks," he said. "I'll take over." He raised his horn to his lips and blew. What came out was an awful squeak.

Roy quickly put the trumpet inside his coat and said: "That's not me."

It was Ray Brown who said, "If it isn't you, who is it?"

One time, Herb and Ray stumbled over what seemed like the ultimate gag to play on Oscar. They were all appearing in Los Angeles at the time, and one day Herb and Ray noticed a sign in a drug store advertising a hair dye that could create any color and could be washed out instantly. Brown is an African-American from Pittsburgh, Pennsylvania; Ellis is a red-headed Texan.

They bought some of the advertised dye and Ray became red-haired and Herb black-haired. Then the trick was to lure Peterson to their apartment to show off their new hair colors and see his reaction to this outlandish gag. They phoned Oscar and insisted he come over to discuss something important before going out to dinner with some friends.

When Herb answered the knock, Ray was sitting in a chair, reading a newspaper. Oscar looked right at them and, without batting an eye, said, "What did you want?"

Ray said, "Don't you get it?"

"Get what? You guys detained me from my dinner. I'll see you tomorrow." Then he left. Oscar maintained—for a full year—that he never noticed anything unusual during his brief visit.

"Now, that's control, isn't it?" commented Herb.

11

MUSIC AND RACISM

Oscar Peterson has been confronted by racism all his life. For example, when he played with the Johnny Holmes Orchestra, he was introduced by and referred to as "the boy at the piano." Oscar's own record company executives employed the same moniker.

Until the 1940s, the word "boy" was used in reference to black males—of any age. The implication was that even adults were not to be regarded as "men," but always as "boys."

In his book *Boogie, Pete & The Senator*, author and jazz critic Mark Miller recreates part of a radio interview Oscar did with an announcer identified only as "Mr. Davis."

Oscar was then eighteen years old. After he had played a number, the interview went like this:

> ANNOUNCER: "Oscar, that was terrific! Tell me, boy, how many hands you got?"
>
> PETERSON: "Just two, Mr. Davis, just two, but I like to make them work hard."
>
> ANNOUNCER: "You're not kidding! Tell me, Oscar, you're still going to school, aren't you?"
>
> PETERSON: "That's right. My folks would tan my hide if I missed a day."
>
> ANNOUNCER: "Your dad would have his hands full there!"

The interview continued in this vein, with a couple of more references to the "boy."

In the 1920s, *The Chicago Defender* made a point of listing, periodically, the names and locations of Canadian hotels and boarding houses where visiting black American musicians were welcomed. Even such internationally renowned jazz figures as Duke Ellington and Louis Armstrong could only stay at "black" hotels while touring—in both the United States and Canada.

As World War Two was drawing to a close, Oscar was in the first flush of fame. He was on his way home from shopping in downtown Montreal, his arms full of packages, when he saw a taxi pull over to the curb. As its male passenger was paying the driver, Oscar moved forward to grasp the still-open rear door. A woman rushed up and said she wanted that taxi. Before Oscar could even reply, the previous passenger turned on him, called him a "dirty nigger" and hit him in the face. Oscar fell to one knee and the woman got into the cab, which then pulled away.

A policeman who witnessed the incident simply turned his back. Oscar, even then six feet, two inches tall and weighing in at about 245 pounds, rose silently and hit the man who had hit him, sending him sprawling. The man got up, called for help from the policeman and took another punch at Oscar. When Oscar hit him the second time, the man had the sense to stay down.

The policeman then told Oscar he was under arrest.

"You turned your back when he hit me," Oscar argued, bending down to pick up his parcels. The policeman said they could finish the argument at the station.

Oscar said: "If you want to take me to the station, you'll have to use that gun." Then he walked away, leaving his assailant and the cop to stare after him.

In May of 1951 Oscar had another direct experience of racism. His trio was appearing in Hamilton, Ontario, at the Hunting Room of the Fischer Hotel. Oscar noticed that Ray Brown was sporting a new haircut. The bass player told him he had gone into a "white barber shop" and had no problem getting a haircut. He told Oscar where the shop was located, so Oscar went there the next day to get his own hair cut. A man at the barber shop told him the place was closed. Oscar went again the next day and once more was told the shop was closed—but a white man followed him in and was immediately seated in a barber's chair.

Peterson returned to the Fischer Hotel and called the police, asking that an officer accompany him to the barber shop. The police declined to interfere. Oscar went again to the barber shop. This time he asked why he was being refused service and was told, "That's my orders." He reported all this to Lloyd Fischer, who owned the hotel, who called the Crown attorney's office.

The story hit the papers—*The Hamilton Spectator* first—on May 5. (It was Gene Lees, then a reporter at the paper and later Peterson's friend and biographer, who reported the story, possibly with the help of Bruce Murdoch, the *Spectator*'s city hall reporter.)

Of course, the news story ballooned across Canada, but, interestingly, did not surface in the United States. There were meetings and protests, there was talk of turning over the licensing of barber shops to the police commission. But by the end of the month (when Oscar and his sidemen were long gone), the story died away.

Early in the summer of 1958, Oscar decided to move out of Montreal and settle in Toronto, partly because he disliked the severe winters in his home town. In addition, he wanted to work closely with his friend Phil Nimmons, who was to write the orchestrations for Oscar's *Canadiana Suite*.

So he moved his wife and children to a section of Scarborough (at the east end of Toronto), but racism again surfaced. Residents of the area talked of getting up a petition to oust the Petersons. Friends urged him to "go public" about this, but Oscar decided against it. In time, the tension cooled and Oscar had no further troubles—at least there.

Lil Peterson, Oscar's first wife, told an interviewer for

Maclean's magazine that when Oscar toured the southern United States with JATP, "sometimes the white musicians he was traveling with would have to bring food out to a car for him" or, she said, "he would have to stand at the back of the restaurant and they'd pass it out the kitchen door."

Oscar said: "I couldn't eat that way. Traveling in the South, it feels like you're not just in another world, you're on some other planet."

"Once," said Lil to Oscar, "you had to play with a tire chain at your feet, to protect yourself in case anyone in the audience came over the footlights to attack you."

Oscar chimed in: "I wouldn't know what to do with a tire chain." But he added that at least one member of JATP kept a baseball bat nearby when onstage in the South.

Traveling through the US South with Ray Brown, Oscar got a lesson in the difference between the "quiet racism" of Canada and the far more brutal kind in the States.

On this night he was driving Ray's car, a Cadillac. Ray was asleep. Oscar needed cigarettes so he stopped at a diner. A police car was parked in front of it. Oscar went in and asked for his brand of smokes from the counterman, producing a $20 bill to pay for them.

"Where did you get twenty dollars, boy?" said one of the cops.

Realizing the gravity of the situation, Oscar said the money was legitimately earned. The counterman gave him his cigarettes and then threw his change on the floor.

One of the cops said, "Pick it up, boy." His hand was on his gun. Oscar was prudent enough to bend down, pick up his money and depart.

Quincy Jones, one of the most charismatic figures in black music for several decades, has similar impressions: "I remember leaving Seattle, going to the South and having to get used to seeing two drinking fountains, for white and colored, in waiting rooms in bus stations—for white and colored—the hotels, the venues we used to play. The general admission was $3.50, but only $1.50 for whites to sit up in the balcony and watch black musicians play. You just got used to it."

"I was shocked," he reported later, "at the overt symbols of segregation." He was especially dismayed at seeing separate washrooms and water fountains marked "For White" and "For Colored."

Wrote Gene Lees: "If he [Oscar] went through the shock of meeting and working with his idols, he also, by all evidence, went through a cultural trauma on touring for the first time in the United States, where the racial discrimination was not tacit and non-violent, but entrenched, obvious, accepted and brutal."

Recalling the earlier days of his long career, Oscar said: "When I went to the United States, I'd go into the studio to do radio shows or television shows and I'd look over and there wouldn't be any blacks in the orchestra, and I knew really that it was a clique thing, everyone had their pets, and they did what they did.

"That is why black musicians had to go the way of the jazz route. We had no other route to go. And I decided that if the only way I was going to make it happen was to frighten the hell out of everybody pianistically, then that's the way I was going to make it; if that's what it took to get attention, then I was going to do my best to do it that way."

Unhappily, racism was a two-way street. Oscar Peterson was subjected to angry criticism when he hired Herb Ellis as his guitarist.

"I would get hate letters in Chicago about Herbie Ellis being in the group—from both sides, just so everybody got their rightful recognition. I'd get hate letters about, 'What is that white cat doing in the band? He can't play nothin'—he's white.' Whatever that had to do with it, I don't know."

Referring to Ellis and bassist Ray Brown, Oscar said: "We really became a close-knit unit. Our friendship became even tighter, and we were criticized for having a white person in our group."

Herb Ellis told me that whenever the trio was on the road—in the US South—he made a point of staying at the "black" hotels or motels with Oscar and Ray Brown. He wasn't taking a stand or making a statement, he said.

"Some of the white musicians stayed at white hotels, and blacks stayed at black hotels," he explained. "But I always stayed with Oscar, because I couldn't see any reason not to. I mean, I wanted to be with him, anyway, and I would have felt— I couldn't handle it."

Ellis explained his attitude about being chosen by Oscar: "It made me very proud. Oscar hired on the basis of your musicality and what kind of person you were. And he made no bones about it. He said, 'He's my guitar player, he's the guy I want.' Black or white, it didn't matter to him."

To which Oscar added: "I don't think color has anything to do with it. I'm black. If you bleached me, I'd still be able to play."

On another occasion, Oscar told interviewer Mike Hennessey: "I've always said that talent of any kind comes in a variety of packages—black, white, brown, yellow, tall, short, fat, thin, monster-like or gentle."

Herb Ellis decided to quit the Oscar Peterson Trio in 1958. He had his reasons: "I drank successfully for a few years, then it became a problem. I had some disastrous bouts with alcohol. I missed concerts. I didn't show up for gigs. One time I was gone for over a month, nobody knew where I was."

Oscar added: "Herbie decided the only way to lick it was to give up the road. He got married and became a session musician in Los Angeles."

That was when Oscar decided to replace Ellis not with another guitarist, but a drummer: Ed Thigpen. "When I joined Oscar and Ray, I had a lot of respect for those two men," said Thigpen. "I was in awe."

In 1969, Herb was reunited with Peterson in Villingen, Germany, for the album called *Hello, Herbie*. Ever since Herb had left, jazz fans had disagreed which Peterson group was better, the one with the guitar or the one with the drums. The matter was temporarily settled with this album, because it offered both. Oscar had Sam Jones on bass, Bobby Durham on drums and Herb Ellis on guitar.

Among the highlights on this album were a lyrical duet between Herb and Oscar on "Exactly Like You" and a sizzling rendition of "Seven Come Eleven," which Charlie Christian and Benny Goodman had co-authored back in 1939, when Christian was with Goodman's sextet.

Norman Granz had some vivid memories of his own regarding racism in show business, which included the world of jazz. He remembered particularly "Bell Telephone Hour" on which Granz featured Ella Fitzgerald. The group accompanying her included guitarist Herb Ellis—the only white musician in the group.

The producer immediately objected to a white man being shown playing in Ella's accompanying group. Granz resisted, made a big issue of it. But in the end, he lost. The producer couldn't get Granz to replace Ellis with a black guitarist, but he had the show's director shoot the sequence in such a way that Herb Ellis was never shown.

One of the black jazz musicians who spoke openly about the anti-white bias was trumpeter Art Farmer. He told Gene Lees: "This whole racial thing is a lot of shit, from all the way down, all the way to the top. And the closer you get to the top the more it disappears. I used to think that way, too."

Farmer remembered asking Miles Davis why he had "those white guys" (Gerry Mulligan and Lee Konitz) in his band. Davis replied: "I don't care what color they are. As long as they can play the music the way it's supposed to be played, that's what it's all about."

Farmer admitted that this experience made him re-examine his thinking: "Where I grew up, Arizona and California, you were damned sure that white people couldn't play jazz. The situation was so divided. Your ears would be closed right from the beginning. You just wouldn't listen to some white person playing jazz, just wouldn't give a damn. It went on and on and on and on. White people playing jazz, it didn't make any sense to me at all. . . . I was a young kid. But, man, look, if you were a black kid coming up in L.A. and went through all that shit out there, I didn't want to hear about no white people playing jazz. You'd go out and play in a club that drew a mixed audience, and the police would come in and close it down. That kind of thing closed my ears."

Eventually, he "got away from that" and it seemed to him "the most stupid thing on earth to think that just because somebody is white, they can't play, and vice versa—that just because somebody is black, they can play."

One time, Dizzy Gillespie was on the Mike Wallace TV show and Wallace asked him if it was true that only black people could play jazz. Said Dizzy: "No, it's not true. And if you accept that premise, well then what you're saying is that maybe black people can *only* play jazz. And black people, like anyone else, can be anything they want to be."

Clark Terry, the great (black) trumpeter, has always been a foe of racism—against black or white. He once formed a big band to teach music to boys in Harlem and, because he couldn't always be present, he got Don Stratton, who was white, to help with the teaching.

"Attendance started falling off," Clark recalled to Gene Lees. "I found out that one kid was a sort of ring-leader in the hate-Whitey movement. He had instigated the kids to not pursue the program any more. . . . I called a little meeting. . . . One of the little dudes had the nerve to say to me, 'Man, we don't want Whitey teaching us our music.' I just gave it up, I got so disgusted."

"A long time ago," Terry also said, "I had a problem with this when I had a big band at Club Baron. The band was about a 50-50 mix. I had people come up to me and say, 'Man, what kind of shit is this, bringing Whitey up to Harlem?'

"I'd say, 'Well, man, Harlem is known as the home of good jazz, and I thought it was up to somebody to bring good jazz back here. In doing so, I picked the best cats I can get, and I don't listen with my eyes. . . . My theory is that a note doesn't give a fuck who plays it, as long as he plays it well.'"

*   *   *

Author/critic Gene Lees once asked Oscar Peterson about his views on Canada and whether the paucity of opportunity in the arts in earlier years forced Canadians to make the most of the chances they did get, and made them skillfully versatile in the process. He cited Glenn Gould, Robert Farnon and Peterson himself as examples. Oscar's thoughtful reply was enlightening:

> I think in Canada we have a little more time in our every-day lives to mature at a slower rate than you do in the United States. I'm not talking about Dubuque, Iowa, but the major cities. If you take a jazz pianist and put him or her in New York City, and start the same person in Vancouver, that person would have in Vancouver a little more rounded seasoning. We're just talking about craft now, not talent. The pressures are not the same [in the two countries]. The competitive factor [here] is a lot lower.
>
> Now that has its drawbacks also. I think, at points, we need a little more competition here, because Canadians tend to be lazy anyway, and self-satisfied.
>
> It's only now that we suddenly look and find out that we're all human beings, and we've got the same kind of greed and bigotry as the rest of the world. We can't point the finger any more, because we're getting ready ourselves to segregate, with oil and the other mineral resources. We find that we have the same *isms* that many people in the world suffer from. And perhaps now we'll grow with a better density as a people.
>
> We were too bloody complacent before this. We'd sit

around and say, 'Do you *believe* what's going on *there*? It couldn't happen here.' It could and it did.

The fact is that jazz musicians—and serious jazz fans—were far ahead of the general public on the matter of desegregation—and had been for years.

I can remember when I was in my teens in the late 1930s, living in New York City, I used to spend every Sunday evening from five to eight or nine, at Jimmy Ryan's, a club on 52nd Street where Milt Gabler (of the Commodore Music Shop and later Commodore Records) used to hold weekly jam sessions. You paid a buck to get in and could nurse a 50-cent beer for a couple of hours. I was a year or two under the legal drinking age, of course, but that didn't seem to matter to anyone—least of all, me.

The bands were always "mixed." You would see Pee Wee Russell (white) playing alongside "Pops" Foster (black), George Brunis (white) with Zutty Singleton (black), Eddie Condon (white) with Charlie Shavers (black), Max Kaminsky (white) with J. C. Higginbotham (black). And all that mattered was the music. As Clark Terry so aptly put it, we didn't listen with our eyes.

In the recording studios, too, "mixed" bands were common. If Eddie Condon or Frankie Newton or Hot Lips Page had a recording date, he would use the best men available—regardless of their color. If the general public were aware of this, it didn't seem to bother them. In the mid-1930s, Billie Holiday, the leading blues/jazz vocalist of her time, recorded one tune with Artie Shaw's band ("Any Old Time"), but she was replaced by Helen Forrest, who stayed with Shaw for several years. When Shaw took the band into the US South, some locals would object to having Billie Holiday featured and would voice their complaint loudly, demanding that Shaw take "the nigger" Billie Holiday off and send out Helen Forrest.

Shaw later hired the brilliant, fiery trumpeter Roy Eldridge, but racist treatment in the US South soured him. He became quite bitter about the way black musicians in white bands would be revered on stage, then reviled in hotels and restaurants. It wasn't worth the glory or the money, Eldridge said, and he finally quit the Artie Shaw band.

But it wasn't until the mid-1930s that a "mixed" band would be presented to and be more widely accepted by the public. It was in 1935, when Benny Goodman was first being referred to as "The King of Swing," that he hired the black pianist Teddy Wilson to form the first Goodman Trio. (Gene Krupa, Goodman's drummer, was the third member.) And this was not just in a recording studio, but in public appearances, first in New York and then across the country. Then Goodman added Lionel Hampton to make it a quartet. And then, in 1939, he hired the incomparable black guitarist Charlie Christian for the Goodman Sextet, and later added trumpeter Cootie Williams, formerly of the Duke Ellington band.

That marked the beginning of the end of racial segregation in the world of swing, which was that era's version of jazz. Whatever else his faults, Goodman deserves credit for being the first big band leader to break the color line.

However, attitudes don't change overnight. Leonard Feather recalled a movie short made in 1950 in which Billie Holiday was featured, backed by a Count Basie group, which included one white musician: clarinetist Buddy DeFranco. He was featured, that is, on the soundtrack. But on the screen, while audiences heard de Franco, they saw Marshal Royal (a black musician who had worked for Basie) playing the clarinet.

Leonard Feather recounts another example. In 1958, Nat "King" Cole appeared in a movie titled St. Louis Blues, in which he played the role of W. C. Handy, a man sometimes referred to as "the father of the blues." In the movie, Cole (as Handy) was given some advice by his father: "Don't play jazz. That's the Devil's music."

In 1981, Oscar Peterson aimed a salvo at the racist practices of large companies during an interview with Gene Lees:

I wonder, if any manufacturers who make products from toothpaste to breakfast cereals, realize that blacks brush their teeth, that Chinese people have been known, believe it or not, to drive an American or a Canadian car, that Pakistanis and Haitians and Cubans and whatever you want to call all the newly welcomed Canadians, all have need of the same products, so that once in a while you might see a Chinese drinking a Coke, or an Indian or Japanese person using a dental product or a black talking about milk being good for you.

The Americans have already made a step. What is amazing, living here in Toronto, with access to the American channels, is to turn on Buffalo and see Tony Dorsett with Seven-up, and Tracy Austin, and John McEnroe. So there's a black in there.

But I come up here and I see three athletes [in commercials] and they're all white. And we have a hell of a lot of black players here, and we have a black coach of the Toronto Argonauts. We have a lot of black players on the baseball teams.

And it amazes me that they have this goddamn complacency in these lily-white agencies that they think that the minorities—and I don't even like that word—are not going to get together and say some day that they're not going to buy the products.

The world has changed. There are no more borders. You can't run home and be safe from the bomb, from the terrorists, from anything. We're all open to anything—certainly to the viruses we're sharing. If we're going to share the ills, I think we should share the good things.

Understandably, Oscar Peterson's sensitivity about racial matters endured. In 1985, he sounded off about the "stupid racism" of beer commercials that excluded minorities from their advertising. Speaking at a conference on minorities and the media, he blasted beer ads that showed only white people joking, fishing or sharing a few drinks at summer cottages.

"I don't believe," said Oscar, "that I'm the only black in this country that owns a cottage. I don't believe that I'm the only black that's gone fishing with his or her neighbor."

Peterson said "lily-white" ads convince ethnic children that consumer "goodies" are not for them, and lead to crime as they grow up and become determined to get their share. "I have seldom if ever seen a Canadian Aboriginal in an ad for any reason but pictorial value, and seldom without a horse. I've seldom seen an Eskimo without an igloo, seldom seen a black not singing or baring his teeth. . . . I believe many kids believe Santa Claus will not bring them any toys, because they seldom see any children of their racial origin receive any toys in those commercials."

(Of course, a spokesman for the Advertising Standards Council immediately replied that bias in advertising was "usually not deliberate.")

One of the most irritating (and mystifying) incidents was the time a "fan" came up to him after hearing Oscar play and went into copious detail about how much he admired Oscar's talent, how fully he had enjoyed hearing Oscar, and on and on. And then he ended it all by adding, "But I could never shake hands with a nigger."

Well aware of the problems posed by racism to any musician, Phil Nimmons says: "I admire, I have to admire anyone who has achieved what Oscar has achieved in the face of such odds—the tremendous drive that an individual has to have and the strength and the insightfulness to maintain some kind of continuity. In that respect, he's had a very rough time."

*   *   *

In 1986, another aspect of racism disturbed Oscar Peterson. In this case, his anger was aimed at the Canadian Broadcasting Corporation.

Sid Adilman, a veteran columnist with *The Toronto Star*,

broke the story: "Canadian jazz pianist Oscar Peterson is threatening to sue the CBC for violating a contract with him and selling a CBC-TV music series he headlined to South Africa.

"The CBC, it was disclosed last week, without public notice banned future program sales to South Africa in July, in protest of that country's apartheid policies.

"The sale of *Oscar Peterson and Friends* took place within the past two years, an angry Peterson told me, 'and it was strictly stated in the contract that the series was not to be sold in South Africa. They admitted to me that it had been done.'

"Peterson strongly supports Bishop Desmond Tutu, the Nobel Prize-winning apartheid foe who argues for economic bans against the country.

"Peterson's Toronto lawyer, Michael Herman, says a decision about possible legal action against CBC 'is imminent. Oscar is very upset.'" (Evidently, no legal action took place.)

Again in the 1990s, Oscar was sounding concerned about racial attitudes in Canada: "I . . . see a hardening of the arteries in people. I see a lot more antagonism among Canadians, and I see, unfortunately, targeting of the new Canadians and many of the ethnics."

On the Canadian political scene, he also expressed concern about the quick rise of the Reform Party (later the Canadian Alliance): "I see the growth of a new party that I'm not crazy about. . . . Right now, they're playing on the nervous system of the country, and that's not the way to build a political party."

Oscar Peterson has never been reticent about expressing his opinions—even when they might be unpopular.

12

OSCAR THE TEACHER

Sometime during the Fifties, a budding musician asked Louis Armstrong how to learn to play jazz. "If you've gotta ask, you ain't got it," replied Satchmo. "Forget it."

Despite that gem of advice, Oscar Peterson and a few of his colleagues decided that the acquired wisdom of their years of practical experience in the world of jazz could be passed along to others. In 1959, the National Film Board produced a two-part film titled *The Performer*, directed by Donald Ginsberg. Herbert Whittaker, then the drama and film critic for *The Globe and Mail*, interviewed several young performing artists for the NFB film. One of them was Oscar Peterson. During the interview, Peterson aired a complaint he has made several times over the years, namely his feeling that some Canadian entrepreneurs tend to take Canadian artists for granted.

"I can remember," he said, "after I had achieved a reasonable amount of success outside Canada, it was almost impossible to get a decent fee in Canada. They'd say, 'After all, you're Canadian.' They seemed to feel that I should do it as a matter of patriotism."

At the end of the segment, as the closing credits rolled by over Peterson at the piano, he played "The Maple Leaf Forever."

It was in that same interview that Oscar revealed (possibly for the first time publicly) that he was planning to start a jazz school in Toronto. "The trio and I [bassist Ray Brown and drummer Ed Thigpen] will be teaching ourselves," he explained to Whittaker. Reed player and arranger Phil Nimmons was also involved in the

94

Advanced School of Contemporary Music, which opened in 1960—in Peterson's home.

Phil Nimmons had been introduced to Oscar in the early 1950s. "I met him and was totally knocked out with his playing, not only technically, but his concept of jazz was mind-boggling," said Phil.

Their relationship was "confrontational" in one sense; they had "a loving diatribe about that," says Nimmons, because Oscar revered Art Tatum, "and my point was that he was better than Art Tatum." Nimmons has always felt that Oscar's harmonic concepts were much more advanced than Tatum's.

Peterson and Nimmons formed a deep and abiding friendship, based not only on common musical interests but also on their mutual sense of humor. When Oscar first moved to Toronto, he stayed with Nimmons, and later Phil would often stay with Oscar.

The Advanced School of Contemporary Music was certainly not the first school in North America to teach jazz. Pianist Teddy Wilson, for example, had been teaching improvisation at the famous Juilliard School in New York much earlier. And the Berklee School of Music in Boston had been around for some time, too. Indeed, there were also thousands of high school and college stage-band programs in existence.

But "the concept of the school," wrote Marguerite de Sackville-Hunt in *Performing Arts* magazine, "was simply to have tomorrow's professional musicians taught by today's professionals, people who were movers and shakers on the touring and recording circuits. And it did draw kids from all over the world, attracted by just such an idea."

When word of the trio's plans to open a school got around, there were requests that it be located in the United States, but Oscar and his colleagues decided on Toronto. "It was a needed thing here," said Peterson, "and Toronto is the trio's home. It was the logical place."

Oscar also felt that Toronto compared favorably with jazz

centers in the States. It ranked with San Francisco, he pointed out, and topped New York at the time. "New York is very quiet right now," he said.

"Finally we decided to do it," Oscar told *Down Beat*. "We didn't have the funds, but it wasn't just a matter of money; we were working and couldn't afford to get a building and everything until we could see what was going to happen. We were a little unsure of the format, so we set up a trial term, using some of the principles we intended to use in the full-scale thing."

The school opened in 1960, in the basement of Peterson's home in Willowdale, in north Toronto. A six-week course was planned. But that same year, a seventeen-week course was held, offering courses in piano, bass and percussion, and composing and arranging. A third session opened that year, running for twenty weeks. (The school later moved to Park Road, in downtown Toronto.)

"It was far too long," Oscar later told *Weekend Magazine*. "We had our regular jobs to do and taking five months to teach really hurt. We couldn't afford the time and neither could most of our students, many of whom were professional musicians themselves."

The faculty put their heads together and came up with a compact, concentrated four-week course that proved an immediate success. "The pace of that four weeks all but killed us," Nimmons later commented. "We didn't want to cut anything out of the courses, so you could imagine how hard we all had to work."

Phil also recalls that the load was very demanding for Oscar, Ray and Ed. "It was very nice of dear old Sammy Berger to book the trio into the Town Tavern. But it was a big job for Ray and Ed and Oscar to work at the club every night and then come and teach all day."

By the time the course was completed, many of the school's forty-six students were pretty tired, but they were satisfied with the results.

In 1961, the ASCM's second year of existence, some forty-four selected students—many of them already experienced working musicians—believed in the idea so fully that they invested twenty weeks (and $525) each in tuition for the privilege of studying under Peterson and his colleagues. Half of them came from the United States, one-third from Toronto and the rest from Edmonton, Montreal and other cities across Canada.

As pianist Brian Browne (head of his own trio even then) observed to *The Star Weekly*: "We learn more from Oscar in an hour than we pick up in a year anywhere else."

Bassist and French horn player Willie Ruff (who later teamed with pianist Dwike Mitchell to form the successful duo called Willie and Dwike) remembered: "The pace was rugged but worth it. Where else could you find better teachers who are also tops in their profession? I come to Canada [from New Haven, Connecticut] because the opportunity to study bass under Ray Brown is certainly a real experience."

There were three female students. One of them, Carolyn Absel, came from Detroit. "I have been playing classical music for years," she said, "but jazz has always fascinated me. I feel that the jazz medium is much more personal and self-expressive, whereas classical music is someone else's ideas and you merely copy it."

When interviewed for *Down Beat* and asked about the methodology of the ASCM, Nimmons replied:

> There is a closer contact between theory and application in every way. In the ordinary academic music school, the student doesn't get a chance to apply what he's learning. This emphasis on application of the theory hasn't happened before.
>
> We find that a common shortcoming in students is a lack of knowledge of basics and a lack of knowledge of the history of music—and, in some cases, a lack of respect for it.

Unfortunately, in the past, I don't think colleges had a direct enough appreciation of it to integrate the history and theory ends of music.

What is our method? I keep coming back to that one word, "integration." Integration of history and theory. Integration of the staff and students. All the students receive the total effect of all the staff. A piano major, for example, is made aware of the problems that the other instruments face.

Clarke Wallace and Louis Jaques were respectively the writer and photographer *Weekend* assigned to do a piece on the ASCM. Wallace wrote: "To jazz buffs this large and smiling native of Montreal is simply the most. And when he announced a few years ago that he and several others would head up the ASCM, jazz musicians could hardly wait to study with this Plato of the piano. . . .

"Even outsiders visiting the school found the pace too fast to keep up. The day staff photographer Louis Jaques and I visited it was no exception. As we approached 23 Park Road, music was pouring from the windows from attic to basement. Most of the students arrived early to squeeze in some practice before classes began.

"Though the schedule for classes was on the notice board, last-minute changes were not unusual. One pupil had asked Ray Brown if there could be a lecture on ear-training. Brown said yes, if he could round up enough who wanted it. Minutes later he found himself up to his ears in an ear-training course."

At 11 a.m. that day, a "music forum" was held and students, assigned to play in trios at the beginning of the school term, showed what they could do as a group, with the four teachers making notes or stopping them to comment.

One student, Rick Osborne of Toronto, went without sleep for the sake of his music studies. He was not a full-time musician, but took his two-week holiday to attend the ASCM. For the final two weeks of the course he was going to wangle some time off. But a staff shortage where he worked threatened to prevent him from attending. Osborne solved this by switching to the graveyard shift, and the number of hours he had to stay awake at work and school nearly killed him.

"What a time that was," he recalled. "I would just finish my shift, grab a bite of food, sleep for an hour, then go on to school. I was certainly the most tired-looking piano player by day—and the sleepiest engineer at night—but I managed to survive."

The heart of the ASCM system was the forums held once or twice a week. For these, each of the approximately forty male and three female students was given an assignment—usually to arrange any established tune he or she preferred, to bring out the results the teachers wanted. Phil has said that holding the forums was Oscar's idea.

"It's the group sound that's important," Peterson stressed, "even when you're playing a solo. You not only have to know your own instrument, you must know the others and how to back them up at all times. That's jazz."

Peterson the teacher insisted on neatness, punctuality and use of proper English instead of "hip" musicians' jargon. Even with such high standards of skill and deportment, only one student (a girl from Los Angeles) was ever expelled. "She thought it was just a lark," Oscar explained, "a big jam session. We're here to work, not fool around."

He remembered another student at the ASCM who had what he called "an attitude." Oscar said, "I had it at the school. I had a kid who came up to me and said, 'Excuse me, Mr. Peterson, but I don't need all that. I'm not here for that. I can do all of that.' So I said, 'Well, what are you here for?' He said, 'I have all that.' So I said, 'Okay, come up here and show me what you don't need. And I'll show you what you do need.' I sat with him and showed him. And he's been a dear friend of mine ever since. He's never forgotten that."

In the early afternoon, pupils would receive instruction on

their own specialty. Later in the afternoon, the students gathered in trios to practise for the next day. Practice sessions were held whenever the students had extra time. Unlike ordinary schools, most students stayed around until 11 p.m., working on a composition, studying beats or playing one of the twelve pianos.

Students were required to become aware of jazz history. Peterson had them listen to records by such major jazz figures as Duke Ellington, Coleman Hawkins, Dizzy Gillespie, Art Tatum and others. Some students objected to this, maintaining they already knew the music—but Peterson still prodded them.

One student, Mike Longo, remembered: "He [Peterson] put the emphasis on two things—how to play and what to play."

Longo also made another observation: "If you examine a Chopin étude, the techniques I learned from Oscar are exactly the same. The left-hand techniques and textures—he put a lot of emphasis on that. Piano is piano. Art Tatum played that way also."

During its three-year existence, the ASCM's staff increased to include Eric Traugott (trumpet), Butch Watanabe (trombone) and Ed Bickert (guitar). There were even a few guest lecturers, including Count Basie. There was also a Music Appreciation Club (MAC) that pupils could attend twice a week. It met in the evenings and was mainly for the public. People interested in learning more about jazz paid a membership fee and attended each week while the school was in session.

"MAC, as we call this club," Peterson said at the time, "is not exclusive, but it is limited. It is held in what used to be the living room. However, we can only cram about fifty people in it, so you can see that tickets sell on a first-come, first-served basis."

At MAC, the faculty worked as a group. Nimmons would offer the evening's theme, and then discussion would follow. Usually someone in the audience would ask how arrangements were worked out, so the trio would supply the answer with a standard tune that everyone would recognize.

"There is a need for a school of this kind," Peterson told writer

Clarke Wallace, "so we wanted to help our profession along a little. And personally, it is so gratifying for us to see that the school is appreciated."

ASCM students included such future professional musicians as Skip Beckwith, Carol Britto, Brian Browne, Wray Downes, Doug Riley, Don Vickery and Bill King. Four volumes of Oscar's *Jazz Exercises and Pieces for the Young Jazz Pianist* were published in the mid-1960s.

The ASCM existed for only three years, and in one of those years, Oscar canceled his annual fall tour to devote the time to the school. It eventually closed only because Oscar's crowded schedule of touring made it impossible to concentrate on the school. After the school closed, Marguerite de Sackville-Hunt wrote: "The school closed three years later when it became apparent that it was impossible to fulfill the obligations of professional musician and professional teacher simultaneously. In terms of time and orientation, the conflicts were just too great for all of them, but for Peterson, the decision was more difficult because he has a natural affinity for teaching."

With years of one-night stands and thousands of miles of travel behind him, Peterson expressed one fervent wish for the future: "I'd like to travel leisurely." He expressed one wish to take his family to Europe, another to write music. But he shook his head at the idea of writing a book about jazz and the jazz greats who had created its history. "I'd like to, but my writing talents are inadequate," he said. Then he laughed and added, "I'd like to try. I got the guts for it."

(Some years later, he connected with Richard Palmer, an English jazz enthusiast, and together they created a slim but interesting biography titled simply *Oscar Peterson*. It was published in England in 1984.)

As for the efforts of the faculty being "appreciated," when one term finished, the class was so grateful it placed a plaque on the office wall. It read "The Class of 1960–61—For the personal sacrifices, infinite patience and good humor shown each of us."

When the 1962 session ended, late in February, Oscar and his trio immediately went to Europe for a round of concerts and a six-week teaching seminar at a West German university. Several students who had met and worked in trios at the ASCM also had plans to tour the continent. "With all the solo jazz we've learned," said bass player Jay Leonhart, "how can we go wrong?"

Oscar told me that Norman Granz was always after him during this time, quibbling, "You've got to make up your mind if you want to be a pianist or a teacher." But the closing of the Advanced School of Contemporary Music did not put an end to Oscar's career as teacher. In 1974, he and Phil Nimmons conducted a jazz workshop at the Banff Centre of Fine Arts in the Rockies. Students clamored for his instruction morning, noon and night. Chatting informally with journalist Iris Fleming during a break, he said: "I think I do have a lot more patience now. I was always too demanding of myself and the musicians I worked with."

After his week of teaching at the Banff Centre, he went fishing in the mountains for a few days. Fishing, photography and astronomy have long been among his hobbies. And he likes to think of himself as a pretty good handyman around the house.

He never worried about his famous hands, according to Fleming. Other people did the worrying. Some of them persuaded him to insure his hands with Lloyd's.

"And that started something," he told her. "The day the policy became effective, I slammed the car door on my hand, and I had one accident after another after that. I canceled the policy and I've had no accident since. How do you explain that?"

Rob Fogle is the knowledgeable host of "Some Experiences in Jazz," heard on CHRY-FM (105.5) in Ontario each Friday from 9 p.m. to midnight. In the summer (2000) edition of *Big Band World*, published quarterly in Ontario and edited by John Dimon, Fogle wrote a warm tribute to the ASCM, where in the summer of 1962 he "was fortunate enough to have been a part of a small group of music lovers involved. It was a thrill to be able to be in a class for several informative evenings with this marvelous musician [Peterson] who was an equally adept 'professor.' "

In the same article, Fogle called up another happy memory: "Another notable event for me occurred in the mid-1960s at Basin Street East in New York City. Oscar was appearing with vocalist Teri Thornton and Woody Herman's Orchestra. Each performed one set with their respective groups. The grand finale was the pianist sitting in with the Woodchopper. Boy! I've never heard the band swing as it did that memorable evening."

Fogle's article ends with this gracious salute: "Although slowed down by a stroke, several years ago, affecting partial use of his left hand, Dr. Peterson continues to dominate the field of today's piano players. The left hand might have slowed him down a touch, now he's only ten times as fast as anyone else playing the 88s."

Among those who sang the praises of the ASCM were (predictably) Norman Granz and Ella Fitzgerald, but also composer/arranger Russell Garcia and the gifted alto saxophonist Paul Desmond. Desmond's tribute was impressive: "The standards set by ASCM cannot help but be of complete benefit to any student who takes advantage of the course offered by this institution."

13

OSCAR AND THE CRITICS

Understandably—perhaps inevitably—not everyone likes Oscar Peterson's music. Some critics—and even some musicians—have been critical of his style and technique.

As far back as 1955, when Oscar was widely regarded as the most gifted jazz pianist around, Bill Coss, then editor of *Metronome* magazine, dismissed Peterson's style as "too much a compendium of others' styles."

Whitney Balliett, the veteran jazz critic for *The New Yorker*, dismissed Peterson's art this way in 1966: "Peterson's playing continues to be a pudding made from the leavings of Art Tatum, Nat Cole and Teddy Wilson. That he stirs it so vigorously fools most of the people most of the time."

And, in his 1981 book *Night Creature*, Balliett was at it again: "Peterson exploded into his solos from his opening melodic choruses. The 'virtuoso' sign flashed incessantly, and it hid the fact that the chief content of his solo was packed into the first eight or ten bars; what came after was largely ornamentation and hyperbole. . . ."

Another noted jazz critic, Nat Hentoff, in a book titled *Listen to the Stories*, included a piece about guitarist Herb Ellis, in which he couldn't resist a swipe at Oscar: "He [Ellis] first became widely known as part of the Oscar Peterson trio in the 1950s. Peterson played a lot of notes, but underneath that prodigious technique, as Miles Davis once told me, 'He didn't know how to swing.' "

Miles Davis was the pioneer who decided to meld jazz with rock—he called it "fusion"—with questionable results. Peterson himself dismissed that development.

And Davis once said Peterson played the blues "as if he had to learn them." Peterson countered: "The blues is an emotion you've either got or you don't—whether you're playing in Harlem or not."

Davis was also quoted as saying he "loathed" Peterson's playing.

According to Geoffrey C. Ward, in his book, *Jazz: A History of America's Music*, which accompanied the Ken Burns television series, "Jazz was in the process of being redefined as merely a form of instrumental pop music. While the mixture of jazz and rock did create something that had not existed before, it also introduced instruments and beats that had nothing to do with swing, the propulsive essence of jazz phrasing. That jazz is a music of adult emotion while rock is focused on adolescent passion created another problem for jazz musicians who tried fusion. They could never get to that teenage feeling of ardent ineptitude and resentment of sophisticated authority because they are not inept and their music is as sophisticated as any performing art that has evolved in the Western world."

But Oscar was never one to take a hit without retaliating. He always had strong views on jazz and, as Greg Quill once said in *The Toronto Star*, "no time for mere poseurs or undisciplined performers." Oscar made no secret of his lack of regard for Davis' music: "I can't abide that fusion crap," he said. "It's neither this nor that."

In his 1955 *Handbook of Jazz*, critic Barry Ulanov referred to Peterson as a "well-trained, slick performer of Tatumesque skill and particular persuasiveness on developing, in a florid style, swinging melodic lines." (Ulanov also wrote that Peterson was born in Toronto.)

In his book *Where's the Melody?*, jazz writer Martin Williams launched a full-scale attack on Peterson:

> There are two inevitable words in any talk about Oscar Peterson: technique and swing. There can be no question about the finger dexterity of Peterson's piano, certainly; he can handle the shortest notes and the fastest tempos. . . . But technique is as technique does. If a reference to musical technique also implies musical expressiveness, then it might be better to say that what Peterson has is facility. Quite often, his dexterity seems to be a detriment. . . . Nor, it seems, can Peterson resist a jazz cliche. . . . One might almost say that Peterson's melodic vocabulary is a stockpile of cliches, that he seems to know every stock riff and lick in the history of jazz. Further, his improvisations frequently just string them together. One has the feeling that Peterson will eventually work every one of them into every piece he plays, regardless of tempo, mood or any other consideration; it will simply be a matter of his going on long enough to get them all in.

Martin Williams also charged that Peterson "would seem to belong to the Thirties," as if that put him in the category of Methuselah. The fact is, Peterson was born in the Twenties, grew up in the Thirties and experienced (and contributed to) the flowering of jazz. His keyboard idols were not James P. Johnson or Willie "The Lion" Smith, but Nat Cole, Teddy Wilson, Count Basie and Art Tatum. Who could ask for better artistic lineage?

Mark Miller wrote a review in *The Globe and Mail* of an Oscar Peterson Trio concert at Toronto's Roy Thomson Hall in June 1988. This trio included drummer Bobby Durham and bass player Dave Young: "Peterson, Durham and bassist Dave Young often sounded as though they had never played together before, which might well have been the case. . . . With Peterson redoubtably in the lead, though, the three men bumped and jostled through several of the up-tempo pieces and were held on course only by virtue of the pianist's unswerving rhythmic strength. . . . The pianist's high standards are in part a matter of making the impossible look and sound easy. It looked like hard work. . . ."

Miller continued, suggesting that Peterson "must continue to live up to his own standards, the standards he set in the 1950s, not too many years out of his native Montreal. His . . . appearance on Friday night at Roy Thomson Hall fell short on precisely his own terms: what would have been a terrific performance from many another pianist was from Peterson simply adequate."

In fairness to Miller, he wasn't always critical of Peterson's playing. Two years earlier, he was generous in his praise of a benefit performance of Oscar's: "'C Jam Blues' is a flip little tune," he wrote in *The Globe and Mail*,

the very model of the simplicity that Duke Ellington turned so often and so easily into a jazz classic. Oscar Peterson first recorded it in boogie-woogie fashion in 1945, and the celebrated Canadian pianist returned to it— in boogie-woogie fashion—on Saturday night at Roy Thomson Hall, as part of the Ellington medley that generally concludes his concert appearances.

Side by side, even forty years apart, these two versions could be the work of only one pianist, so well-formed was Peterson's musical personality even at age twenty, and so consistent has that personality been in the years since. Of course, there's so much more to Peterson's piano jazz now than the vigorous boogie-woogie that dominated those first youthful recordings. But the personality is the same: voracious, extravagantly confident, dominant if not domineering, and altogether larger than life.

Peterson's latest Toronto performance was, in most respects, a generous one. His trio's two-and-a-quarter-hour concert was a benefit to fund a jazz scholarship in his name at Toronto's York University, where Peterson has been an adjunct professor since the fall of 1985, overseeing workshop ensembles as his touring schedule allows.

Some critics never tired of sniping at Peterson. The noted and highly regarded Marshall Stearns, for instance, wrote his survey book *The Story of Jazz* in 1958—nine years after Oscar made his spectacular Carnegie Hall debut and began touring with JATP. Yet in that book there is only one mention of Oscar, and that in a laundry list of pianists' names that also included Bud Powell, Billy Taylor and Thelonious Monk.

In Leonard Feather's book *The Pleasures of Jazz*, published in 1976, there are several mentions of Oscar Peterson, but all in a chapter about Norman Granz.

Max Jones, the British jazz critic for *Melody Maker*, England's premier jazz periodical, wrote about the JATP tour of 1953 in a book called *Jazz Talking*, which was published in the year 2000, several years after his death in 1993. But his only mention of Peterson had to do with Jones' helping Peterson and Granz see "such sights" of London as Westminster Abbey.

That same year was when Ken Burns aired his monumental series, *Jazz: A History of America's Music*. The mammoth, 490-page book of the same title that accompanied the series was written by Geoffrey C. Ward, who had previously worked with Ken Burns on his two earlier and quite successful series, *The Civil War* and *Baseball*.

In Ward's book, Peterson receives four mentions:

On page 204, he is mentioned, but only peripherally, in an Art Tatum anecdote.

On page 331, there is mention of the fact that Miles Davis disliked Oscar Peterson's playing.

On page 393, Oscar is one of fifteen people in a group picture of the Jazz At The Philharmonic troupe arriving in Honolulu on a tour of Hawaii.

And on page 458, Oscar is again in a laundry list of Norman

Granz personnel. This time, he is referred to as "the Canadian-born pianist, Oscar Peterson."

At that, he was lucky. Maynard Ferguson got only one mention. And Oliver Jones didn't make the list at all.

And then there was Patrick Scott, a Toronto columnist who was so wedded to Dixieland that he regarded anything in jazz that happened after 1920 as heresy. Scott almost made a career of reviling Peterson.

On the other hand . . .

More than a few jazz musicians (including younger ones) have taken a different view of Peterson.

Herb Ellis: "I've played with a lot of people, and a lot of piano players. I've never played with anybody who had more depth and more emotion and feeling in his playing."

Ray Brown: "To play with and for Oscar Peterson is very demanding. It doesn't take very much to upset Oscar on stage. He and I would get into it once in a while, if he had anything to bitch about. Herb and I spent too much time honing up for him to have anything to bitch about. We were keeping that group damn near waterproof. Herb and I tightened it up to the point where it was waterproof."

Peter Appleyard: "Whenever I get depressed, I choose between the classics and Oscar to cheer me up. Oscar wins hands down."

Billy Taylor describes Peterson as "not only a virtuoso pianist but a remarkable musician." He adds: "The thing I admire about him is that he is always growing."

Andre Previn doesn't hesitate to call Oscar "a genius." He explains: "If it is possible for any interpretive artist to be labeled thus, Oscar Peterson is a prime contender. His imagination during his improvisations is dazzling, his virtuosity is guaranteed to turn all other pianists a lovely shade of envy-green, and his taste is impeccable. He can swing harder than the biggest of big bands and play more delicately than a lute."

Marian McPartland, on whose long-running radio series,

"Piano Jazz," Oscar was a guest, recalled her early exposure (in the 1940s) to Peterson's playing:

> At that time, I never dreamed that a year or so later my husband Jimmy and I would be playing a date in Toronto as the opening group for Oscar and Ray Brown. It was for a week at the Colonial Tavern, the premier jazz club in Toronto. I was both thrilled and terrified—the idea of being on the same program with Oscar and Ray was exciting, but I was nervous at having to play in front of them myself. Yet somehow I survived it! Oscar and Ray are great human beings, and they were so encouraging that I need not have worried. They lifted my spirits. It was sheer bliss listening to them night after night, and I learned so much.
>
> In those days I was playing with Jimmy's group, and later, in the Fifties, with my own trio at the Hickory House. I remember Oscar came to see me there—he even sat in with my trio [Joe Morello and Bill Crow]. It was always such a pleasure to hear him play and to talk with him—he is an extremely literate, charming, and witty guy. At a later date I went to hear Oscar, Ray and drummer Ed Thigpen at Basin Street East, and once again I was in awe of his prodigious talent—the loose, loping swing, the glittering runs and arpeggios, his breathtaking speed and precision. One sometimes tends to overlook the fact that there is a great deal of emotional depth and passion in Oscar's playing—it is overshadowed by the towering technical equipment that is so much a part of him. . . .

Nor is it only musicians or critics of his own era who revere Peterson. Herbie Hancock, a considerably younger—and decidedly more modern—pianist, regarded Peterson as "the greatest living influence on jazz pianists today."

The British jazz critic Benny Green wrote in 1984: "Peterson today stands as one of the greatest soloists of all time, a player whose technique never obscures the lucidity of his thoughts or the wonderful buoyancy of his execution. What Earl Hines began forty years ago with his discovery that the pianist's right hand was itself a solo instrument reaches its final consummation in Peterson."

And Oscar has taken a stand, too, in this debate about jazz: "The trouble is, people these days are confused about what real jazz is. I saw a tribute on TV to saxophonist Benny Carter, and they had David Sanborn come up and collect some award. Now, good as he is, what has David Sanborn got to do with Benny Carter? So many young players are deluding themselves that they're making jazz statements in rock and pop music. It can't be done. There's only one way to make it in jazz: take a stand, swim with it or sink."

In September 2000, *Maclean's* magazine featured a cover story saluting twenty-five Canadians it deemed worthy of attention. Among those thus honored were former prime minister Lester B. Pearson, James Naismith, the YMCA teacher who invented basketball in 1891, and the noted (and widely respected) novelist Margaret Atwood.

Also included among those thus recognized was Oscar Peterson, the only jazz musician on the list. The *Maclean's* tribute reads, in part: "He quit school early. Playing professionally from the age of 16, Peterson developed the flowing, technically exquisite style that became his hallmark.

"With his left hand, he plays a 'walking bass,' or 'boogie,' and with his right a syncopated swing. In Oscar's case, the right hand not only knows what the left is doing, but approves and cooperates. . . .

"Every conceivable international honor has come his way, from eight Grammys to Oscar Peterson days in Florida and California to the Order of Canada and France's Order of Arts and Letters. In 1999, he flew from suburban Toronto (Mississauga), where he makes his home, to Japan to accept the Praemium Imperiale; this year, he is to go to Aachen, Germany, on Nov. 10 to receive UNESCO's International Music Council Prize."

As he steps up to accept the honor bestowed upon him by UNESCO, the number of albums he has recorded exceeds two hundred. This is, perhaps, a sufficient answer to his detractors.

14

OSCAR AND THE VIKING

"I've never liked working with TV," Oscar said once, in 1992. "I don't think it's a sensitive medium. TV people are so obsessed with what *they* do, that they often intrude, distract both the performer and the people who've paid money for a special, intimate experience. My personal obligation is to my audience. And so, I haven't been TV's best friend."

When he said that, he was in the midst of producing his own video, *In the Key of Oscar*, in which he traced his career via a train ride and reflected on the jazz scene as he had experienced it.

In his words is the implication that his dislike for television dates back twenty years to a TV pilot he had done in Vancouver—an experience that soured him—and Norman Granz—on the medium.

Originally, this pilot for a projected television series starring Oscar was to be videotaped in Los Angeles, and I was to be its writer. The producer and director was Jorn Winther, a handsome, blond-haired Dane.

I was sent to Toronto to meet with Oscar and discuss, in a general way, the pilot. We had a pleasant session with no difficulties. Oscar wanted to open the program with the Largo, the second movement of Antonin Dvořák's *Symphony from the New World*, which had been the basis for the beautiful song "Goin' Home," and which Oscar had played for me when I visited him. But Jorn was dead set against this; he wanted something livelier. Oscar finally agreed to open with the lively "March Past" from his own *Canadiana Suite*, which satisfied Winther. Peace reigned.

But in that summer of 1973, the Writers Guild of America West (there's also a WGA East, based in New York) called a strike over securing residual rights for script writers in future sales of programs through cable, videos, etc. Nobody likes strikes, but I was a member of WGA West, so I had to go along with it.

I was on picket duty outside the Paramount Pictures studios on Gower Street, along the western border of the huge plant. Like all other movie studios, Paramount was virtually a graveyard by this time. Even before the strike only a few TV series were being filmed there and no feature pictures. The entrance to which I was assigned to do picket duty was hardly used at all. Nevertheless, the Writers Guild felt it important that pickets patrol every entrance, just in case some scribbling scab should try to sneak in.

On the first day of the strike, Steve Allen (who was a member of the Writers Guild, as well as other craft unions) was picketing nearby. Being a big name, he inevitably attracted the attention of TV news crews covering the strike. He spoke with them, but only about the strike and the reasons for it—no jokes, no memorable quips. He was there as a striking writer and did a good job of telling the TV interviewers what the issues were all about.

I was paired with a writer named Alan Leavitt. It turned out we were both transplanted New Yorkers, so it was pleasant talking with him as we paced slowly back and forth along Gower on a hot, sunny day. We were required to picket for four hours, from ten in the morning until two in the afternoon, at which time we would be relieved by a fresh team of striking writers.

At about noon this day, a sleek Jaguar pulled up and a young man leaped out and engaged Leavitt in conversation. He was an agent, I learned, and my colleague was both his friend and his client. After they chatted for a few minutes, the agent asked jokingly, I assumed, if we'd like to join him for lunch. "Oh, sure," said Leavitt, "just put down the signs and go off to lunch. If you were a real friend, you'd send some lunch over for us."

The agent laughed, waved goodbye, hopped back into his Jaguar and drove off.

The next day, promptly at noon, a small white catering truck pulled up at the entrance where we were picketing again. The driver came over to us and explained that the agent (whose name I never did catch) had, indeed, sent over lunch for us.

As we gaped in amazed delight, the man proceeded to bring out a handsome wicker picnic basket, from which he produced two quite elegant lunches: cold lobster in scooped-out pineapple halves, a tossed salad with a vinaigrette dressing, hot, crusty French bread and a decidedly respectable chilled white wine—all served with real crystal, sparkling cutlery and laundry-clean linen napkins.

Alan and I dropped our signs against the ancient Paramount wall, sat on the two folding canvas stools the caterer provided at the bridge table he produced, and devoured this delightful lunch, feeling a bit like Laurel and Hardy in one of those comedies where fortune suddenly smiled on them.

"Imagine," said Leavitt, as we munched our lunch, "if a television news crew happened to come by now and shot some footage of this. I can see the story on the six o'clock news: 'Starving Writers on Picket Duty!'"

A writer friend of mine, Neal Marshall, said later that where he was picketing during the strike a woman passed by with her little daughter, who wanted to know what the men with the signs were doing.

"They're on strike," the mother explained.

"But why?" whined the tot.

"They want more money for the shit they put on television," said the mother.

Out of the mouths of moms, yet.

The strike lasted for four months. Don't ask who won. I doubt that anyone did. However, the very fact of this strike presented a problem for Jorn Winther: he was all set to do his pilot with Oscar Peterson, and now, all of a sudden, he couldn't.

It was Jorn (among others) who realized that Vancouver, British Columbia, was not under WGA jurisdiction and therefore writers could legally work there. He soon cooked up a deal with BCTV, the private TV station based in Vancouver, whereby he could go there to shoot a series of pilots—one of them the Oscar Peterson project. I was hired—along with Tony Hudz, a young Vancouver writer Jorn had recently met—to write the Peterson pilot.

I knew Jorn well by then. I had written "The Barbara McNair Show" for two years, with Jorn as producer/director. That was when we nicknamed him "The Viking," mostly because of his blond good looks and mock-imperious air.

While Winther was a very good director—fast, precise, imaginative, even daring—he was not as good a producer, mostly because he had no appetite or patience for the paperwork and the wheeling/dealing involved.

Tony and I were flown to Toronto for meetings with Oscar at his Mississauga home. The pilot was to be done in two parts: the first in "Oscar's Music Room," in which he would play a bit, then introduce his guest for an informal chat. The second half of the show would be a straight concert, with Oscar's trio and the guest performing several numbers in front of a studio audience.

Things went smoothly, both at the meetings in Toronto and later during rehearsals at the BCTV studio in Vancouver. The guest for the pilot was Carmen McRae, an old pal of Oscar's and one of the most compelling jazz singers around. (When she got angry, Carmen had the earthy vocabulary of a stevedore, but never mind—she could sing up a storm.)

Taping day, however, was a different story. The first half was fine. Oscar opened with "March Past," and then Carmen was brought in for some talk and informal music-making. That segment went beautifully.

That evening, the concert portion of the pilot was to be taped. Jack McAdam's elegant set took up most of the studio. Oscar and his two sidemen were on a raised, circular stage with a classical Greek decor—as described in an earlier chapter. It was a beautiful sight, and the musicians, of course, were in a mood to play for the sizable and eager studio audience.

But things soon bogged down. I was on the floor during the taping, but soon I was called up to the control booth—Jorn was not happy. He wanted Niels-Henning Ørsted Pedersen, Oscar's brilliant Danish-born bass player, to turn to the camera and smile at a specific point during the performance, so that Jorn could get a close-up shot of him. (The third member of the trio was the taciturn but brilliant guitarist Joe Pass, who was not much of a smiler.) I tried to tell Jorn gently that Oscar would not be receptive to such an idea. But Jorn insisted, so down I went to the floor for a quick *tête-à-tête* with Oscar. I relayed Jorn's instruction and, as I feared, Oscar wasn't interested.

"Tell him," he said, "that jazz musicians don't turn and smile for the camera. We just play our music and we don't go in for that kind of direction."

Up I went and reported this to Jorn, who still insisted he wanted a "reaction" from Niels-Henning Pedersen for this shot. Down I went for another conference with Oscar, whose good humor was wearing thin.

Back upstairs I went with this response, but Jorn said he "needed" the shot. I told him I didn't think Oscar would agree to it, but Jorn insisted. Once again, I was the reluctant bad-news messenger; once again, Oscar refused—this time a little more curtly.

We finally got the number shot, to nobody's complete satisfaction. Oscar never did ask his bass player to smile for the cameras and Jorn never did understand Oscar's reluctance to do what the director wanted. What it boiled down to was that, for all his experience with other TV variety shows, Jorn simply did not recognize that jazz musicians were not like actors or dancers or other "directable" performers; they did their thing, without interference, and expected the director to just take his shots as best he could—while they played as best they could.

Next, Oscar introduced Carmen, who came out to generous applause to sing, as only she could, a beautiful standard ballad, "Imagination." Unfortunately, one of Jorn's cameramen, sitting on his huge crane camera, was always on the lookout for an unusual shot. When he saw what he wanted—in the middle of Carmen's song—he loudly ordered his crew to swing the crane around. The crane missed Carmen's head by a few inches. She was completely unnerved by the narrow escape. We had to stop tape, let Carmen pull herself together and do another take of the number. Frankly, I was surprised she didn't let loose a string of expletives. How Carmen got through the second take is beyond me, but she did.

After the taping of the show, I went up to Oscar's room in the Denman Place Inn for a talk and a few drinks of Scotch. He was still furious, cursing Jorn, swearing never to do television again. He wasn't mad at me and I certainly agreed with him that, whatever his talents as a variety show director, Jorn just did not understand jazz musicians. Oscar and I sat up most of the night and we killed the bottle of Scotch, but Oscar did not get over his dejection.

I can still remember some of what he said.

"I don't think you have to belabor it by having the musicians stand on a mark or sit in a certain position. Just as the music is improvised, a lot of the TV shots have to be.

"One of the big things television people haven't realized about jazz is that when people come to a jazz concert, they buy a ticket and they sit. The seat doesn't give them a head shot, it doesn't give them a shot between the legs of the piano player. They sit and they listen to the music and they see the group from whatever seat they're sitting in. Now granted, television, because of

NLC

The first Oscar Peterson Trio broadcast live by CBC Radio in Montreal in the early 1940s. Austin Roberts is on bass and Clarence Jones on drums.

Oscar on record, Montreal, 1940s.

A confident young Oscar Peterson, late 1940s in Montreal.

Oscar admired Nat King Cole for his vision and success. This photograph was taken backstage at a concert in 1957. In the mirror, you can see JATP founder, Norman Granz.

The First Lady of Song, Ella Fitzgerald,
in concert in Stockholm, 1952.

Oscar's mentor, Art Tatum, at the piano. Helen McNamara
and Alex Barris look on.

PAUL HOEFFLER

Oscar Peterson and Ray Brown in 1957.

PAUL HOEFFLER

The Oscar Peterson Trio, with Ray Brown on bass and Herb
Ellis on guitar, at the Ridgecrest Inn, Rochester, NY, 1957.

Louis Armstrong. In 1957, Norman Granz produced an album, *Louis Armstrong Meets Oscar Peterson*, on which Oscar plays a subdued piano behind Armstrong's vocals.

Oscar Peterson in concert in 1959. He would soon open the Advanced School of Contemporary Music in Toronto.

Oscar on CBC TV's "Take 30" in 1979.

A shot from an Oscar Peterson Superspecial on CBC TV.

Oscar and Dizzy Gillespie review an arrangement for "Oscar Peterson Presents" on July 14, 1980.

The inimitable Dizzy Gillespie.

Governor General Roland Michener presents Oscar with the
Order of Canada on April 11, 1973.

Oscar Peterson is installed as Chancellor of York University, September 13, 1991.

Ray Brown, 1996.

Oscar Peterson waves to fans during a concert at Roy Thomson Hall on April 11, 2000. In honor of Peterson's 75th birthday, Verve Music established the "Dr. Oscar Peterson Jazz Scholarship," to be awarded to a student currently enrolled in the Jazz program at Concordia University in Montreal.

Celebrated Japanese pianist Makato Ozone visits Oscar Peterson at his home.

Oscar receives the Bösendorfer Award from Christian Hoferi, Vice President Sales and Marketing, at the inaugural National Jazz Awards held in Toronto on February 24, 2002. The award is the first of its kind and recognizes Oscar as the "Musician of the Century."

Oscar responds to a standing ovation at the Jazz Awards.

An historic moment: Dave Young on bass and Oscar at the piano. Oscar played an excerpt from his *Canadiana Suite*.

Dave Young and Oscar Peterson respond to a standing ovation follwing their performance.

In a pensive moment.

Oscar relaxing at his Bösendorfer.

the advantages of moving cameras around, should give you a little more flexibility. But by the same token it should not impair the artist; it shouldn't cause him any discomfort at all."

Another thing that Oscar said he was bothered by about that night was the time and effort spent on rehearsing. As Milt Jackson once commented, "You rehearse all the soul out of it."

That night, Oscar also talked about another criticism he had about television's approach to jazz. He felt that the medium's concentration on the picture came at the expense of sound quality. This seems a strikingly obtuse approach when you're doing a musical program.

Incidentally, I've heard the same complaint from other musicians involved in television. Tommy Banks, the gifted Edmonton pianist and band leader, who has done a great deal of TV on both the CBC and private stations, has expressed the same concerns.

During some tapings of TV shows, he told me, the directors would call a halt if there was a camera or technical problem, but never if there was a musical problem—it just didn't seem to matter.

"Sometimes," Tommy told me, "if somebody blew a bad note, the taping would go right on. We'd have to yell out 'Shit!' to make the director stop tape and do it over."

Anyway, the day after shooting the pilot, we all left Vancouver. Oscar reported the unhappy experience to his manager, Norman Granz.

I never saw that pilot, but it did air. What's more, Oscar and his trio and various guests did a thirteen-week series for CTV (of which BCTV was an affiliate) in Vancouver. The series was called "Oscar Peterson Presents," and among the guests featured were Count Basie, Joe Williams, Dizzy Gillespie, blues shouter Joe Turner and the gifted English couple, Cleo Laine and John Dankworth.

But nobody connected with the pilot was involved in any way in the series. When Granz heard about the unpleasantness in Vancouver, he insisted on a totally different team for the ensuing series. And I can't blame either Oscar or Granz for cleaning house.

Oscar told me later that the series had gone well. Some changes were made. The "Music Room" was kept and used only for the trio. But that segment was shortened, allowing more time for the concert portion with the guest.

Jorn Winther did go on to do another TV series for CBC in Toronto and yet another one for the BBC in London.

15

OSCAR SPEAKS OUT

Nobody could ever accuse Oscar of being reticent in expressing his views on the piano, on jazz, on music in general, on critics, on other jazz pianists—even on the world around him.

As far back as 1954, in an interview with *Metronome*'s George Simon, Oscar sounded off about what he regarded as the short-comings of some of the younger jazz musicians.

"I wanted to quit," he told Simon, "because I thought that maybe I was too far behind the times."

Speaking of some of the younger jazz players, he said:

> Honestly, I heard some of them, but I couldn't understand what they were playing. . . . Too many of the ultra-modern groups have no feeling for jazz. Many great modernists don't have the spark and soul of a great jazz musician. Soul is, after all, initially an honest feeling. You must play something you believe in. I'm disappointed in a lot of the new modernists. The study of the classics is not enough. It can't make you swing. It can't give your music a soul. And the attitudes of some of those guys! Insincerity in music reflects insincerity as a human being.
>
> I wonder, too, how the average listener is going to get anything out of some of the things the ultra-modernists play, if I can't. I honestly try, but sometimes it's just beyond me.
>
> And you know who knows less about jazz than those

guys? Some of the critics. I'm against those who encourage musicians when they, themselves, don't really understand what the musicians are trying to play. Both they and these musicians who aren't completely honest in what they're doing are really hurting music and its young audiences. The kids don't understand it and yet they feel that because somebody they look up to says it's good they've got to like it. As a result, we're getting a sort of mass-hysteria about modern jazz that's doing nobody any good.

Peterson has always been realistic in his view of jazz and jazz musicians, and believes in the sobering realization that nothing is forever. This realization was formed early, and he expressed it to *The Globe and Mail*'s Kay Kritzwiser in 1961: "One of the biggest aids to the success of a jazz personality is the recording. But it's also a matter of what you do. If a man sticks to one restricting format until it's run into the ground, that's no good. He can rise overnight with one recording and die next week. If the average jazz artist uses his head and at the outset of his career realizes that he won't play as well at fifty as he does at twenty-five, he won't be in a line-up outside the Salvation Army when he's fifty."

Oscar has also been critical of other jazz pianists in general— and in some cases of specific musicians.

"Too many jazz pianists limit themselves to a personal style, a trademark, so to speak," he once said. "They confine themselves to one type of playing. I believe in using the entire piano as a single instrument capable of expressing every possible musical idea. I have no one style. I play as I feel.

"To play as you feel means that you must master the piano and not let it master you. It also means that you must make use of everything that has been done before, in the classics as well as in jazz, adding your own creative ideas."

At times, Oscar has been willing to express his opinions of other pianists, not all of whom have impressed him. Among them have been Horace Silver, Errol Garner and Ahmad Jamal.

In a 1959 interview for *Down Beat*, Oscar offered this analysis:

> Each of these men is confined for a certain reason. Errol because he's a stylist. We will never hear what he might have done if he'd studied. Horace pursues primarily the linear approach. Ahmad sticks to the type of absurd singing lines that he uses. All these men are pursuing one line of the instrument's potential. . . . A lot of these pianists don't have the basis to start with. Because a man is working within one esthetic framework, that's not to say he shouldn't, therefore, use the rest of the scope of the instrument. . . . I think this is why a lot of artists never grow. One thing that has made me, subconsciously, never want to become as commercial as Ahmad or Errol is that I don't want to be confined to only one part of what I do.
>
> Let's face it. Basically, jazz piano is an instrument that most pianists have forgotten. A piano can be as subtle as a French horn in the distance or as driving as the Basie band. When I am working, it's a challenge, not a chore. But I'm not afraid of the instrument. I love it.
>
> You should be able to build. You shouldn't build to a summit only to fall off. That is another thing wrong with much jazz piano. When the pianist shifts into high, often he's used up all he's got to get there.

While others developed by changing the music, the same article pointed out, Peterson, "more modestly," confined himself to the task of trying to become a better instrumentalist.

In 1977, a piece in *The New York Times* said of Peterson: "His improvisations never cohered in the manner of, say, Keith Jarrett." It didn't take Oscar long to respond: "I am not pleased with the so-called pianists I hear today," he told Marsha Boulton of *Frontlines*. Referring to Keith Jarrett, he told her: "He's shucking [faking]. Keith Jarrett has got everyone buffaloed. I think he's probably very intelligent in that he's found a swatch of people who want to go along with this particular thing he's doing, but I've heard too many players do it better. And I say the same thing of Chick Corea. The best player of all those guys is Herbie Hancock. Any time Herbie wants to, he can wipe all those new players out. He's the talent of the day."

Another Peterson reflection on pianists: "Pianists must be taught. If a man has no technique, if he has been self-taught, you'll hear it said that he has an open mind. On the contrary, he has grooved himself. But the classical-trained musician has been trained to take in new aspects, new materials."

Some of the "fans" who revered Peterson for staying in Canada later turned against him all the more violently because he did not live up to their expectations, or because he did not develop along what they considered to be the correct aesthetic lines.

But Peterson has had his defenders, too. Frank Conroy wrote in *Quarter Notes* in September 1981: "Peterson is not a great creator of jazz. . . . He is a great executor—which is every bit as rare as a creator—whose life has been spent immersed in the music of the jazz masters for whom he feels the most affinity. When Peterson brings his intelligence and skill to bear on the ideas of Charlie Parker, Ellington, Waller, Hoagy Carmichael, and some others of that era, he is, after all, reviving and honoring a golden age. The music was good then, it is good now, and it is fitting that there be someone to play it.

"Peterson's solos are far from empty. They contain reflected emotion, referring back to other players or to jazz itself. It is artful music, with its own particular pleasures. He does not so much discover—he reveals."

"Over the past ten years in particular," said *Quarter Notes*, "perhaps because of all the concert work, he seems to have increased his control over the piano. His dynamics have improved, affording him greater range, and it seems easier for him to make the instrument sing."

Oscar offered this reflection: "Most musicians have this burning ambition to say certain things musically. If they can do that, then they'll just go into it deeper. They enlarge on it. . . . But audiences have changed, have become much more individualistic. They don't just go to hear jazz. They go to hear certain musicians. They know what they like."

In Len Lyons' 1983 book *The Great Jazz Pianists*, Oscar wasn't timid in discussing jazz audiences. Lyons led him into it this way: "You have a reputation for being skeptical of the seriousness of jazz audiences."

"Well," replied Peterson, "I really started to take aversion to one aspect of the jazz world, and that was the general conception that if you come into a club, you don't necessarily have to pay attention. Occasionally, when people are noisy, I'll turn to them in anger and say, 'Would you act this way at a classical concert?' It would seem like a form of snobbishness on my part, but I don't think there's any need for different outlooks toward the different forms of music. It doesn't matter whether you're going to hear jazz or [violinist] David Oistrakh at Lincoln Center."

Peterson can sometimes get impatient with jazz critics, too, as he indicated in the interview with Kay Kritzwiser: "Jazz doesn't have to be that controversial, that confusing. We get all these overnight geniuses and the pseudo-critics supposedly explaining what the musician is playing. It doesn't really need that explanation. The ill-informed jazz critic or reviewer spouts off and confuses the honest listener all the more."

Having traveled as widely as he has—from Stockholm to Ghana, from Dublin to Athens to Tokyo—Oscar has views on the portability of jazz, as he told Kay Kritzwiser: "Jazz doesn't differ from any other art form. It is accepted or rejected in the same way as art and literature. But I feel it is more readily accepted in Europe. There is more interest. This is understandable because jazz is America's folk music. Therefore there is more curiosity regarding it in Europe."

But there are differences from one country to another: "The

French are more vociferous in their likes and dislikes. The Scandinavians are very polite. I think GIs may have influenced the Germans because there's generally great fervor in their acceptance. In Japan, it's fantastic. There's an almost fanatical interest."

Jazz, Oscar expressed, is "very environmental," and despite a passion for jazz, Europe produces few first-rate jazzmen. "European men can't give jazz the same authenticity. It isn't part of their origin," said Oscar. "It hasn't nurtured their talent, for example, the way it did my generation."

But Japan, he felt, was another story. "Maybe it's because of their imitative bent," he said, "but they have some wonderful musicians there. There's a woman recording here in North America—Toshiko Akiyoshi—who is tops."

Peterson expressed confidence in the future of the jazzman, partly because improved recording techniques—hi-fi and stereo—resulted in educating a more discriminating audience.

"And the jazzman has become a much more studied musician," he said. "There's no such thing now as a man playing by ear. Musical requirements are much stricter. Youngsters coming up realize they must study and improve in order to grow as the music grows."

But in 1991, he expressed some misgivings about the state of jazz in his native land: "From my standpoint, the Canadian jazz scene seems very fragmented. I've been invited only once to play the festival here in town [Toronto]. No one's even consulted me about how to improve it and that comes down to local politics."

Oscar fired another salvo in 1998, this time at the talk of a swing "revival": "There are too many people out there who wear zoot suits, pork-pie hats like Lester Young and play what they think is swing," he told Geoff Chapman. "It's like part of the jazz community that's lost its imagination, which has become involved with rock entities and innocuous singers in the hope of making a greater impression. They have demeaned their worth and the impresarios and presenters have taken over.

"I've stopped performing at jazz festivals where there isn't any jazz, like Montreux, and I pick my appearances very carefully. I won't have any part of subterfuges.

"And as for the people who think they're playing swing, well, I'm embarrassed. It's like seeing me as a parody of Mick Jagger. Playing jazz is not part of the Vegas and showbiz tradition. Playing to the marketplace takes away from the music.

"It angers me to see it and hear it. Look how much Count Basie could do with just a nod of his head. His bands really did swing. But it's like the awards that are handed out these days— they don't mean anything, although they used to be for a lifetime's production. Now it's just a big business thing."

And Oscar has taken his shots at the music business, too. In August 2000 he told *Digital Journal*: "The record companies are too materialistic. There's a story going around that there is a song writer who wrote a song and wanted it on a particular vocalist's album and to get it on that album cost him $350,000. But what does that tell him about the context of his song? Don't they care about how good it is or how bad it is? It's sell, sell, sell. I think that if this was the case many years ago, there may not be classical music and that is a frightening thought.

"I have been very fortunate because over the years, because of my successes, I have been able to walk a pretty straight line to do what I want to do. People are forced to venture into other media because they want to get on the label: what about the artistic end of it? Where does that fit? I want to do something because I really want to do it. I don't do something because I think it will sell 30 million albums. I couldn't care less. If it sells one, it sells one."

*   *   *

Peterson has always been fiercely competitive. "I used to say to the guys that at our worst we have to sound better than the best guys out there. It was a piano era, wasn't it? With Shearing, Garner, Wilson, Horace Silver . . . . Somehow we became in that shuffle what I call the crutch group. And I mean at the door. At the beginning, we may not have sold out the room every night.

But whenever we came to town, we established a level that only got better. . . . But the funny thing is that the money never went that way. For whatever reasons the nightclub owners would say, gotta have the trio back, love Oscar. Norman [Granz] said, 'Never mind love. Pay him.' We couldn't break whatever the price barrier was.

"If you want the truth on where you stand, ask the help; don't ask the owner, ask the help. They turn in all the tabs. I got tired of the help in all the clubs saying, 'You'd better be getting top money, because we don't do this kind of business.' We obviously quit playing certain clubs. . . . I decided I was going to wipe every piano player around if that was the only way I was going to get my just due. And I went for broke. I played some sets in the London House [in Chicago] and other clubs with Ray and Ed Thigpen or Ray and Herb, and Herb used to say: 'Jesus Christ, I don't know what you're trying to prove."

But Oscar was very proud of his various trios: "I thought we had the steam. And we did have it. . . . Yeah, we were pressure groups. I kept the pressure on them. And because of keeping the pressure on them, it made for a belief and an approach in the group whereby everyone became self-sufficient creatively. Ray Brown believed in what he was doing, so much so that Ray Brown made himself into what he is today in the movie studios and recording field."

In 1991, Peterson spoke of his trios' work: "It's music which is not pretentious or esoteric. We just make statements about how we feel on that particular night. Some people try to get very philosophical and cerebral about what they're trying to say with jazz. You don't need any prologues, you just play. If you have something to say of any worth then people will listen to you."

Another instance of Peterson's competitive spirit was cited by Gene Lees. On a night when the trio was opening for Count Basie, "Oscar said to his sidemen, 'They got more guys, but that's all. They're not taking nothin' from this band.' That's the way he thought. To hell with Count Basie's orchestra. You understand, they were our closest friends in the world, but on the bandstand, Oscar takes no prisoners."

At about that time, one Toronto critic, covering a Peterson concert at Roy Thomson Hall, reported: "Time and again Friday night the speed of Peterson's right hand inventions and the sheer effortless daring of his chord clusters and fanciful flourishes squeezed deep sighs and gasps of awe from an audience clearly attuned to his repertoire."

The piece ended with gracious this salute: ". . . it was Peterson's barrelhouse piano that won the day. Interspersing solos with [Dave] Young and [Bobby] Durham, he laid down blues grooves so wide and deep that fans rocked in their seats and cheered whenever his impossible right-hand stretches, doubling time with each pass and unimpeded by occasional swipes at his face with a towel, finally arrived back at the original rhythm and theme with almost prophetic inevitability. This is the Oscar Peterson for whom the jazz world stands in awe. Long may he boogie."

16

OSCAR
THE COMPOSER

Peterson has always been a great student of jazz and a piano virtuoso. Because of this, people tend to overlook the time he has spent composing. While he has never tried to *lead* jazz in bold new directions, he has with age become more of an experimentalist, taking greater risks and attempting greater innovation.

And while others developed by changing the music, Peterson, more modestly, confined himself to the task of trying to become a better instrumentalist.

In the end, Peterson's wisdom is evident. Aware of the nature of his gifts, he resisted strong pressure from those who wanted him to be an innovator and dedicated himself instead to celebrating jazz, with energy, honesty, intelligence and obvious love. He's been doing it for forty years, and he has prevailed. Noble work, to be sure.

In other words, he determined to become the best Oscar Peterson he could be.

"You deepen," he told journalist Peter Goddard in 1984, while making an appearance in Ottawa. "Over the years you deepen in what you're trying to do. You don't just deepen as an artist. You should deepen as a person. You change your objectives. And if you do that, your work has to change."

Goddard added that his own understanding of Peterson had also deepened. "He seems to be aware of his place in jazz now," he wrote. "He seems to understand that he's become one of those figures of respect, the ones—like Art Tatum—he once admired, when he was that hot-shot wonder piano player out of Montreal thirty years ago. He's working on material he wouldn't play before. He's re-working stuff he played as a kid . . . he's expanding. And his playing now has a breadth, a grandeur at times, that comes with growth other than age. I find myself listening in a new way, too—not to be bowled over by technique, but to be moved."

After leaving Ottawa, Oscar returned to Toronto with his trio for an appearance with the re-formed Modern Jazz Quartet. Goddard commented: "It may not be the Toronto International Festival's first, or only, salute to jazz. It may be the festival's classiest night, though."

Then, after a club date in Washington, DC, he was back in Ottawa, rehearsing at the National Arts Centre for a CBC special designed to celebrate the 450th anniversary of Jacques Cartier's arrival in Canada from France. Also on the special would be two of France's better-known jazz/pop pianists: Michel Legrand and Claude Bolling, the latter of whom had written a series of classical/jazz works for the likes of flautist Jean-Pierre Rampal and cellist Yo-Yo Ma.

As Goddard wrote, ". . . it's Peterson who's at the heart of it all. You could sense this throughout the day before his arrival. The others rehearsed. Bolling, just in from Paris . . . repeated over and over some of the complex runs of 'Oscar for Oscar,' a piece he'd written for Peterson."

For a man who is known throughout much of the world as a dynamic improviser at the keyboard, Oscar Peterson has done his share of composing, too. In 1974 Iris Fleming wrote this about Peterson: "He has always had a phenomenal memory. It made school easy for him in Montreal, where he was born, and it meant he could get away with hardly any practising when he was forced to take piano lessons. He could run through a piece once or twice and know it. His father would return after several days at his railway-porter job and praise his son for practising well."

Oscar's sister Daisy came to realize that he had not really practised that hard but, instead, had memorized the pieces he was
expected to "practise" and then simply played them—from
memory!—at his next lesson.

By 1980, Oscar had begun to broaden his interests. Said
Norman Granz: "And these new interests will be a measure of
the kind of musician he really is. Think of it. He's been playing
for thirty-five years. Yet he has this interest in composing. I
know a lot of other great players who after so much time simply
kept to their playing. Lester Young played beautifully throughout his life, but he didn't compose. Oscar can!"

Probably his best-known long works are his *Canadiana Suite*,
recorded in 1964 with Phil Nimmons and his Nimmons 'n' Nine
Plus Six (Nimmons also wrote the arrangements), a nine-part
suite brilliantly portraying different areas of the country, known
by their song titles as "Place St. Henri," "Wheatland,"
"Hogtown Blues" and "March Past," and his later *Trail of
Dreams*, introduced to the world in April 2000 at Toronto's Roy
Thomson Hall, with Oscar leading his own quartet backed by a
twenty-four-piece string section under the direction of Michel
Legrand. This was a suite of twelve pieces that also celebrated
different parts of his native land.

Oscar's group consisted of guitarist Ulf Wakenius, bassist and
vocalist Niels-Henning Orsted Pedersen and drummer Martin
Drew. The quartet played the first half of the program, and then
the string section came onstage to complement Peterson's quartet for the premiere of the *Trail of Dreams Suite*.

The *Trail of Dreams Suite* was commissioned by Nicholas
Goldschmidt, artistic director of Music Canada 2000, which
invested $2.3 million in new creations by more than sixty Cana-
dian composers. It would be performed across the nation during
that year.

"It was a little difficult to get to grips with the idea, so the suite
partially depicts the trail," Oscar told Geoff Chapman in April
2000. The twelve tunes were inspired by the Trans-Canada Trail,

a 16,000-kilometer trail spanning the country that was soon to be completed.

Chapman wrote: "The *Trail of Dreams* may well be the jazz highlight of the first year of Canada's new century."

Covering that concert for *The Globe and Mail*, Mark Miller wrote:

> Consider, for a moment, Oscar Peterson the composer. If those four words don't roll off the tongue quite as readily as Oscar Peterson the pianist, there's good reason. For the past forty of his seventy-four years, the celebrated Canadian jazz musician's writing has served his playing—so commanding has that playing generally been. Simply put, his tunes set up his solos. The tunes didn't necessarily amount to much, but such solos . . .
>
> Composer and pianist were centre stage on more equal terms Tuesday night at Toronto's Roy Thomson Hall, as Peterson's quartet gave the world premiere of his *Trail of Dreams Suite*, with a twenty-four-piece string orchestra under the direction of the distinguished French conductor and arranger Michel Legrand. The suite, performed in the presence of Governor General Adrienne Clarkson and Deputy Prime Minister Herb Gray, is one of sixty-one works commissioned by Music Canada Musique 2000 in honour of the millennium.
>
> It must be said of this changing balance between Peterson's writing and playing, that his piano work is no longer what it once was. Reliant now almost exclusively on one hand, his right, its defining qualities have to varying degrees diminished in recent years—that extraordinary drive, that indomitable sense of swing, that astonishing articulation and that exquisite touch.

Referring to the suite, Peterson said: "I decided that certain tunes could be about places in Canada that were important to me. The other compositions reflect areas of Canada that give it a real personality and speak to the picturesque, and photographic, scenic qualities of places through which the trail passes."

Most significant to Peterson is the final piece, "Anthem to the New Land," which salutes the newly created territory of Nunavut. As he told Geoff Chapman, "That happening was very pleasing to me. It's really important and shows how Canada has matured. Another favorite is 'Harcourt Nights,' which reminds me so much of the happy times when I had a cottage there [in the Haliburton Highlands], while Banff is such a beautiful place— hence 'Banff the Beautiful.'"

The opening tune, "Cookin' on the Trail," has a sly double meaning. "Cooking" is jazz slang for a band in top form, but Peterson said the number's name also echoed the times when as a Montreal schoolboy he went camping near Burlington, Vermont.

Many other pieces have obvious geographical implications, like "Morning in Newfoundland," "The Okanagan Valley," "Manitoba Minuet" and "Ballad to P.E.I."

Two others, noted Chapman, needed explanation.

"The French Fiddler" is a tribute to Montreal fiddler William Gerard, whom Peterson listened to as a youngster. "He was a wonderful jazz violinist who never became known. I think his musical spirit reflects the people of the Quebec area," said Oscar.

"Dancetron" was composed "to recreate the effervescent joy of the Acadian people," said Peterson. "It has an incredible score, just like the others, because Michel [Legrand] has done a magnificent job."

Incidentally, it bears noting that Peterson's poignant "Hymn to Freedom," which was to become a favorite with many audiences, was originally part of his *Canadiana Suite*. This suite was nominated for a Grammy award as best jazz composition of 1965; it was recorded by Peterson's trio and also by Oscar with Nimmons 'n' Nine Plus Six. Versions of "Hymn to Freedom" were recorded in the 1980s by Oliver Jones and Doug Riley.

Oscar once discussed the background to the song: " 'Hymn to Freedom' was written during the upheaval years of the Sixties, when it seemed there was going to be a huge and very awful confrontation in America. I wrote it with hope—when everyone joins hands in harmony, that's when we're free. That's the essence of freedom."

It was in 1981 that Oscar took on an unusual and somewhat challenging project. He felt compelled to compose a work for the marriage of Lady Diana Spencer to Prince Charles—even though he would be so busy touring that he had to turn down an invitation to attend the royal wedding on July 29. Among other commitments, he was to appear at the Kool Jazz Festival in a Carnegie Hall concert titled "The Magnificent Oscar."

"It wasn't something that was planned," he told Peter Goddard at the time. "I'd gone from Japan to Australia on a tour and everybody was talking about the wedding. Who knows why, but they're crazy about it over there. Well, the next time I started to do some writing I found the ideas about the wedding coming out in the music."

The suite's sections were titled "Announcement," "London Gets Ready," "When Summer Comes," "It's On," "Heraldry," "Royal Honeymoon," "Jubilation," "Lady Di's Waltz," "Let the World Sing" and "The Empty Cathedral."

The last piece was partly Norman Granz's doing. Granz, still Oscar's manager at the time, heard what Oscar had written and suggested that Peterson had to write something about St. Paul's Cathedral, that the suite wouldn't be complete without something about the place where the wedding would be held.

There have been other Peterson compositions worth noting. In 1979, he completed his *African Suite*. In 1984 he wrote his *Easter Suite*, and also composed *City Lights* for Les Ballets Jazz de Montréal and composed and performed works for jazz trio and orchestra on commission from Bach 300 (premiered with the National Arts Centre Orchestra in 1984) in celebration of Bach's 300th birthday, and for the 1988 Winter Olympics in

Calgary. Rick Wilkins has served in several instances as Peterson's orchestrator.

In his biography of Peterson published in 1974, the British critic Richard Palmer wrote of the *African Suite* that "it started as an individual song dedicated to the imprisoned South African black nationalist leader Nelson Mandela and his wife Winnie. The project has expanded, and still awaits completion, but two pieces have appeared on record, namely the tribute to Mandela, 'Fallen Warrior,' and the evocative 'Nigerian Marketplace.' Musically, these pieces are more ambitious, in both structure and harmonic texture, than Peterson has written before. The lines are long and muscular, and they make central use of Niels Pedersen's formidable singing power, a compositional feature first evident on the lovely 'Night Child' (1978), which Oscar wrote to celebrate the birth of his son."

Among his other works for jazz groups over the years are "Hallelujah Time," "Blues for Big Scotia," "The Smudge," "Bossa Beguine," "A Little Jazz Exercise," "Trippin'," "Mississauga Rattler," "Samba Sensitive" and a variety of informally conceived blues.

Parts of Peterson's suites (for example "Nigerian Marketplace" from his *African Suite*) have been played and recorded as independent pieces. Oscar also wrote and recorded "Blues for Allan Felix," heard in the Woody Allen film *Play It Again, Sam* in 1972. He has composed scores for the feature film *The Silent Partner* and the film documentaries *Big North* and *Fields of Endless Day*, the last-named an NFB-OECA history of blacks in Canada. His score for *The Silent Partner* received a Canadian Film Awards "Genie" in 1978.

As the decade of the Eighties opened, Peterson was starting to devote more of his time to writing. "I never was one to be on the road all the time; I couldn't handle those 365-days-a-year tours. Even so I never found enough time to write except a few songs or so. Being at home has allowed me to get into more involved pieces. I've just written a twenty-minute piece for Les Ballets

Jazz of Montreal, and I have some film scores I'm interested in after doing *Silent Partner*. I'm at the point now in my life where I'll refuse to do anything unless I have the time."

It was during the summer of 1981 that Oscar was to be involved in a project with the distinguished film director Robert Altman, whose films then included *Nashville* and *M*A*S*H*, both big successes. Altman had contacted Peterson to discuss the possibility of Oscar's doing the score for a project based on the history of Harlem's famed Cotton Club. "But he [Altman] eventually pulled out of the project," Oscar later reported. "The studio wanted to turn it into a gangster film and Altman wanted no part of it."

(Three years later, director Francis Ford Coppola made a film titled *The Cotton Club*. It had a large cast headed by Richard Gere and a score crammed with Duke Ellington music. But it was neither a critical nor a commercial success.)

In 1984, musician André Previn reported: "In recent years the Canadian virtuoso [Peterson] has devoted more time to composing. ABC television invited him to compose music for a couple of television pilots, which he performed with Milt Jackson, Joe Pass, Jake Hanna and John B. Williams."

Four years later, Greg Quill wrote about Oscar's concert at Roy Thomson Hall, in *The Toronto Star*:

> Though he finds freedom mostly in more-or-less rigid blues structures and rhythm patterns, Peterson offered several surprises in Friday night's two-set concert. The recent composition, "The Love Ballade," for example, juxtaposed with the rollicking profane stride of "Cakewalk," was a delicate, classically-inspired piece whose gentle, symmetrical theme, stated at the beginning and end on solo piano, was overlaid during the middle section with sheets of elaborate filigree until it became a sparkling, brittle web.
>
> Peterson also revived "Night Child," a simple, joyful

romance in honor of his eleven-year-old son Joel, who was in the audience.

"Nigerian Marketplace," from the composer's long-awaited *African Suite*, was a departure from the otherwise basic rhythms of Peterson's repertoire. Its simple melody, stated first by bassist [Dave] Young, floated airily over a loping African feel when [Bobby] Durham settled in, and provided Peterson with myriad opportunities to display his assured grasp of polyphonics, his dazzling precision and a breathtaking degree of separation between the functions of the right hand, a freewheeling improvisation instrument in itself, and the left, a virtual anchor, swinging economically and metronomically between structural chords.

Though it's his abilities as a composer that set Peterson apart from many of his peers who prefer to interpret existing standards, he did work with several classics of the jazz repertoire Friday night, including Duke Ellington's "Take the 'A' Train" and "Mood Indigo." In one piece he even seemed to meld half a dozen standards in a far-ranging construction that evoked shadows of "Who Can I Turn To?" and Gershwin's "Rhapsody in Blue," with each new turn suggested solely by the harmonic aftertaste of the previous section. Whether spontaneously invented or carefully premeditated, the sheer brilliance of Peterson the composer was nonetheless evident.

*   *   *

One of Oscar Peterson's loves is another form of composition. For many years, photography was more than a hobby—it became an addiction. "He didn't just buy a camera," said his friend, trombonist Butch Watanabe, "he bought a whole system." And he would replace his equipment as soon as something new came along, manifesting his passion for gadgetry. "I'm afraid of the cameras," Oscar once said. "Every hour I spend with them is an hour away from the piano."

"Photography has always been a love of mine," Oscar said. "I am into the digital aspect of cameras and I use several cameras and digital cameras. It supplants the darkroom; it's an immediate darkroom. When time is of the essence, that answers the question. You also don't have to carry around boxes of film all the time; you have little cards that you just stick into the camera that allow you to do what you have to do."

When I interviewed him in February 2001, he recalled the fun he always had with cameras. "I used to have my own darkroom kit on the road," he recalled. "They used to call me 'The Astronaut' on Jazz At The Philharmonic."

Yes, he loves cameras and cars—and gadgets, which led him later to synthesizers. "Canada's best-known jazzman synthesizes his sound," proclaimed a heading that ran in *The Toronto Star* on May 1, 1982. Roy Shields, who wrote the story, went on to describe Peterson's newest toy: "And his synthesizer is not the garden variety, either. His is a Synclavier H Digital Analysis/Synthesis Option. When seated at it, he resembles a mad scientist in a science-fiction movie. The console is huge with a background wall of connecting cables that might intimidate a Bell engineer.

"With his Synclavier, Peterson can compose music that is automatically transformed by a computer into written form on a video screen for other instruments. And these scores are then available as printouts or can be sent digitally by telephone to other musicians or members of his quartet around the globe."

"When synthesizers first came out," said Oscar, "I was leery of the sounds I heard because they were in their embryonic stage. But now they are valid instruments with voices and sounds of their own."

To those who still view them as weird, music manipulators, Peterson replies with a smile and a shrug: "It's a little like somebody fighting the piano; it's a little late, they're here."

*　*　*

Peterson has always been generous in reference to musicians and composers he respects. One man he reveres is Duke Ellington, and he told me of an incident that occurred when Duke was appearing on Jazz At The Philharmonic.

One night after the concert, as instruments and luggage were being packed for the next stop on the tour, he and Ellington were left alone on stage and Duke asked Oscar to play something on the piano. "So, I sat down," Oscar recalled, "and at that time, I was in the throes of learning a tune of his called 'Lady of the Lavender Mist.' So I began to play it and Duke was sitting, listening, and he said, 'What is that?' I thought he was kidding. I said, 'Don't you remember that? It's 'Lady of the Lavender Mist.' Don't you remember that?'

"You know what he said? He said, 'I don't worry about what I've written. I worry about what I have to write tomorrow.' "

17

OSCAR
AS COLLABORATOR

Given his standing in the jazz community, Oscar has never wanted for outstanding musical collaborators.

He was proudest, understandably, of the trio he led longest, with Ray Brown on bass and Herb Ellis on guitar. In 1991, Tim Perlich, writing for *NOW Magazine*, looked back at that group: "Peterson's trio, featuring bassist Ray Brown and guitarist Herb Ellis, went on to become the quintessential trio of the jazz-smitten '50s. What placed the inseparable upstarts a cut above the other trios of the day was not only their ability to anticipate each other's rhythmic changes, but to dramatically share improvisations rather than support a lead player.

"Their tastefully swinging sound, characterized by its dynamic sense of flow, also made the group the perfect accompaniment for the sub-colorings of saxophonists like Coleman Hawkins and Ben Webster."

It was in 1969 that Oscar made a recording titled *Hello Herbie*. The liner notes (written in German by Wolfgang Dohl and translated into English by Clay Sherman) offer this explanation of the title: "It's usually said that the really essential things in jazz happen in the United States. There have been few exceptions to this rule. One such exception happened last fall in the middle of the Black Forest in Germany: the reunion of Oscar Peterson and Herb Ellis.

"Ever since Oscar replaced the guitar in his trio with drums—
it was in November 1958—fans have been discussing which of
the two lineups is more important. It now becomes a moot point
since we have the Oscar Peterson 'dream combo' with both
guitar and drums. [Bobby Durham was the drummer.]

"Herb and Oscar's old friendship was immediately renewed in
Villingen. Oscar called out 'Hello, Herbie' as the guitarist
walked into the studio, and this greeting became the title of this
album."

In the mid-1970s, Peterson and Norman Granz embarked on
an ambitious project. On Granz's own Pablo label, Oscar made a
series of five albums, each featuring a different trumpeter. The
trumpeters in question were Clark Terry, Roy Eldridge, Dizzy
Gillespie, Harry "Sweets" Edison and Jon Faddis. Their accompaniment was provided by Oscar, playing either piano or organ.

Some time later, Pablo issued a kind of sampler titled *Jousts* on
CD, which consisted of pieces recorded by Oscar with those
different trumpeters but not included in the earlier releases. Each
of the trumpeters (except for Jon Faddis) was represented by two
numbers to show off his style, technique and inventiveness. The
sole Faddis contribution (co-written with Oscar) is an eight-
minute item called "Oakland Blues," and gives young Faddis
ample space to show off his abilities—and potential—quite effectively, with fine support from Peterson.

Clark Terry opens *Jousts* with a lightly swinging item, "Danish
Pastry," which he and Peterson co-wrote. After each man solos,
they do some neat four-bar trading back and forth, then swing
on out to the end.

Terry also closes the CD, with a mellow old-timer, "Trust in
Me," which starts off simply enough, with Clark in a bluesy
mood and Oscar supplying his usual perfect backup. But it
builds into a fairly fiery finale.

Oscar is on organ for Roy Eldridge's two numbers, "Crazy
Rhythm" and "Summertime." The reliable "Little Jazz" Eldridge
displays his trademark daring. The man simply could not back

away from a challenge, especially on his first outing, "Crazy Rhythm." He is relatively subdued (for Roy) at the beginning of "Summertime," and Oscar's work on the organ is appropriately low-key. But Roy could never resist tossing in a few higher-register notes, just in case you might forget that he was capable of hitting them cleanly.

Dizzy Gillespie uses a mute on "Stella by Starlight," but that doesn't hamper him in the least. He plays in a moderately restrained way, but there's no mistaking John Birks Gillespie's dexterous technique and the amplitude of his ideas. Oscar, too, supplies expert accompaniment, as well as some lovely solo work. Dizzy's work on his second tune, "There Is No Greater Love," again with mute, is—well, muted, but it serves the mood of the tune. Oscar's work, both behind Dizzy and in solo, is outstanding. And Dizzy heats things up very subtlely later in the cut.

Harry "Sweets" Edison chose the familiar Ellington tune "Satin Doll" as his first choice. As might be expected, "Sweets" is able to pump plenty of fresh ideas into the Ellington oldie, and Oscar certainly keeps pace with him. Edison's other contribution is another evergreen, "Makin' Whoopee." Using a mute, Harry has no trouble playing strongly on this workhorse. As Benny Green wrote in his liner notes: "For forty years, Edison has seemed to dance with death by withholding the ending of a phrase until it threatens to breach the cohesion of the next one, but a consummate sense of time always sees him through."

What a marvelous idea it was for Oscar (and to give him due credit, Norman Granz) to go into studios in Los Angeles, New York and even London, England, with these trumpet kings and give us all such joyous jazz.

"That all of the hornmen succeed to the extent that they do in this most difficult of formats," wrote one reviewer, "is due largely to the intelligence, insight and experience of Peterson. No mere self-effacing accompanist, he brings to his responsibilities the same degree of intensity and involvement as do the trumpeters.

It should suffice then to say that few pianists of any era ever displayed as little dependence as Peterson does here on the resources of a rhythm section."

There's one more trumpet artist that Oscar worked and recorded with, who is not mentioned above because the two didn't record until later. This was Freddie Hubbard, who recorded with Oscar in 1982. (The album, called *Face to Face*, was reissued as a CD in 1997. Also in this group were guitarist Joe Pass, drummer Martin Drew and bass player Niels-Henning Orsted Pedersen. In his liner notes, Norman Granz described Hubbard as "probably the greatest of the post-bop players. His devil-may-care attitude is: try anything. If it works, fine; if not, and you fall on your ass, at least you've tried—Roy Eldridge's credo all the way: TAKE CHANCES! On top of that he has incredible chops.")

There are only four cuts on this CD, Hubbard and Peterson each contributing one. Freddie wrote "Thermo," and Oscar wrote "Tippin'." The first cut on the CD, written by Miles Davis, is titled "All Blues," and while Hubbard's work is certainly impressive, so is the bass playing of Ørsted Pedersen, and of special interest is the back-and-forth trading by Hubbard and Oscar. The Peterson contribution is a sizzler, taken at breakneck tempo and featuring, among other things, some all-out piano work by Oscar. Equally rewarding is the group's warm version of "Portrait of Jennie," a lovely ballad written in 1949 by film composer Dimitri Tiomkin, given a warm and tender treatment here, showing off Hubbard's sensitivity to the material, as well as Oscar's ability to remain in the background when accompanying another artist. And Joe Pass's guitar, neatly backed by Pedersen's bass, is also well worth paying attention to.

In 1975 Oscar took a group of musicians with him to play at the prestigious Montreux Jazz Festival in Switzerland. The group was billed as the "Oscar Peterson Big 6." His five sidemen were Milt Jackson on vibes, Joe Pass on guitar, Toots Thielemans on harmonica, Louis Bellson on drums and Niels

Pedersen on bass. For the record made that night, British critic Benny Green's liner notes included this glimpse of Oscar: "The night began, as a great many successful nights do, with the Blues. . . . By the time Joe Pass had completed his solo and Milt Jackson had taken over, the other musicians were starting to lay little riffs behind the solo line, which is always a good sign, and after Oscar Peterson had ended his solo with a little ten-fingered impromptu composition, he could hardly bring himself to stop playing, and so pecked hungrily at the keyboard behind Niels Pedersen's bass solo."

In December 1974, Oscar and Count Basie got together in Los Angeles to make an album together for the Pablo label. It was called *Satch and Josh*, and Granz felt compelled to explain (in a "Producer's Note" on the back of the LP sleeve) the reasons for this. "Satch" was Satchel Paige, of course, the great black baseball pitcher, and "Josh" was Josh Gibson, the equally impressive black baseball hitter.

The point of the album title was an anecdote concerning a momentous confrontation between the two men on the baseball diamond—when Satch declined to let Josh get a hit, even though the latter pleaded with the former because Satch's mother was in the grandstand, watching the game.

In the Granz album notes: "The point that Basie was making is that in this album, he places Satch for Oscar Peterson and himself, modestly, for Josh Gibson, but the truth of it is that in this album Oscar not only achieves his strike-outs but at the same time Basie hits his home run."

What I find most intriguing about the "Satch and Josh" combination is the way these two giants of the keyboard—so different from each other in style and approach—show their mutual respect for each other. Basie shrewdly keeps the rhythm going when Oscar solos, and Oscar gallantly refrains from trying to demolish the Count by flaunting his own flamboyant style.

The *Satch and Josh* album was successful enough that three

years later, Peterson and Basie did a second LP titled *Satch and Josh . . . Again*, also for Pablo, and also, of course, a hit. Peterson and Basie eventually made five albums together in a short and incredibly creative period between 1974 and 1978.

On the first two albums, Peterson and Basie were aided by Ray Brown on bass and Herb Ellis on guitar. Both men had been with Oscar in his most famous trio, back in the 1950s and 1960s.

In 1964, first Ed Thigpen and then Ray Brown left the Peterson group, simply because they had become exhausted by all of the touring. Brown had been with Oscar for fifteen years. "That's longer," said Brown, according to biographer Richard Palmer, "than most guys stay with their wives."

＊   ＊   ＊

I remember interviewing the Count back in the mid-1970s, in California. Movie biographies of various jazz figures had been made and I asked Basie if there had been any talk of a movie about his life. He told me he didn't know, but that he was working on a book about his life. I asked him how it was coming along. "Oh, fine," he said. "I've been working on it for fifteen years now. I guess I've got about eight pages done." (Count Basie died in 1984, his book still not completed. He had teamed up with writer and jazz critic Albert Murray, who fortunately completed the book, which was published in 1995.)

While we discussed the matter of movie biographies about jazz musicians (e.g., Goodman, Krupa, et al.)—this was only a few years after Diana Ross had starred in *Lady Sings the Blues*, a highly fictionalized and steamy movie allegedly depicting the life of jazz singer Billie Holiday—the Count expressed some doubts about how much should be revealed concerning the personal lives of musicians. "Sometimes," he said, "I think the skeleton should stay in the closet."

Basie liked to compare himself and Peterson to Satch and Josh. The Count was the ultimate minimalist among jazz pianists, but he had great respect for Oscar's keyboard wizardry, and I remember his talking about himself versus Peterson. Oscar, in turn, would call up memories of his friendship with Basie.

"We were on tour somewhere, in Germany, I think, and one night my phone rang. I was asleep. And it was Basie—he had that little lisp—'Thay, lithen here,' he'd start, and I knew who it was. I said, 'Base, why aren't you in bed?' He said, 'Have you got your radio on?' I said, 'No, Base, I was resting.' He told me to turn on the radio, right away. Didn't say what station or anything, but he insisted I turn on the radio. I said, 'Why, Base?' He said, 'There's some fool tearing up the piano, just like you. You oughta listen to him.' You know who it was? It was Horowitz."

Another special memory Peterson has is this: "We had the pianos facing each other, every night. He'd say, 'Don't go out there and act like a fool out there.' He'd give me a lecture. He'd say, 'Now, remember who you're out there with. It's not Horowitz; it's me.'

One night, he said, 'Now remember, if I play something, you answer me, and be nice when you answer.' Norman would be laughing. One night, Basie came out carrying a baseball bat. And he played the first eight bars or whatever it was and then he took out the baseball bat and showed it to me. It was like a threat."

Oscar added: "God, I loved that man."

In reflecting on Peterson, Basie had said: "Now, that's that monster, and I'm poor Josh. Norman Granz has had Oscar's group and my band do quite a few things together over the years, and as a special little novelty after Oscar's segment of the program, Norman has brought the two of us out, and we used to do three things together. We'd play a few bars each, and he'd play a chorus, and I would stumble through one, and he'd catch me stumbling along and pick me up and help me. He was wonderful.

"But some nights he'd forget, and I'd have to hit the piano real hard to let him know I was still there, so cut it out and don't get carried away. He was wonderful. But he was also terrible.

Sometimes I'd just think about how I was going to have to be with that monster that evening, and my whole day was ruined."

Basie said he was "always happy" when Granz had them appearing on the same concert.

"I just sit there in the wings, just looking and listening," he said, "because what he does is really incredible. I mean, it's impossible for anybody to sit down at the piano and think that fast. Impossible. You can't think that far ahead. So he just puts his hands on the keyboard, and his fingers will just play. He doesn't even look at the piano. . . . And I am sitting there, looking at him out there smiling because his fingers have just played something he wanted to hear."

*   *   *

In 1983, I had the pleasure of meeting and interviewing both Ray Brown and Herb Ellis, on different occasions, in Toronto. I had known Herb Ellis for a long time. I first met him in 1948 when he was with a group called the Soft Winds, along with pianist Lou Carter and bass player John Frigo. Ellis, Carter and Frigo comprised three-quarters of the rhythm section of the Jimmy Dorsey Orchestra (Ray McKinley was the drummer), until they quit to form the Soft Winds. Carter was not only a good pianist and composer (he wrote two good songs for the group, "Soft Winds" and "Detour Ahead"), but he even had a second persona—that of a New York taxi driver who came up with some very funny monologues. But the Soft Winds had a rough time getting enough work, so when Oscar offered Herb Ellis a job, he took it.

When I interviewed Herb, I was doing a regular piece for CBC Radio's "Variety Tonight." Four nights a week, I did brief pieces, about ten minutes each, spotlighting some musician or performer—two records separated by a short biographical sketch. On the fifth night, I did thirty-minute interviews—including some music—with well-known musicians.

Herb and I got talking about his first European tour with Jazz At The Philharmonic, with "Stuff" Smith, who played amplified violin and also sang and clowned.

"Having been to Europe a few times before," Herb told me, "being with Oscar, when you go on stage with Oscar, he expects the best from you, which is only right—and he expects your equipment to work properly.

"Well, having the different electrical current over there at that time, you had to take two amplifiers and you had to have a converter and different plugs, all kinds of stuff.

"So I had two amplifiers and a converter, and I was ready for all situations. God forbid, if one didn't work, I had another one. And I had cases for them, cases built especially for them, with foam rubber.

"Stuff played electric violin, and he went over. He had a little funky amplifier. He had no converter—I had to go get one for him. He had nothin'—no case, no cover. It had tubes in it, too.

"And they shipped that thing on the airplane and it would come rolling down with the baggage— Ka-plunk! It never failed to work, and I had trouble all the way through the tour. Ask Ray Brown about that."

Ray came to Toronto a few months later, in July 1983, and I invited him to our CBC studio for a talk. Just before coming to Toronto, he had played the closing night of the Montreal Jazz Festival. He appeared with Oscar, Herb and the Modern Jazz Quartet. To date, Ray had spent fifteen years with Oscar Peterson, four of them teaching at the Advanced School of Contemporary Music. I asked him if he enjoyed it, and he said he did—for four years.

"Different projects get my saliva going," he told me, "then I drift away from it."

He also did studio work for some sixteen years, he said, but that "got to be a drag, finally."

Brown told me his "Number One Man" was Jimmy Blanton,

the gifted young bass player with the Duke Ellington band in the very early 1940s (who, like the revered guitarist Charlie Christian, died very young).

"That's what made me play the instrument, the way he played it, the sound he got out of it," Ray told me. "It was intriguing enough to catch my ear and my eye. The ear tells you that's what you have to do. I used to stand outside bars and listen to the juke box. Jimmy Blanton changed things—definitely. He revolutionized the instrument. It's so beautiful to lay down the time and the beat for the soloists."

I asked Ray if he had ever played the cello, as I had heard.

Yes, he had. "I just changed the tuning around so it would be less difficult for a player to play," he said.

Then he reminded me that it was Oscar Pettiford who had popularized the cello in jazz. And, he added, "Percy Heath has my cello," he added. "I sent it to him."

Ray was the original bass player with the Modern Jazz Quartet—with John Lewis, Milt Jackson and Kenny Clarke. "I was one of the founding fathers of the group," he added, with justifiable pride.

Brown was no longer a working musician. He had turned producer and managed Quincy Jones, who, he said, "took me to some places I'd never been."

Ray managed the Modern Jazz Quartet for a time, touring England and Europe. Then, with a grin, he added: "This gives me the opportunity to *not* bother with the garbage-can gigs."

Ray Brown had one more thing on his mind he wanted to pass along to me: "Young people today are prone to take one thing at a time—usually rock and roll. If you can get their attention for jazz, then you're doing something."

* * *

Another outstanding artist Oscar worked with was the late jazz violinist Stephane Grappelli. Along with Joe Pass, Mickey Roker and Niels-Henning Pedersen, Grappelli recorded an album in

1979 in Copenhagen, titled *SKOL*. As usual, the producer was Norman Granz, who had earlier recorded Grappelli, Pass and Pedersen at the Tivoli Gardens in Copenhagen, Denmark. For *SKOL* he added the services of Mickey Roker and Oscar Peterson; it features a "touching solo" by Oscar and "an incredible virtuoso demonstration by Grappelli."

Of particular note is the haunting rendition of "Nuages," an almost seven-minute version of the Django Reinhardt tune, which opens with a Joe Pass guitar solo, followed by the masterful Grappelli and then some relatively low-key Peterson piano. Also worthy of attention is a rollicking version of that old workhorse for jazz musicians, "Makin' Whoopee," on which everybody seems to be having a ball.

Another auspicious occasion was in 1980, when Oscar appeared as a guest on Marian McPartland's long-running "Piano Jazz" radio series over National Public Radio in the United States. (It was actually a production of South Carolina Educational Radio but was carried by many public radio stations.)

When those magical half-hour radio shows were issued as a CD some years later, Marian wrote the liner notes, in which she recalled: "I was quite terrified about doing the show with Oscar, but I was also thrilled about it. And as it happened, it turned out to be great fun. I think I even said (jokingly), 'Please leave a few notes for me.' It was almost too much to bear to have Oscar Peterson all to myself. . . . He creates a different kind of emotion, a heady excitement, because of this overwhelming capacity to dazzle and generate exhilaration. At times it's almost as if he's driven by a force greater than himself that makes him play at an almost impossible speed, but when he changes pace and performs a reflective piece one can hear the tender side of Oscar, the voicings he uses that are his alone."

Clearly, both Oscar Peterson and Marian McPartland had a ball on this occasion. It is there in their warm conversation and in their playing—either solo or in duets, of which they did two:

"Falling in Love with Love" and Duke Ellington's "Cotton Tail."

*   *   *

Another of Oscar's appealing collaborators was Roy Eldridge, known as "Little Jazz," the diminutive but fiery trumpeter whose passion for playing jazz equaled his dazzling technique. Roy was Oscar's guest on a radio series the pianist did for CBC in the early 1980s titled "Oscar Peterson and Friends." The half-hour show had drummer Bobby Durham and bassist Ray Brown rounding out Oscar's trio, plus a guest each week. When he had Eldridge on, Oscar introduced him by saying Roy didn't represent jazz history, but "*is* jazz history."

No less a taskmaster than Norman Granz said he regarded Eldridge so highly because "he's not afraid to take risks." That was true enough. Roy never held back; he was fiercely competitive, always ready and willing to "cut" any musician he played with—or against.

The two musicians had met, years before, on the very night in September 1949 that Granz introduced Oscar at Carnegie Hall. On that program, Oscar talked about Roy's "true jazz sound" and "the way you play ballads." Then he got Eldridge to play "Talk of the Town," which was delivered with his customary passionate, soulful fearlessness.

You'll forgive me, I hope, if all this sounds a bit over-the-top, but I have to confess that Roy Eldridge is my favorite jazz trumpeter. Some critics liked to describe Roy as "the bridge" between Louis Armstrong and Dizzy Gillespie—a description that Roy always rejected. "I was never trying to be any bridge," he commented. "I was just out to play the best I knew how."

In the early 1980s, while I was doing a regular spot on CBC Radio's "Variety Tonight," I had occasion to go to New York to do some interviews of musicians. Roy was playing at some club (I think it was Jimmy Ryan's, at its newer location on 54th Street). Roy was then in his seventies and, to my dismay, wasn't playing nearly as well as he had for so many years before. It was disappointing to see and hear this giant of jazz past his peak. But, I reasoned, I could still listen to his many brilliant records and remember fondly how deeply his playing had moved me when he was in his prime. (Roy died in 1988, at the age of seventy-seven.)

But of all the artists Oscar Peterson has worked with in his spectacular career, the one I tend to associate with him is the late (and marvelous) Ella Fitzgerald. Ira Gershwin, the reticent brother of the more aggressive George, once paid Ella the ultimate tribute: "I never knew how good our songs were," he said, "until I heard Ella sing them."

Perhaps I associate Ella with Oscar so closely because I saw them perform together so many times, usually in JATP concerts, including the first JATP at Toronto's Massey Hall. I remember asking Ella for her earliest recollections of Oscar Peterson.

"I think it was a club in Toronto he was playing in," she said. "We used to go around there and catch him all the time, and I was just amazed at the way he was playing."

Years later, Ella again talked about Oscar: "He's way up there so far that you can't say what he is, because he does all of the things."

Another totally unsolicited tribute to Oscar came from contralto Maureen Forrester, who was born in Montreal five years after Oscar. "I would tell my mother I was going to the Youth Centre and I'd go off to Westmount where Oscar was playing. I was always impressed with his improvising because you could tell he had a classical training, because it was so incredibly beautiful."

18

OSCAR GETS AROUND

In his 1974 book *From Satchmo to Miles*, jazz critic Leonard Feather wrote, tongue in cheek: "The requirements for glamour in jazz too often include eccentricity, limited technical scope (supposedly compensated by 'soul'), a personal background of sexual problems, and a tendency to show up for the Wednesday matinee at midnight on Thursday. By these standards, Oscar Peterson was a cinch to be voted Least Likely to Succeed."

Throughout his long, busy, fruitful career, Oscar has played with a variety of sidemen. Most memorable, of course, are Ray Brown, Herb Ellis and Ed Thigpen. He also recorded with a lengthy list of other notable sidemen—from the series of albums he did with trumpeters such as Roy Eldridge, Dizzy Gillespie, Clark Terry, Harry "Sweets" Edison, Freddie Hubbard and the young Jon Faddis, to his memorable collaborations with Count Basie, to his work with Benny Carter, Coleman Hawkins and Stephane Grappelli, and the larger Montreux Jazz Festival group, which included Milt Jackson and Toots Thielemans.

In 1979, Oscar played a concert at Tivoli Concert Hall in Copenhagen, leading a group that included Joe Pass, Niels-Henning Ørsted Pedersen, Mickey Roker and the superb jazz violinist Stephane Grappelli. Later he said of Grappelli: "I love the way his bow skims over the notes, like a stone bouncing over the surface of a gleaming lake."

He also commented on Grappelli's "beatific smile, with a hint of devilish mischief."

Oscar was always gracious and generous in praising the work of musicians he worked and recorded with. From one interview, in the early 1980s, Oscar was asked which musicians he admired most. He began to reel off the names of some of his favorites— Clark Terry, Zoot Sims, Lester Young, Coleman Hawkins, Ella Fitzgerald. Then he recalled pioneering jazz trumpeter Clifford Brown, who had seemed destined for great fame. "I was on my way to a Chicago engagement in 1954. When I got there, I was told, 'You're opening. Clifford Brown is dead.'" Brown had been killed in a car crash at the age of twenty-six.

While he loved to play with sidemen, it was the prodding of Norman Granz and Duke Ellington that influenced him to play more solo piano. "Duke and Norman Granz were really responsible for me playing more solo piano," Oscar remembered. "Duke used to bug me—lovingly bug me—night after night, when we'd play tours together. He'd ask, 'Why don't you go out there and burn up the piano for us for a while?' He said he loved my trio— no matter who was in the trio, he'd say he loved it. But he'd say, 'But, you know, people sometimes like the caviar without the eggs and onion.'" (The "eggs and onion" meant his two sidemen.)

He followed Ellington's suggestion and (temporarily, at least) broke up the trio. "It was a challenge," he recalled years later. "It opened up a whole new world to me. I could play with whomever I liked and wherever I liked." Among those he worked with during that period were Cleo Laine and John Dankworth, and his old friend Count Basie.

Hans Georg Brunner-Schwer, owner of MPS Records, had been an admirer of Oscar's work for years. Beginning in 1961, he invited Oscar once a year to visit Brunner-Schwer's home in Villingen, Germany, to have a select group of appreciative guests hear Oscar's trio play.

In the mid-1960s, when Oscar's contract with an American record company had run out, Brunner-Schwer said he would like to issue some of the material of Oscar's that he had recorded on his label. Oscar agreed and flew to Villingen to help select and edit the tapes. But it turned out there was not enough usable material to issue (because some of the material had already been released on other labels), so Brunner-Schwer suggested Oscar make a solo album—which Oscar wanted to do, anyway.

Oscar's piano solo album, titled *My Favorite Instrument*, was the fourth and final Oscar made in Germany for Brunner-Schwer.

In his liner notes, Gene Lees wrote: "It's an album I consider long overdue. Only in a solo album would Oscar be able to show the full scope of his playing. Tatum felt that rhythm sections got in the way. They do, too. The piano, for good or ill, is a self-contained instrument.... Anyone who hasn't heard him playing alone cannot know how gigantic his playing is. This record makes that possible.... I am tempted to say this is the greatest jazz piano album ever made. And maybe it is. But it's more than that. Said one fascinated musician, on hearing it, 'This surpasses jazz.' Yes, it does."

In *The Globe and Mail*, jazz critic Mark Miller wrote: "Over the years, Peterson's solo piano has become the model of consistency, and the model of his very personal approach to music. The pianist in Peterson holds sway over the jazz musician, and conceives any given tune as much in terms of the instrument as the tradition...."

The album has a lot to recommend it, not the least item being the realization on the very first tune, "Someone to Watch over Me," that Oscar serves as his own rhythm section.

Among the highlights on *My Favorite Instrument* is his sensitive grasp of the multi-faceted aspects of Johnny Green's "Body and Soul," long a favorite among jazz musicians partly because of its harmonic intricacies. And when he plays the old Rodgers and Hart song "Little Girl Blue," you sense that he truly reveres not only the tune and the harmonies, but the lyrics, too.

The other three albums Peterson recorded in Germany for Brunner-Schwer were titled *Action, Girl Talk* and *Tristeza on Piano*. His sidemen varied only slightly. On *Action*, the first album in the series, he recorded with his two standbys, Ray

Brown and Ed Thigpen. Of the six tracks on the album, Joachim Ernst Berendt, who wrote the liner notes (translated into English by John Wilde) noted: "It's striking how Peterson's music has become soloistic in character. Originally, in the trio with Barney Kessel or Herb Ellis on guitar and Ray Brown on bass, the basic concept was more that of the combo, rather in the tradition of the idea of 'integration' introduced by John Lewis with the Modern Jazz Quartet."

Girl Talk, the second album in the series, had Ray Brown as bassist on some cuts, Sam Jones on others. And Bobby Durham and Louis Hayes split the drumming chores. This time, there were only five cuts, the last of which was a three-tune medley: "Girl Talk," "Robbins Nest" and a Peterson medley consisting of "I Concentrate on You" and "Moon River."

Wrote Egbert Hoehl in his liner notes: "His masculine keyboard touch corresponds to almost explosive ornamentation in phrasing. Despite all the dynamics, a boundless desire for improvisation, a sublime artistic technique, however, the structure of his play (i.e. the over-all conception of harmonic means, phrasing, rhythms, etc.) remains translucent and tight. And in the sphere of intuition Peterson leaves no murky corners."

For *Tristeza on Piano*, the third volume in the Villingen series, Oscar again had Sam Jones on bass and drummer Bob Durham. The title ("tristeza" means sadness) is a nod to the Brazilian influence that propels at least some of the music involved.

Joachim Ernst Berendt wrote in his liner notes: "You hear 'Tristeza' everywhere. Soon you are singing along and you find that with this song, you start to understand Brazilian music, although you never stop marveling at how it is possible to sing over and over again of 'tristeza,' of sadness, with so much joy and ecstasy."

"Tristeza" was composed by Edu Lobo (who is sometimes called "the Bob Dylan of Brazil") and was originally a carnival hit, although it soon became an evergreen of the "Desafinado" class. "Desafinado," composed by Antonio Carlos Jobim, was the first bossa nova hit played and recorded by Stan Getz (who had heard the recording made by Brazilian singer Joao Gilberto).

Jobim is represented on Oscar's *Tristeza* album by "Triste," one of Jobim's most beautiful compositions. Oscar plays it in fast bossa nova rhythm, making it into a masterpiece for piano, bass and drums.

Michel Legrand's "Watch What Happens" begins as an unaccompanied piano solo before Sam Jones and Bob Durham join in and quickly transform it into a samba, with Oscar swinging along in a bluesy vein.

The album ends with "Fly Me to the Moon," on which, according to Berendt's notes, "Oscar begins his scintillating finale like a Mozart piano sonata before Bobby Durham's brush introduces a feather-weight swing. Sam Jones brings in the required intensity and Oscar himself hammers out the theme with all the precision and power of the whole Basie orchestra."

For anyone who is interested, I have a kind of little game, a method of tracing Oscar Peterson's development over his enduring career. To do this, you simply listen to the following records, ranging over forty-five years of Oscar's career. Here they are:

ONE: *Oscar Peterson Beginnings—1945–1949*. This is a double CD reissue, originally on the RCA Victor label, offering sixteen tunes on each disc. These were all recorded in Montreal, with various sidemen: bass players Bert Brown, Albert King and Austin Roberts, and drummers Frank Gariepy, Russ Dufort, Mark "Wilkie" Wilkinson and Roland Verdon. Discussing Peterson's evolution, even then, the liner notes mention that "Peterson soon transferred his allegiance from classical music to jazz, more especially at first to boogie-woogie, a style calling for a strong, agile left hand and an unfailing sense of rhythm. Some tracks on this album . . . bear witness to Peterson's ability in this direction, while at the same time revealing that he had already extended his musical language beyond these particular frontiers."

TWO: *The Oscar Peterson Trio at the Stratford Shakespearean Festival*. This album, made in 1956 for Norman Granz's Verve label, was recorded on the Shakespearean stage at the Stratford Festival, with Ray Brown and Herb Ellis. Most of the tunes recorded were standard popular songs ("Falling in Love with Love," "How High the Moon," "Swingin' on a Star" and Ellington's "Love You Madly"). But there are a few surprises, too, such as Django Reinhardt's "Nuages"; "Noreen's Dream," written by Oscar and dedicated to Phil Nimmons' wife, Noreen; and "Daisy's Dream," which Oscar dedicated to his sister. Peterson's liner notes ended with "As for myself, I have never felt more relaxed and at ease at a recording session than I have at this one, and I feel that it shows in my playing."

THREE: *Ella and Oscar*. This album was recorded for Norman Granz's Pablo label in 1975, with only the bass of Ray Brown supporting the singer and the pianist. "The pianist plays as hard as usual," said one evaluation of the album, "but instrumentalist and vocalist bring out the best in each other, and there are at least three near-classics in 'Mean to Me,' 'How Long Has This Been Going On?' and 'Midnight Sun.' "

FOUR: Finally, I suggest *Last Call at the Blue Note*, recorded live at the New York club of that name in March 1990 and issued on the Telarc label. It was the last of three albums cut by the reunited Peterson Trio. Before it came *Live at the Blue Note*, which won two Grammys, and then *Saturday Night at the Blue Note*, which won another Grammy. Featured this time was the reconstituted Oscar Peterson Trio (i.e., Ray Brown and Herb Ellis) with the addition of drummer Bobby Durham. There are only seven cuts on the CD, two of which are sections of Peterson's *Canadiana Suite*, originally recorded and released in 1964. These are "Wheatland" and "March Past." The latter, as Peterson has said, was originally written for the Calgary Stampede, and he got a charge, later, out of seeing and hearing his tune played by a

Queen's Guard band in England. "It was quite an honor," he said, "the kind of recognition I haven't always had at home."

But this CD also has two lengthy and impressive medleys. "It Never Entered My Mind" and "Body and Soul" form one medley. The other offers "Our Waltz" by David Rose and two Peterson originals, "Adagio" and "Bach's Blues." In his album notes, Donald Elfman wrote: "*Last Call* features the unique blend of lyric, rhapsodic and virtuosic brilliance that so consistently informs the writing and playing of Oscar Peterson. The classic trio sound is augmented by another former associate of Oscar's—drummer Bobby Durham—and the group once again demonstrates an athletic swing complemented by an innately communicative approach to music."

Elsewhere in the liner notes, Herb Ellis is quoted: "They [the trio] had a lot of arrangements. It was awesome. But that period was one of the highlights of my life and career. The challenge that Oscar put on me and put on Ray and put on himself. So you couldn't have qualms about it; he made it as hard for himself as he did for everybody."

And Peterson himself is also quoted in the liner notes: "You have to have those years of experience. Jazz is a matter of being mature in your choice of what you play and create. . . . I played with everybody from the old school (swing) to what was then the new movement (bebop). I learned a lot. I'm still learning. That's what it takes."

It was Quincy Jones, a true titan in the history of American popular music, including jazz—trumpeter, arranger, bandleader, producer, guru—who may have most aptly summed up the value of Oscar Peterson.

"I remember Benny Carter saying, 'Get up from the piano. Oscar is in the house,'" Jones said. "And it's true. I mean, who wants to be at a piano when Oscar is there? Find something else to do."

19

OSCAR AND BROADWAY

Despite an early remark by Oscar that he "didn't know" many Broadway show tunes, he turned out quite a few albums devoted to the music of various Broadway shows and/or their composers.

For example, for either the Clef or Verve labels, he recorded works by Cole Porter, Irving Berlin, Duke Ellington, Jerome Kern, Richard Rodgers, Harry Warren, Vincent Youmans, George Gershwin, Jimmy McHugh and, certainly not least, Leonard Bernstein.

He also recorded albums of various Broadway shows, among them *On the Town* (originally a Jerome Robbins ballet with music by Leonard Bernstein), *My Fair Lady* (Lerner and Loewe), *Fiorello!* (Jerry Bock), *Porgy and Bess* (George Gershwin) and *West Side Story* (Bernstein again).

To look at an album devoted to the work of a particular composer, the first one Peterson recorded, in 1959, was *Oscar Peterson Plays the Cole Porter Song Book*, for the Verve label. Ably assisted by Ray Brown and Ed Thigpen, Oscar features an even dozen Porter tunes, including an easy, relaxed rendition of "In the Still of the Night" (from Porter's 1937 show, *Rosalie*) and a swinging "It's All Right with Me." Also attractive is a saucy, almost suggestive interpretation of "Love for Sale." Next comes a breezy "Just One of Those Things," from the 1935 Porter show, *Jubilee*. "I've Got You Under My Skin" was from the Eleanor Powell movie *Born to Dance*, and was reprised in

Broadway Melody of 1940, sung and danced by Fred Astaire and Eleanor Powell.

Also in the show's score was "Begin the Beguine." Although the critics generally liked *Jubilee*, they had some reservations about the music. So, apparently, did Porter, his producers and his publishers. When the songs were first issued (in sheet music), two that became Porter classics were not included: "Just One of Those Things" and "Begin the Beguine."

When Porter wrote "I've Got You Under My Skin," he marked it "beguine tempo," possibly because he was still under the influence of "Begin the Beguine," which he had written the year before. But Lawrence D. Stewart makes an interesting point in his liner notes: "Oscar Peterson can also be the purist and helpfully restore a song's forgotten charm. Listen to his treatment of 'I've Got You Under My Skin.' " While Ray Brown and Ed Thigpen re-establish the haunting quality of a beguine, Stewart adds, "Oscar Peterson uses the piano to convey us on a melodic and exotic excursion."

Although "Begin the Beguine" was to become one of Porter's most enduring hits, it was dismissed when it was introduced. Moss Hart commented: "I had reservations about the length of the song. Indeed, I am somewhat ashamed to record that I thought it had ended when [Porter] was only halfway through playing it."

Although it was one of Porter's two favorites among his compositions (the other was "Love for Sale"), "Begin the Beguine" might well have been totally forgotten but for a recording, late in 1938, by Artie Shaw and his orchestra. Shaw had just been contracted by RCA Victor to record for its Bluebird label. He was strongly advised to record Rudolph Friml's 1924 song "Indian Love Call," which Shaw wasn't crazy about. He finally consented, but only on condition that for the other side of the 78 rpm disc he be allowed to use "Begin the Beguine."

"I just happened to like it," he later explained, "so I insisted on recording it at this first session, in spite of the recording manager, who thought it a complete waste of time and only let me make it after I had argued it would make at least a nice quiet contrast to the 'Indian Love Call.' "

Shaw's recording sold two million disks, becoming one of the largest-selling instrumental recordings by an American band in recording history. "That recording of that one little tune," Shaw said, "was the real turning point in my life."

Despite its success in the Shaw version, "Begin the Beguine" was not "covered" (copied or repeated) by other bands, except for its interpolation in a few motion pictures (e.g., *Night and Day*, a screen biography of Porter in which the songwriter was played by Cary Grant). It's anybody's guess as to whether this odd disinclination to cover Shaw's record can be attributed to a lack of interest in the Porter song or perhaps the realization that no attempt could equal the popularity of the Artie Shaw version. In any case, and for whatever reasons, Oscar did not include "Begin the Beguine" in his Cole Porter disc.

Probably Porter's most enduring hit song is "Night and Day," introduced by Fred Astaire in the 1932 show *The Gay Divorcee*. Porter said he was inspired to write the song after hearing Mohammedan calls to prayer in Morocco and that the "drip, drip, drip" of the verse was suggested by the comment of a hostess annoyed by the sounds coming from a broken downspout (this according to Gerald Bordman's book, *American Musical Theater*, published in 1978).

"Why Can't You Behave?" came from Cole Porter's biggest Broadway success, *Kiss Me Kate*, based, very loosely, on Shakespeare's *The Taming of the Shrew*. Oscar gives it a smooth, tender treatment, as he does the next tune, "I Concentrate on You." But the tempo picks up on the album's last tune, "It's De-Lovely," which came from the score of Porter's 1936 show, *Red, Hot and Blue*, which starred Jimmy Durante, Ethel Merman and newcomer Bob Hope.

As usual, Peterson didn't mince words when discussing his music or recordings. Here are some excerpts from a 1983 interview with Len Lyons:

> LYONS: "What albums do you think should appear in a selected discography of your recording?"
>
> PETERSON: "I'd have to cite *The Trio* album in Chicago, on Verve, and the new Pablo album also called *The Trio*. The *Night Train* album because we accomplished what we wanted in terms of feeling. I'd cite the *West Side Story* album because it was a departure in terms of material from what the trio was doing at the time. Then there was *My Favorite Instrument*, the first solo album I did for MPS."
>
> LYONS: "Are there albums you're dissatisfied with?"
>
> PETERSON: "I won't be coy with you. In all the years I've been with Norman Granz, I've always had the option to kill something if I didn't like it."
>
> LYONS: "I wanted to ask you about *West Side Story* and the other show music albums, because many people consider it a commercial departure and criticized it on those grounds."
>
> PETERSON: "To the contrary, that album is one of the biggest challenges I've taken on musically. I said no to the idea at first for the exact reason you're citing. I didn't want to get into the Showtime U.S.A. bit. But as I listened to the *West Side Story* score over and over, I realized it represented a new challenge. It was one of the roughest projects we tackled, and it came off differently from the other show albums."
>
> LYONS: "Leonard Bernstein's music impressed you?"
>
> PETERSON: "That's right. I don't consider him to be the same type of jazz writer as Benny Golson or Duke Ellington. I don't think we have anything in the jazz world comparable to that, structurally speaking."

LYONS: "I've never considered Bernstein a jazz writer at all. I've always thought of those compositions as show tunes."
PETERSON: "I feel they have a jazz context."

Another show whose score appealed to Peterson was *Porgy and Bess*, sometimes described as an American folk opera. The genesis of its musical score was a long and tortuous trip. DuBose Heyward had written his novel *Porgy* in 1925. George Gershwin was interested in turning it into a musical, but the Theater Guild had other plans. The Guild wanted Jerome Kern to do the music, with the idea of starring Al Jolson in the musical, an idea whose demise should still be celebrated. But Heyward, reminded of Gershwin's more serious ambitions, held out for Gershwin. The show, of course, became an American classic.

Peterson was so enamored with the score that he recorded it twice, three times if you count his inclusion of the song "Porgy" in his *Tristeza* album in 1970.

The first time Oscar recorded "Porgy" was for Verve in 1959, of which it was noted "Peterson makes the session so forcibly his own." His second recorded version, in 1976, has Oscar playing clavichord instead of piano, leading one observer to comment that this was "nothing more than a way of freshening up rather stale performances."

Oscar again explored the music of the Broadway theater, also in 1959, with a Verve album featuring music from two hit shows, *My Fair Lady* (Lerner and Loewe) and *Fiorello!* (Jerry Bock).

It was in 1962 that Oscar Peterson, with Ray Brown and Ed Thigpen, recorded some of the songs from Leonard Bernstein's smash hit musical drama, *West Side Story*. This is one of my favorite Peterson albums, as *West Side Story* is one of my favorite musicals. (It had, after all, a pretty respectable ancestry, being based—albeit loosely—on Shakespeare's *Romeo and Juliet*.)

By the time Peterson got around to it, the music to *West Side Story* had been recorded by practically every kind of musical organization in every kind of context except possibly a march. The show had opened on Broadway in 1957 and was produced as a successful movie in 1961.

"Peterson's problem was clear-cut," in the view of Don Cerulli, who wrote the liner notes, "to present a jazz version of the score without losing the essence of the music or the identity of The Trio." As Peterson said between takes at one of the recording sessions, "Basically I would say this is the first album of its type of the music from *West Side Story*. It's a very different album. And it's primarily different because the music is an arranger's delight. We are approaching it more obviously from the player's standpoint—the improviser's standpoint. It's the same way we approach all our things.

"This goes along with my belief that anything within the jazz medium should contain proper room for improvisation, or what we call the creative impact.

"We have tried to give it a very definite proximity to an open, blowing type of jazz, which is what we do. And in doing this, we had to make necessary deviations, musically speaking, in some cases, while still being conscious of not destroying the Bernstein framework.

"I found it pretty difficult to approach the music from this aspect. The reason, I would say, was that the balance between the musical image of The Trio and the musical image of *West Side Story* was an almost infinitesimal thing."

The trio had its rough moments preparing for the album. They had not worked before audiences since the previous October, but had been teaching at the Advanced School of Contemporary Music. After classes, they would get together and run through some of the music.

The album has no patchings, no splices, no choruses cut out. It was recorded as you hear it.

The album is an absolute gem. It opens with "Something's Coming," done in a robust, ambitious manner, swinging in just the right places. Next comes the haunting ballad "Somewhere," sung longingly in the show by the two leads, Maria and Tony. The Peterson version features Brown bowing the main theme, and Oscar's sensitivity to the song's meaning. It finishes with a soaring climax.

"Jet Song," the white street gang's strident, boastful anthem, is done in a light, swinging mode, somewhat different from the original context of the song. "Tonight" is brighter than might be expected, not the tender, longing love song of Tony and Maria, but a well-constructed arrangement.

"Maria," perhaps the score's prettiest melody, gets a light, airy treatment, with a subtle Latin beat, but it builds to a moving climax, again with the light Latin rhythm. "I Feel Pretty" is given a lively treatment without ever losing the tune's original simple charm. (Peterson's four-bar breaks at various points during the piece led one of the recording engineers to comment: "Someday, that guy's hand is going to fly off at the wrist while he's doing that.")

The album ends with "Reprise," a kind of epilogue, or highlight of the highlights of the Bernstein score, the music compressed into a capsule that says, unmistakably, this is the sound of *West Side Story* and the Oscar Peterson Trio.

As Cerulli said in his liner notes, "This is a trio in which the unit sound is always superb. This is also a trio in which three remarkable soloists use every portion of their creativity to produce that unit sound. And the overall concept is always that of the improviser."

Peterson also revered the music of George Gershwin, as shown by his two recordings of the *Porgy and Bess* score. Over the years, he recorded many of Gershwin's songs, from "I Got Rhythm" (written in 1930) to "Love Walked In," written in 1938, the last year of Gershwin's all-too-short life.

In 1996, Norman Granz's Verve label reissued two of Oscar's Gershwin collections on a CD titled *Oscar Peterson Plays the George Gershwin Song Book*. There are twenty-four Gershwin melodies crammed into this gem of a CD, equally divided between two different Peterson trios—although that remarkably strong bass player Ray Brown is on both of them.

Both trios had been heard earlier, of course, on LPs, but on this CD the later group (Oscar, Brown and drummer Ed Thigpen) is heard first. This was originally recorded in Chicago in 1959. The second dozen, with Barney Kessel on guitar, was recorded in Los Angeles and first issued in 1952.

The CD begins with a beautifully subdued Oscar offering, "It Ain't Necessarily So," indicating Peterson's reverence for the music of Gershwin. Three of the Gershwin tunes appear twice: "It Ain't Necessarily So," "Oh, Lady Be Good" and "Love Walked In."

It's interesting to compare the different versions of, say, "Love Walked In." The later (1959) version is treated pretty much as a simple ballad. The earlier (1952) treatment, with guitarist Kessel in place of Thigpen, swings along gently.

"Oh, Lady Be Good," in the 1959 edition, is given a distinctly bluesy mood, taken at a markedly slower tempo than one is accustomed to hearing it (especially after Ella Fitzgerald began using it as her scat-singing anthem), but the tone and mood are irresistible.

The 1952 edition of "Oh, Lady Be Good" (with Kessel) is also taken at a leisurely tempo, but Oscar gets into improvising earlier in the game and seems to be having more fun with it.

As for "It Ain't Necessarily So," again the earlier (1952) seems a bit less reverent than the 1959 version. And on this one, Barney Kessel is allowed a brief solo. As for Ray Brown, he is his usual Gibraltarian self.

A pleasant bonus is the free-and-easy Peterson version of "Somebody Loves Me," a song, by the way, for which brother Ira did not write the lyrics. They were done by Buddy De Sylva and Ballard MacDonald.

Unlike the flamboyant, confident, outgoing George, Ira was rather shy, modest, even self-effacing. Despite his often brilliant lyrics (heard in "S'Wonderful," "I've Got a Crush on You,"

"Embraceable You" and "But Not for Me"), he lived in George's shadow for much of the first half of his life. (He was born two years before George but outlived his brother by some forty-five years. The soft-spoken Ira Gershwin died in 1983, at the age of eighty-seven.)

After George's tragic death in 1937 of a brain tumor, Ira was idle for several years, until he teamed up with Kurt Weill to write the score of *Lady in the Dark* (1941), his irresistible lyrics overshadowing Weill's music to "My Ship." After that, he went on to write many more lyrics to go with music by such as Jerome Kern, Harold Arlen, Harry Warren and Arthur Schwartz. He even worked with Vernon Duke in 1938 to complete a song for *The Goldwyn Follies*, the movie whose intent to have an all-Gershwin score had been blocked by George's death the year before.

I remember hearing a lovely story that perfectly illustrated the difference, in temperament and personality, between the famous Gershwin brothers.

Both George and Ira were at a Beverly Hills cocktail party on this particular Saturday in the mid-1930s. There were some eight people at this late-afternoon gathering and they all enjoyed themselves so much that it seemed like a good idea to go on to dinner somewhere. George went into another room to phone one of the classier restaurants in the area (a favorite hangout for the Hollywood set), but returned with the sad tidings that the place was all booked up.

The shy Ira then volunteered to try his luck and went to the phone in the other room. He came back in a few moments and said, "Okay, we're all set, but we have to get there fast."

George, among others, was amazed. "How did you manage that?" he asked his brother.

Said Ira: "It was easy. I mentioned your name."

Oscar told me a Gershwin story, too. While he was in Los Angeles, Norman Granz invited him to go "for a walk." Somewhat reluctantly, Oscar agreed. Where they went was to visit Ira Gershwin, who still had his brother George's piano. Ira invited

Oscar to play the Gershwin piano and, somewhat tentatively, Oscar did. When they were leaving, Ira presented Oscar with a book of his, a collection of his own lyrics.

Once they were outside, Granz looked at the book Ira Gershwin had given Oscar and felt a bit slighted. "He put the *figure* in yours. He didn't put it in mine," he complained to Oscar, who had no idea what Granz was talking about.

So Granz explained. Ira Gershwin autographed many books, but only in certain ones—those to be given to somebody he felt was special—he would draw a little figure of a man in tails, taking a bow. Oscar got one of those.

20

THE AMSTERDAM SCAM

The year 1994 brought one of those rare oddities in the careers of Norman Granz and Oscar Peterson. That was the release of a CD, on Granz's Verve label, titled *The Oscar Peterson Trio at the Concertgebuow*. A subtitle pronounces, "Recorded in Amsterdam, Holland." The recording came about through a fan of Oscar's who attended the concert. Norman Granz relates: "In the spring of 1958 I made a concert tour through most of western Europe which was called 'An Evening with Ella Fitzgerald and the Oscar Peterson Trio.' It never occurred to me to record the concert in Europe as I had for so many years with Jazz At The Philharmonic in America. Fortunately, a rabid jazz fan in Amsterdam recorded the concert that I presented at the Concertgebuow and afterwards presented me with the tapes. On these tapes is some of the most exciting jazz, and certainly the most exciting trio music that I've heard in years. This album is the best of that taped concert at the Concertgebuow as played by the Oscar Peterson Trio."

Originally released as an LP on Verve (MGV 8268) in 1958, a CD was issued in 1994.

The liner notes on this CD are eyebrow-raising. They were written by one Reuel V. Lubag, described as a jazz pianist in the Pacific Northwest "who works with Ernestine Anderson."

Lubag writes, "The LP's title, *The Oscar Peterson Trio at the Concertgebuow*, has been a red herring since its original issue (Verve MGV 8268). The music actually came from a concert at

171

the Civic Opera House in Chicago. Further, the bonus tracks on this CD are from an LP that was titled *The Modern Jazz Quartet and the Oscar Peterson Trio at the Opera House* (Verve 8269), but they came from a concert at the Shrine Auditorium in Los Angeles. Oscar Peterson and his trio did perform at the Concertgebuow in Amsterdam—at a midnight concert on April 12–13, 1958. No recording of this concert has been found."

(For what it's worth, the *Encyclopedia of Music in Canada* lists the Concertgebuow album with no reference to its having been recorded at the Shrine Auditorium in Los Angeles.)

Quite apart from the mini-scandal suggested by Mr. Lubag, the music on the *Concertgebuow* CD is quite pleasant, from Oscar's speedy workout on "The Lady Is a Tramp" to the smooth, laid-back rendition of Benny Carter's "When Lights Are Low." And there is even a lively Peterson original, titled "Evrev," which points up—apart from the otherwise thoroughly satisfying music contained—a bit of a problem Oscar used to have in those days, that of humming/singing along with his playing.

In fairness, it should be pointed out that Peterson neither invented nor monopolized this sometimes distracting practice. The much revered maestro Arturo Toscanini actually sang his way through a recorded broadcast of *La Bohème*, and the venerated cellist Pablo Casals "grunted out an ad lib self-accompaniment for an album of Bach suites for unaccompanied cello," according to Joseph Roddy. It was, as always, a habit that some musicians got into, obviously without realizing that the same microphone that was picking up their playing could also pick up this humming/singing, to the consternation of recording engineers and producers.

Peterson did eventually cure himself of this distracting habit, although it is difficult to imagine the sort of concentration and willpower it must have taken to break such an ingrained (and subconscious) habit.

Perhaps the answer came through his actually singing on recordings. There are, to my knowledge, two albums of Peterson vocalizing. The first was a 1953 Clef album titled *Oscar Peterson Sings*, a ten-inch LP with, typically for the time, precious little liner-note information. Oscar is accompanied by bass and guitar and one can only assume the sidemen were Ray Brown and Herb Ellis—but there is no mention of them in the liner notes.

Oscar's singing is neither wonderful nor terrible—perhaps what one might expect if, say, Frank Sinatra tried playing jazz piano. Peterson's singing is never out-of-tune, but there is a tentativeness about it, a lack of confidence that sometimes comes through. He is comfortable enough with such light-hearted material as "I Can't Give You Anything but Love" and "I Hear Music," but on the heavier and more demanding ballads—"I'm Glad There Is You" and "One for My Baby," for example—the uncertainty is more evident.

Peterson did not sing again—at least on records—until 1965, on a CD titled *With Respect to Nat*. His one-time idol, Nat Cole, had died early that year. It was Cole's trio, after all, that Oscar had used as a model when he formed his own group—not the first one, with Ozzie Roberts and Clarence Jones, but the much more famous, long-lasting trio with Ray Brown and Herb Ellis.

A "discographer" named Brian Rust displayed his abysmal ignorance by writing that while Cole made many recordings "there is virtually no jazz music on any of them." This is patent nonsense. I have, in my own limited collection, a ten-inch Capitol LP titled *King Cole at the Piano, with Rhythm Accompaniment*.

There are several pretty and relatively unadorned ballads on the LP (e.g., "Moonlight in Vermont," "These Foolish Things"), but there are also several examples of Cole's interest in and ability to play jazz quite capably, thank you. They include "How High the Moon," one of the jazz anthems of the time, a lively Cole original called "Cole Capers," and another marvelously executed Cole item called "Blues in My Shower," which has long been a favorite Cole recording of mine.

The Nat "King" Cole Trio of the 1930s was quite successful—

strictly as an instrumental group. It was a nightclub owner in Los Angeles, I believe, who instructed Nat to start doing some singing, because "the customers like it." Cole obliged and managed to keep a balance for a while, but then he began recording vocals, and some of these songs—"Route 66," "Nature Boy," "Mona Lisa," etc.—became such huge hits that Cole gradually moved away from the piano and began working as a stand-up singing star. I can still remember the two occasions when I saw Nat Cole in person. The first was at Loew's Uptown Theatre, in Toronto, which then still had stage shows as well as movies. This would have been in the very early 1950s. The second was somewhere around 1964, at Toronto's O'Keefe Centre (now the Hummingbird Centre). On both occasions, he did not sit at the piano but did his stand-up vocal act.

The first time I can recall seeing Cole on television was on his NBC TV series, "The Nat 'King' Cole Show," sometime in 1956 or 1957. Even then, he did his singing standing up. And, by coincidence, on this occasion he was accompanied at the piano by his guest star, Oscar Peterson.

Nat King Cole died in February of 1965. That same fall, Oscar's album *With Respect to Nat* was issued. The affection and respect Oscar always felt for Cole is evident in the twelve songs he does—some with just rhythm accompaniment, several with a big band, with arrangements done by conductor Manny Albam.

But what shines through mostly is Oscar's vastly improved self-confidence in his own singing. The respect for Nat so clearly stated in the album's title is evident, but he is no longer intimidated by Cole. It's as if he's saying, "Never mind how Nat sang it, this is how I do it."

To get back to the *Concertgebuow* CD, Mr. Lubag's notes offer some points of interest, mostly via a conversation he had with guitarist Herb Ellis.

For example, Mr. Lubag asked Ellis if Oscar had been "using Nat Cole's trio as a model."

Ellis: "Ah, no. Well, maybe, in a way. Oscar was fond of Nat's playing, as we all were, but, no, ours was much more complicated than Nat's, and we swung a lot harder, but not necessarily better."

Another exchange in this conversation reflects Oscar's strong sense of competitiveness.

Lubag: "Nat's was a more laid-back approach and yours was definitely jumpin' on it right away."

Ellis: "Yeah, because I remember we played a concert opposite Count Basie one time . . ."

Lubag: "The full band?"

Ellis: "Oh, yeah! Years ago. There were other people on the show, so I remember Oscar said to Ray and me, 'Ah, you know, we gotta, we really want to nail it tonight,' he said, 'because the rest of those cats can fight it out for second place—'cause we have first.' And he was serious."

And one more exchange between interviewer and interviewee:

Lubag: "How was the experience working with Oscar at this particular time, let's say, as compared to working with him now?"

Ellis: "Well, it was very thrilling, but as I said, very difficult because the arrangements were so hard! But he made them hard on himself also, not only on you. And he expected your best every night, which he certainly should! Now there are hardly any arrangements, we just play the songs mostly."

Lubag's notes also make reference to five bonus tracks on the CD. These are titled "Should I?," "Big Fat Mama," "Back Home Again in Indiana," "Joy Spring" and "Elevation." According to Lubag, these bonus tracks are from an LP that was titled *The Modern Jazz Quartet and the Oscar Peterson Trio at the Opera House* (Verve 8269, claim Lubag's notes).

The *Encyclopedia of Music in Canada* lists no such record. The closest thing I can find to it is a Verve CD titled *The Modern Jazz Quartet Plus*, issued in 1987. The MJQ personnel were, as usual, John Lewis, Milt Jackson, Percy Heath and Connie Kay. On this

CD, they are joined by Ray Brown and Oscar Peterson.

However, Peterson and Brown are heard (along with the MJQ) on only two of the ten tracks: "On Green Dolphin Street" and "Reunion Blues," the latter written by Milt Jackson and the former, of course, by the noted film-score composer Bronislaw Kaper.

"On Green Dolphin Street" was recorded in New York in 1961 and is notable for Peterson's marked restraint, much as if he were on his best behavior, as a respectable guest should be in the sedate home of the low-key, laid-back MJQ.

"Reunion Blues" was recorded in Villingen, Germany, in July 1971, when Oscar spent some time there recording for Hans Georg Brunner-Schwer. It features Oscar with Milt Jackson, Ray Brown and drummer Louis Hayes. Once again, Oscar is pretty much on his best company behavior, clearly not making any effort to steal the spotlight, although he seems a bit freer and willing to show his mettle in this austere company.

21

OSCAR SALUTES
HIS PEERS

Oscar Peterson was never one to take his colleagues for granted. Throughout his long career, Oscar has always been generous in giving due credit to the importance to him of the various musicians who have worked with him. (It should also go without saying that Peterson has acknowledged the importance of Norman Granz to his life's work and success.)

I think it's worth focusing some attention on a few of Oscar's recordings on which he graciously bestows laurels on the musicians with whom he has worked.

Much as he loved Herb Ellis—as witness the happy reunion of Ellis with Oscar and Ray Brown in 1990 at New York's Blue Note Club, which resulted in three very listenable CDs—Peterson was happy to have a drummer in his trio.

His first drummer after Ellis left was Ed Thigpen. (Later, he had Louis Bellson, Martin Drew and then Bobby Durham.) But it was Thigpen who first gave Peterson that extra boot that seemed to energize the trio.

Between 1959 and 1962 (apart from the Broadway show albums mentioned earlier), the Peterson-Brown-Thigpen combination made several albums, most of them for Norman Granz on the Verve label, that show off quite effectively what a great trio that one was.

The first of their outings was *A Jazz Portrait of Frank Sinatra*, recorded in 1959. This gave Oscar an opportunity to salute a fellow artist for whom he had great admiration and respect. Peterson wrote the liner notes to the album: "For years I have been an ardent admirer of Frank Sinatra. I've been thrilled by his singing and I've respected the taste that goes with his singing. As a musician I've further admired his choice of tunes and as a fan I've recognized that certain tunes are forever, at least in my mind, inextricably linked with Sinatra, both by usage and interpretation and by that special magic that is his alone. This album is not only a tribute to Frank Sinatra, but also my emotional interpretation of the feelings I get when I hear him. I have tried, therefore, to paint as well as I can a portrait, told in my personal terms, of Frank Sinatra."

The tunes he chose to play certainly succeed in evoking vivid and welcome memories of Sinatra. They include, among others, "You Make Me Feel So Young," "Learnin' the Blues," "Witchcraft," "It Happened in Monterey," "The Tender Trap," "I Get a Kick Out of You" and "Birth of the Blues." Listening to these expertly played tunes, one cannot help but think that Sinatra would have been quite pleased with the way his work is presented.

Two years later, *The Sound of the Trio* was released, again with Brown and Thigpen. In his liner notes, Dom Cerulli referred to "the sound of Oscar Peterson's magnificent piano, Ray Brown's extraordinary bass, and Ed Thigpen's remarkable drums. But, more than that, it's the sound of all three meshing together in the act of jazz."

There are only five (longish) cuts on the LP, but there is plenty that's worth hearing. One of the highlights is "On Green Dolphin Street," originally a movie theme. Jazz players adopted it because it suits their imaginative improvising, as is certainly the case with the Peterson Trio. Oscar noted the "almost deceptive, classical type beginning" that soon turns into a pulsing affair.

The first tune, "Tricrotism," was written by the late Oscar Pettiford, and in this outing Ray Brown makes bass playing sound like such a snap that it's easy to understand his great and lasting influence on many of the younger bass players who came after him.

"Thag's Dance" features Ed Thigpen (whose nickname is "Thag"), and Oscar noted: "I wrote this one for Thag and I meant it to sound like a soft-shoe dance, to show off the intensity of his perception of taste and level." And Thag certainly does that admirably.

"Ill Wind" is, according to Peterson, "a salutary thing to Art Tatum. It's a musical reminder of the way he would handle this type of thing. We used to discuss this at great length." Oscar plays the first chorus alone and out of tempo, but Cerulli's notes point out "how skillfully he establishes with his left hand what the trio will do *before* they join him for the second chorus."

Dom Cerulli also pays this tribute to the group: "As jazz groups go, The Trio is a remarkable instrument. Its members have been together for more than three years. They know each other, and they know almost instinctively how to get where Oscar wants them to go. Oscar is the leader, of course, but he is also a valuable member of the trio. He picks the tunes and plays the primary melodic instrument in the group. But he is not the featured soloist who has a rhythm section backing his playing; he is one-third of three musicians who seem to think as one, play as one, and still retain identity and individuality."

Recorded live at the London House in Chicago, the album lives up to its title—*The Sound of the Trio*—and it achieves its goal: to give the listener a chance to hear all three members of the trio, and to demonstrate again, as if it were needed, that each man is so vital to the group's success. Also in 1961, Oscar, Ray and Ed made another Verve LP, again at Chicago's London House. This one is called simply *The Trio* and offers a variety of tunes, including "In the Wee Small Hours of the Morning," "Chicago," "The Night We Called It a Day," "Whisper Not," "Sometimes I'm Happy" and "I've Never Been in Love Before."

The last-named song was from Frank Loesser's memorable

score for the long-running Broadway show *Guys and Dolls*. On the Peterson version, you can still hear Oscar doing his involuntary voice sound effects. It's done in a medium tempo, but how Oscar swings! (This was long before the great trumpeter Clark Terry did his celebrated, and very funny, item called "Mumbles.")

The album also offers a rare glimpse into Oscar's thinking via the following liner note: "Although I usually abstain as much as possible from adding to the conglomeration of words generally found in liner notes, I find it necessary at this time to make special mention of two specific tunes contained herein.

"Our version of 'Sometimes I'm Happy' was done as a particular musical salute to one of the geniuses of the jazz world, Lester Young. The idea of including segments of his musical phraseology in the original record along with those of Slam Stewart was definitely premeditated, as we felt that this gave the selection the necessary chronological validity. The inclusion of the tune 'Chicago' was done as a musical salute to one of our very favorite metropolises and also to one of its favorite sons, Marty Faye."

In his understandably laudatory liner notes, Don Gold wrote of Peterson: "He is one of those rare, accomplished musicians able to translate to his instrument the most elaborate thoughts his mind creates. Fortunately, his mind is a storehouse of invention. As a result, with the technique he possesses, he knows few bounds. . . .

"For those who have neglected Peterson and friends—or taken them for granted—this set should be an ear opener. In their own neatly-delineated groove, the Peterson Trio succeeds in filling the air with the richly rewarding sound of surprises. For those, like myself, who have been regularly moved by the creations of this group, this outing will serve to reinforce a basic belief. Without a trace of starry-eyed idealism or a single axe to grind, it is possible for me to assert that this is the finest trio in jazz, headed by a pianist whose artistry never fails to enrich my life."

The fourth album in this group is called *Night Train* and was recorded in Los Angeles in 1962. This album gives Oscar an opportunity to feature the work of several composers he admires. First of all, Duke Ellington is represented by "C Jam Blues," "I Got It Bad and That Ain't Good" and "Band Call." Duke's son Mercer wrote another tune on this LP, "Things Ain't What They Used To Be." There is also Hoagy Carmichael's "Georgia on My Mind," Milt Jackson's "Bag's Groove" and Sy Oliver's "Easy Does It." Benny Moten is recalled with "Moten Swing," which suggests (to me, anyway) that Oscar might have had Count Basie on his mind when he chose it, since Basie came out of the Moten band.

Again, Cerulli notes: "There is a virility about the greatest jazz which is immediately recognizable, and it is this quality in his work which contributes so vastly to Peterson's position as the outstanding pianist of his generation. It asserts itself at the crucial moments with unfailing constancy. After the theme statement of 'Band Call,' when Peterson moves into his improvisation, his relaxation is quite sublime. There are hints of limitless untapped power and dazzling melodic invention, and as the solo gathers impetus, it becomes clear that the player is a mature master of his art."

Amen to that. But was there ever a doubt?

There's one more LP that I think is worth mentioning. This one was done in 1965, but not with Norman Granz (who had temporarily moved out of the recording scene). It's called—aptly enough—*Eloquence* and was recorded at the Tivoli Gardens in Copenhagen, Denmark. There are eight cuts on this album, all of them longish. As usual for that time, Oscar is aided and abetted by Ray Brown and Ed Thigpen.

Of special interest, in my view, is "Django," the haunting John Lewis tune dedicated to Django Reinhardt. Oscar gives it a highly individualistic treatment, featuring his light-as-a-feather touch, and if it doesn't remind you very much of the Modern Jazz Quartet version, that's okay—this is Oscar playing and Lewis himself later told him how much he loved it.

Another high point in the album is "Autumn Leaves," an old standard given a fresh approach here that, while perhaps it's a little irreverent, it's refreshing to hear Oscar swing lightly through this chestnut.

On the liner notes, Oscar heaps lavish praise on Ray Brown: "We will never see another bass player like Ray Brown. Not too many guys are so musically unselfish. He has expanded his talents beyond anyone I've ever heard of. Ray has extended the basic meaning of the use of the instrument—his harmonic and rhythmic concept when playing for someone is out of sight. There are so few who possess the feeling he has when he plays. . . ."

And quite appropriately, Brown is given a good opportunity to bear out Peterson's praise in a fairly lengthy and totally enjoyable bass solo.

Eloquence, indeed.

22

OSCAR AND THE FACES OF INDIFFERENCE

Despite his international acclaim and considerable honors, Oscar Peterson has long had one ongoing complaint. Peterson has felt for years that he—and Canadian artists generally—has been taken for granted in Canada.

As far back as 1969, he was expressing concern about "Canadiana," as this notable interview, conducted while on tour in Rome by *The Toronto Star*, reveals:

> Everybody beats the drum for Canadian Consciousness, but the French Canadians are more interested in splitting off from Canada and everybody else is interested in being English or American or what have you than in being Canadian . . . which is a shame. I want to see Canada live up to all it really could be.
>
> Like, I'm invited to a Command Performance for the Queen in England, President Nixon has asked that I do a concert at the White House. But I don't get any requests from Trudeau. It sometimes seems pretty hopeless getting through to Canadians that, yes, we Canadian artists do exist.
>
> I've been touring throughout the world for twenty years now. And I get met at the airport and I get somebody to help with passport and visa problems when I'm performing

in Poland and Czechoslovakia. And that help is always from the American embassy.

I mean, just the other night, someone from the U.S. embassy came backstage [in Rome] to say he enjoyed the music, and that he didn't want to bother me or anything, but just wanted to say hello. And then today I got an invitation to the American embassy. It's embarrassing, because somewhere along the way, I have to say, you know, like, um—I'm not American. About that time they say, "Oh, Canadian. Oh. Where are your embassy people?" And that's when I feel about this high. Honestly.

He saw posters for his Rome appearance announcing "The World's Most Famous Jazz pianist," and in the local press he was referred to as "America's grand old man of the piano." What bothered Oscar was not that everybody else thought he was American, but that apparently Canadians thought so, too.

A couple of years later, in 1971, Peterson talked about the need to live up to his billing and for solid musicianship in his groups. He scorned the notion that just because jazz is a relaxed musical form, sloppiness can be tolerated. "I guess I'm a stick-in-the-mud on this matter of the caliber of performance," he said. "I've been that way with every group I've had. You carry a responsibility on stage with you and the audiences know this."

The same interviewer asked him if he felt audiences are important.

"Certainly the response is important," he replied, "in the sense that I am interested in reaching my public. The reaction has its effect on the whole group. But there is also the matter of loyalty to the music itself, and I won't ever sell out to the audience. A lot of artists have made that mistake, but I look at people like Ellington, proving himself again and again, and the issue becomes quite simple. You have to be yourself and deliver an honest performance."

After a performing trip to Europe in 1970, Oscar said: "There was no doubt about it—people wanted to listen to jazz performers who remained true to the fundamental principles of the music. The *avant garde* got nowhere."

Once, in 1975, when I talked with Oscar backstage during a JATP tour, the subject of film biographies of jazz musicians came up. Red Nichols, Benny Goodman and Gene Krupa had already been used as subjects of movie biographies. He had not been impressed by the treatments.

"Jazz has not really been taken seriously [by film makers] until fairly recently," he said.

Our talk reminded him of a happy experience on American television, which he remembered because of the respect offered him. When he was a guest on "The Danny Kaye Show," Kaye greeted him when he arrived at the studio, and then asked: "What would *you* like to do?"

Some years later, he was again voicing the complaint about the public's perception of him. "I've achieved a funny kind of status in Canada," he told *The Globe and Mail* in March 1980. "Most of it comes because I went to the United States and other places, and as a result of Canadians having seen me repeatedly on the TV shows of people like Johnny Carson, Merv Griffin, Dick Cavett, Jonathan Winters and André Previn, where I'm almost always introduced as 'the Canadian pianist,' I think that has weighed heavily with Canadians.

"I've never had a series of my own on the CBC. . . . That seems strange—everybody else has. Tommy Hunter, Anne Murray, Jack Kane. . . . And yet I'm going back to England this summer for my third series in London. So you kind of wonder why?"

(Somebody at the CBC must have been reading the paper. Oscar was signed to a CBC series, *Oscar Peterson and Friends*, to begin running that fall. The "friends" were his weekly guests, such as Dizzy Gillespie, Mary Lou Williams, Buddy DeFranco, Roy Eldridge and Jimmy Rowles.)

* * *

Jazz has long been universally recognized as an "American" art form. No argument here—except that "American" implies North American, and not just the United States of America. Yet, somehow, Canada seems to have been left out in the cold or, at least, out of the equation.

I guess it should be pointed out, in fairness, that this American indifference to Canada is hardly limited to the world of jazz. To most "Americans," I fear, Canada is just that vast, cold wasteland "up there somewhere" north of Michigan or North Dakota or New Hampshire.

Admittedly, the overwhelming majority of important jazz musicians have been "American," in the sense that they were born, trained and practised their art in the United States—from Buddy Bolden to Dizzy Gillespie, from Coleman Hawkins to Lester Young, from Jellyroll Morton to Count Basie and, yes, from Bessie Smith to Sarah Vaughan. (For the moment, we'll leave out such "foreign" phenomena as Django Reinhardt, George Shearing, Toots Thielemans, Marian McPartland and Stephane Grappelli.)

Yet, Canada has not been an artistic desert when it comes to producing worthy jazz musicians. A few who come to mind are Gil Evans, Maynard Ferguson, Rob McConnell, Guido Basso, Jane Bunnett, Dave McMurdo, Ron Collier, Trudy Desmond, Pat Riccio, Rick Wilkins, Renee Rosnes, Doug Riley, P. J. Perry, Sonny Greenwich, Chris Gage, Wray Downes, Molly Johnson, Ian McDougall, Herbie Spanier, Holly Cole, Bert Niosi, Cliff McKay, Trump Davidson, Jimmy Reynolds, Pat LaBarbera, Bobby Hales and, of course, Oscar Peterson himself.

Somehow, though, the American jazz press has always shown a regrettable indifference to the contributions of most of these musicians—even when they had the temerity to leave their native country (usually temporarily) to visit and play in the United States.

When I speak of the American jazz press, I mean, of course, the two largest, most successful, longest-running publications in that category: *Down Beat* and *Metronome*. (For purposes of comparison, two leading Canadian periodicals have done better by Oscar. *Coda*, which has long been run by jazz critic John Norris, has, over the years, published a number of stories on Peterson, including one in an issue that had his picture on the cover. And *Big Band World*, which is edited by John Dimon, featured a handsome piece on Oscar in its summer 2000 edition, and in the past has done feature stories on, among others, Dal Richards, Mart Kenney, Rob McConnell, Robert Farnon, Teddy Roderman, Johnny Cowell and Percy Faith, as well as articles by trombonist and author Murray Ginsberg.)

In my not-exactly-comprehensive collection of articles about Peterson in these revered publications, by far the most extensive (and favorable) article appeared in *Metronome* in October of 1954, written by George Simon. That piece (also quoted earlier in this book) included this mild outburst from Peterson: "I may be disliked, I know, for the rest of my life for some of these things I've been saying, but I had to get it off my chest. Imagine, some of those musicians actually put Art Tatum down with an imbecilic statement like 'he's not modern.' "

I also happen to have, in my sketchy home library, ten year-books put out by *Down Beat* and *Metronome*—actually five of each. These yearbooks purport to cover activities, achievements, recordings and other supposedly useful information regarding "the jazz scene" during the previous year.

Now, get a load of the sort of treatment received by Oscar Peterson in these yearbooks. The earliest mention of Peterson that I have is in the 1953 *Metronome* yearbook. This comes under the heading "Discography of the Year" (presumably 1952, since this yearbook came out in July 1953). The discography is arranged alphabetically, and Peterson gets one listing, for some early Mercury recordings he made. But, then, so do such Scandinavian musicians as Lars Gullin and Bengt Hallberg, and there's also an album called *New Sounds from Sweden*.

(Remarkably, despite serious efforts, I have been unable to

find anything in either of these prestigious publications about Peterson's triumphant introduction to the American jazz scene in September 1949 at Carnegie Hall.)

The 1954 *Down Beat* yearbook, celebrating that magazine's twentieth anniversary, ran a year-by-year rundown of "the musical scene of the last two decades," in which the only mention of Peterson (for 1950) was the following: "One of the musicians to watch, according to scouts, was Oscar Peterson, the Canadian pianist." (It appears, however, that nobody at *Down Beat*—or anywhere else in the trade journals—took the trouble to "watch" or, for that matter, listen.)

In the 1955 *Metronome* yearbook, Oscar Peterson was one of three Canadian musicians listed in the discography section. The other two were Maynard Ferguson and Paul Bley—both of whom had moved to the United States by then.

The 1956 *Metronome* yearbook was almost all Peterson's—in the sense that Bley was no longer mentioned, but Ferguson was. The yearbook's discography listed *The Music of Harry Warren*, an album Oscar recorded with his trio of that time, with Herb Ellis and Ray Brown.

Down Beat's 1957 yearbook is a bit of a curiosity. It contains a section titled "Jazz in the East" (it's followed by "Jazz in the West," but never mind). In the "East" section there is a picture of Peterson playing the piano. Under his name are the words "A Delight." This section runs for six pages and several thousand words in its presentation of jazz personalities, but there is no further reference to that "delight," Oscar Peterson.

The *Metronome* 1957 yearbook features an article titled "Jazz Around the World," which starts out with this statement: "Jazz is becoming a broad belt of understanding reaching out from the United States to all sections of the world."

The article goes on to mention Swedish pianist Reinhold Svennson, English saxophonist Johnny Dankworth, Belgian tenor saxophonist Bobby Jasper, French bassist Pierre Michelot, Italian pianist Rudolfo Mussolini, German pianist Jutta Hipp,

French guitarist Sascha Distel, Mexican pianist Mario Patron, Swedish baritone sax player Lennart Jansson and numerous others. Guess what? A well-known Montreal-born pianist isn't even mentioned anywhere in that "broad belt."

For its 1958 yearbook, *Down Beat* did a slightly unusual thing. It ran a "Critics vs. Readers" poll. This was published as a kind of comparative table, with critics choosing their favorite musicians on each instrument "versus" readers on the other side. There were comparisons on all jazz instruments—trumpet, trombone, clarinet and three saxophone categories, bass, guitar, etc. The winners and runners-up under the piano category are interesting to note. Both critics and readers chose Errol Garner first and Oscar Peterson second. Only in third place was there a variance of opinion: critics chose Thelonious Monk, readers opted for Dave Brubeck.

Incidentally, of the forty-five or so musicians mentioned in the polls—either by critics or readers—the only Canadian musician who registered was Oscar Peterson. Now, *that's* recognition by an American magazine—and its well-informed readers.

The 1958 *Metronome* yearbook ran a brief piece on Ray Brown, mentioning that he played with the "Peterson Trio," and there was a brief mention of Herb Ellis, to the effect that he "represented hill-billy jazz." As for Oscar, there was a picture of him. The caption read: "OSCAR PETERSON SWUNG WITH THE BEST OF THEM."

Sadly, the American ignorance of so much as the existence of Canada went on and on. For example, the *Down Beat* yearbook for 1962 did its hip readers the favor of printing a listing of "Jazz Societies," along with their addresses. These ranged, alphabetically, from Alabama to Wisconsin.

And then, no doubt in an effort to be both helpful and worldly, there was a separate section headed "Overseas." The first listing under this heading was Roasaria, Argentina. (My *Canadian Oxford Atlas of the World* lists it as "Rosario," but never mind.)

The second "Overseas" listing is for the Yardbird Suite in Edmonton, Alberta. I wonder what sea that was over.

But the same 1962 *Down Beat* yearbook also contains a piece titled "The Teaching of Jazz," in which Gene Lees wrote about various post-secondary schools that offered courses of study on jazz. Lees, bless him, managed to work in a good-sized piece about the Advanced School of Contemporary Music, which by 1961 was in its second year of existence.

At times Oscar's sense of humor has come to the fore in the face of adversity—in the form of the sometimes obtuse questions of interviewers. He told me about one of his favorite instances of this, which occurred somewhere in South America (probably Brazil) when he toured there in 1970. Oscar was told he should let this individual interview him, because he was *the* jazz critic, the one person Oscar must talk to. So he agreed. When the appointed time came, the interviewer asked him: "So, tell me, how long has jazz been dead?"

Oscar replied: "Well, if that's true, what are you doing interviewing me?"

Peterson can also get annoyed at the long-running Canadian inferiority complex. "You know, I paid my dues because of that," he told me. "I was, in certain quarters, an outcast because of that. You know, 'Canada? Come on.' That's okay, I can take that. But this attitude we have, that unless it's stamped U.S.A., we can't buy it. We're killing a lot of talent that way. It's worse now than it's ever been. We're so inundated with everything that isn't Canadian that we can't handle our own heritage, I don't think."

We talked a bit about politics, too. Oscar feels a deep sense of respect and admiration for Prime Minister Chrétien. Once, he wrote Mr. Chrétien a letter of support about some public issue and, to his surprise, Oscar got a telephone call from the prime minister a few days later, thanking him for his letter.

Like most of us, Oscar has political opinions and is not afraid to voice them, but he doesn't abuse the privilege. He doesn't see it as his mission to persuade people to like (or dislike) any political party or, for that matter, any politician.

"I express my views when I vote," he said. "That's what voting is for."

But he has no wish to actively enter the murky world of politics. "I'd rather face Art Tatum," he says, laughing.

The politics of race get a rise from Oscar once in a while. He told me this story about Dizzy Gillespie, when on tour in the US South. The bus carrying all the musicians stopped, and Dizzy got out and announced he was going into the restaurant for something to eat—this despite numerous signs about "white" and "colored" water fountains, washrooms, etc. Dizzy walked in and sat at the otherwise deserted counter. A waitress (white, of course) hovered some distance away, and finally approached Dizzy and said: "I'm sorry, but we don't serve niggers in here."

Dizzy replied: "I don't blame you. Give me a steak."

23

OSCAR
AND THE JAZZ LADY

One Saturday afternoon late in January 1949, I was attending an afternoon cocktail party at the home of Helen Beatty and Eddie Palmer. She was the editor of the women's pages of *The Globe and Mail*, where I worked, and her husband, Eddie, then worked at Canadian Press.

It was at that party that I first met Helen McNamara. By an uncanny (and happy) coincidence, my first music column—called "The Record Album"—had appeared in that morning's *Globe and Mail*, and Helen's first column, titled "McNamara's Bandwagon," had been published in that afternoon's *Toronto Telegram*. That seemed reason enough for us to become friends: our shared interest in jazz. And so we did.

Helen, I was to learn, was a remarkable woman. Born in Galt, Ontario (in 1919), she was stricken with polio when she was two and a half years old. Over her childhood she was separated from the family for long stretches of time, her youngest sister, Barbara Klich, remembers. Helen was often a patient at a Shriners' Hospital. Experimental surgery was conducted, which left a long scar on her leg, but all to no avail. Helen had to wear a leg brace and walk with a cane; for a time she even had to use crutches. But that neither stopped nor even slowed down her activities. She drove a car, she traveled to Europe twice and she carried out all her daily tasks.

She was the daughter of Beatrice Duncan and Joseph McNamara, the eldest of five children, four of them girls. The McNamaras lived in various small Ontario towns but eventually settled in Toronto in the 1930s.

Joseph was born in Canada in 1888. There was always music in the McNamara home. Joe had been in vaudeville, traveling on the "Keith Circuit" as a soft-shoe dancer. He also taught himself to do commercial art. He came to love jazz. Helen's Uncle Walter, only a few years older than herself, was also quite a jazz fan.

Barbara Klich recalls Helen's musicianship. "She would play piano and my dad would sing. He had a very nice voice, and if she would play something at a faster tempo, he would dance." Barbara also remembers Willie "The Lion" Smith, one of the great stride pianists, playing at the McNamara home.

Visiting musicians, most of them from the United States, would go to the McNamara house for a good home-cooked meal made by Mrs. McNamara. "She made enormous pots of chili con carne or baked beans," Barbara recalls. It happened so often, she added, that "to this day, I can't eat chili."

Joe McNamara was very supportive of Helen, as was her mother. Barbara remembers her mother saying, "Don't you ever say that Helen is 'different.'" "That helped make Helen more independent."

According to Barbara, Helen had pride. "In her mind, she was not disabled; she never had any sense of self-pity." Mr. McNamara died in 1963, and Mrs. McNamara in 1984. From 1963 until Mrs. McNamara's death, Helen insisted on looking after her mother.

Helen attended an elementary school located at Bay and Wellesley streets. At the time it was probably the only school in Toronto that was equipped with a ramp for students who had disabilities.

Next she went to Bloor Collegiate Institute and was assisted by her sister Marie, who carried her books from floor to floor—there were no ramps or elevators or facilities to assist handicapped people. Helen took secretarial courses in short-hand and typing at a small business college as well.

Helen loved to learn. Her father drove her to the University of Toronto, where she studied at night school for many years. Even in her fifties and sixties, she was studying French and art. Marie, the second oldest sister, used to carry Helen's books to school.

Her first job was with the Crippled Civilians (on George Street in downtown Toronto), where she worked in a secretarial position. She then went to work in the Women's Department of the *Toronto Telegram*. Following that stint, she moved to the paper's Entertainment section, where she worked for years as a reporter and columnist. In her spare time, she free-lanced, her work published in *The Montrealer* and *Jazz Panorama*, and in England's *Melody Maker*. She also wrote for *The Canadian Composer* and was a major contributor to *The Encyclopedia of Music in Canada*.

She and her friend Marion Madgett O'Hara worked on a jazz newsletter and also at CBC Radio on various jazz shows. Later, in 1973, she wrote a book (with Jack Lomas and with a foreword by veteran disk jockey Elwood Glover) titled *The Bands Canadians Danced To*. It was a thoroughly researched, entertainingly written book, with many outstanding and rare photographs, from "Captain" Plunkett's Dumbells (of First World War vintage) and the Romanellis to Guy Lombardo, Bert Niosi, Art Hallman and Moxie Whitney—and even such visiting American bands as the Duke Ellington and Woody Herman orchestras. The book also served to evoke happy memories of such popular venues as the Palace Pier, the Palais Royale, the Brant Inn in Burlington and Dunn's Pavilion at Bala, Ontario.

One reviewer of Helen's book commented: "This beautifully illustrated history of the Canadian dance band scene from the Twenties to the Sixties is an obvious labor of love. McNamara and Lomas have brought to life a virtually gone-forever era in a manner guaranteed to captivate anyone who ever danced or listened to big bands in this country."

In her book, Helen paid tribute to Cy McLean, the talented pianist from Sydney, Nova Scotia, who became the first black musician to crash the Toronto musicians' union, whose imperious and racist president, Walter Murdoch, had decreed: "Niggers are not allowed here."

Cy had brought his ten-piece band from Nova Scotia to Toronto in the early 1940s and hit the brick wall known as Walter Murdoch. But in late 1944, Cy's little band played at the Club Top Hat, along the Lake Ontario shore. The band stayed there for three years.

It is typical of Helen's writing, incidentally, that racial prejudice had no place in it. Among other things, one of the most admirable achievements of jazz, over the years, has been its role in breaking down racial barriers.

In 1946, "Goodie" and Harvey Lichtenberg and Mike Lawrence bought the old Scholes Hotel on Toronto's Yonge Street and turned it into the Colonial Tavern. The next year, Cy McLean brought a trio into the Colonial and the club did well enough that McLean was succeeded by a parade of more famous, American musicians—Muggsy Spanier, Jack Teagarden, Phil Napolean, Bobby Hacket and Red Norvo.

Goodie Lichtenberg recalled: "Cy and his musicians were decent guys whose music attracted a lot of nice people to the club. Cy was always cheerful and displayed a positive attitude about life in general. A wonderful guy."

That was the turning point not only for McLean but for other black musicians in Canada. Cy's reputation as one of Canada's most talented jazz musicians is best illustrated by an incident involving the world-famous pianist Earl "Fatha" Hines. When Hines was appearing at the Colonial, he had to fly back to New York for a television appearance. The pianist Hines chose to take his place was Cy McLean.

Even though he died in 1986 at the age of seventy, and even though his music may be lost to present-day listeners, his legacy as a kind of anti-racism pioneer has been of some benefit to a younger generation of Canadian black musicians. Consider the number of outstanding black Canadian musicians whose acceptance by white audiences was helped in part by the bold invasion of Toronto by Cy McLean: Oliver Jones, Wray Downes, Sonny Greenwich, Joe Sealy, Archie Alleyne, Russ Little and Frank Wright. Plus Oscar Peterson.

All this background, by the way, was first brought to light in Helen McNamara's book, *The Bands Canadians Danced To.*

Helen was also a gifted artist, working in pen and ink, watercolors and pastels. Among others, she did various sketches of Duke Ellington and a lovely pencil sketch of her friend, singer Phyllis Marshall. I have and treasure a copy of the Phyllis Marshall sketch.

She was a great fan of the Duke Ellington and Count Basie bands, but her favorite in the Basie band was the rotund blues singer Jimmy Rushing, sometimes affectionately referred to as "Mr. Five by Five." She got to know Rushing quite well, spent many hours with him and eventually wrote a full-length biography of Rushing. Unfortunately, she was unable to find a publisher who felt Rushing was worth a biography.

A year or so after our first meeting, Helen and I put together an idea for a jazz radio program featuring records and chatter. It was to be "structured" but not scripted. We took the idea to station CKFH (Foster Hewitt's station) and the station manager agreed to put our show on the air as a weekly Saturday afternoon series. We were paid the lavish sum of $5.00 a week each.

We did the program for a year. We would meet during the week to plan the next program. Each Saturday, Helen would get into her small car—an Austin Mini, as I recall—come by and pick me up and off we'd go to do our little jazz show.

After a year, we went to the station management to ask for a raise. We were refused. So we quit CKFH and took our program (which we titled "Tributes in Tempo") to CBC Radio, and did the weekly program there for another two years—for $60.00 per week each.

Helen also wrote a CBC Television special featuring Duke Ellington. (I still remember that Byng Whitteker, who hosted that program, had been across the street at the Celebrity Club for a rather wet lunch, just before the taping. The Duke was quietly amused at Byng's fumbling-mumbling interview, but he got through it with his usual grace.)

Barbara once told me, "I was amazed at the recognition Helen got everywhere." On one occasion, Helen went to a Duke Ellington concert. She was spotted in the audience and the entire Ellington orchestra gave her an ovation.

I have nothing but the fondest memories of those years of working with Helen. One of them concerns the great Art Tatum. Helen and I had both gone to see Tatum at the old Club Norman, where he was then holding forth nightly. Because we wanted to do a radio show about Art, we arranged to meet him one afternoon to walk back to his hotel and talk with him. Tatum, you may recall, was almost totally blind.

On the day Helen and I were walking with him and his "road manager" (who was really there to look after Tatum) to his hotel, he stumbled while crossing the street and fell down. Instinctively, I moved to help him up, but the manager grabbed my arm and shook his head, "no." He knew, as I didn't until then, that Tatum wanted no help; he would get up on his own.

During the late 1960s and 1970s, Helen and I more or less lost track of each other. For one thing, in the spring of 1969, I moved to Los Angeles and worked as a television writer there for the next seven years. After that, I spent close to a year working in Vancouver, with Tommy Banks, P. J. Perry, Oliver Gannon and many other fine Canadian musicians.

But after I returned to Toronto in 1978, Helen and I resumed our friendship. She was still living at home with her mother, somewhere near Victoria Park Avenue, and I recall visiting her there a couple of times.

Barbara remembers that Helen always spoke highly of Oscar Peterson, both as a musician and as "a gentleman." Helen also wrote about Oscar on several occasions, usually in *The Telegram*. "He works toward perfection," she wrote of him in 1970, and then quoted him: " 'Craftsmanship,' he says, 'is essential to creativity and to a good performance. How many really bad performances have you ever heard on the concert stage in classical music? We [in jazz] should apply the same standards. It takes years of study to learn an instrument to the point where you can go out and perform.' "

"He has interests outside music," she also wrote of Oscar. "He's a first-rate photographer, an expert on sound equipment, a connoisseur of cars, but music is his life. It takes him thousands of miles away from home each year, but a couple of times a year he gets home to Toronto."

It was in 1984, after her mother died, that Helen went into a kind of depression. She suffered tremors, had difficulty remembering things, couldn't understand what a five-dollar bill was. It soon developed that she was a victim of Parkinson's disease.

In 1991, she was admitted to the Salvation Army's Grace Hospital, at Bloor and Church streets in Toronto. Billy O'Connor (who died in November 2001) visited her from time to time.

In June 1995, when Marian McPartland was in Toronto for a three-night gig at one of the jazz clubs, she asked me about Helen. She knew, through correspondence with me, that Helen was not in good health. So the two of us went to Grace Hospital to visit her. Despite her weakened condition, Helen was very touched by McPartland's thoughtfulness.

Two years later, in 1997, I got a phone call from Billy O'Connor, who had known Helen even longer than I had. Billy told me that Helen was in a bad situation. He told me that Helen's sister Barbara was having a tough time keeping up with the costs of helping to make Helen comfortable. (After some two decades with *The Toronto Telegram*, which folded in 1971, her pension was less than $75 a month.) Together we came up with the idea of mounting a benefit concert to raise money for Helen, the money to be put into a trust to be administered by Barbara.

We immediately set about asking various musicians if they would appear and play—for no money, and with the approval of the musicians' union—at the concert. Every musician we approached readily agreed to bring their own groups to play. We had a full program: seven groups, led by Peter Appleyard, Guido Basso, Jim Galloway, Rob McConnell, Ed Bickert, Moe Koffman and Phil Nimmons.

Special mention should be made of bass player Steve Wallace, who played with several of the groups, and also of pianist Bernie Senensky. Pianist Gary Williamson was originally supposed to appear (with the Nimmons small group), but then he said he might have to leave early if some other (paying) job turned up for later that same night. So, just to play it safe, I called Bernie Senensky, although I had never met him, and asked if he might be available. Luck was with me: Bernie had a relative who had suffered from Parkinson's, so he was sympathetic and willing to join our roster of stellar jazz musicians for that night.

I booked the Du Maurier Theatre at Harbourfront Centre (which could seat a few hundred people) for the concert. That venue, incidentally, also gave us a break on renting their facilities. Next, I thought we would need some sort of printed program, so I folded a sheet of typing paper (8 1/2 inches by 11 inches) in half to plan a program. Then it occurred to me I might be able to sell the back page to somebody for an ad. I had never sold—let alone designed—an ad before, but I gave it a shot. Happily, the CBC quickly agreed to pay for that ad. I realized I might do better, so I did some phoning around, and before I knew it, we had a twelve-page program. Several record companies agreed to take out ads, as did venues such as Montreal Bistro, Barootes, The Silver Rail and the Toronto Men's Press Club. We even got ads with personal messages from musicians such as Marian McPartland and George Shearing.

Marian's ad was typically warm: "To Helen McNamara—Dear, Dear Helen—You have been one of my great friends since I met you at the Colonial Tavern in the Fifties. I cherish my memories of you and your fine writing and our good times together. Marian McPartland."

Shearing's ad read: "Having known, respected and admired her work for many years, George Shearing enthusiastically salutes Helen McNamara."

And there were ads and messages from personal friends and colleagues like tailor and jazz buff Dave Caplan and former *Telegram* colleague Bert Petlock. There were even ads from Long & McQuade, the musical instrument dealers, *The Toronto Sun* and *CARP News*, the seniors' periodical now known as *Fifty-Plus*.

And through several record companies, we were able to get (free) a number of jazz CDs, which we sold for ten dollars to the concert-goers.

In the spring of 1997, I attended the annual awards gathering held by *The Jazz Report*, since I was, for a decade, a regular contributor to that publication. That was the year when bassist Dave Young was named Musician of the Year, and Oscar Peterson was there to present the award.

In his presentation, Oscar paid lavish tribute to Young, crediting Dave with helping him regain his confidence as a musician; this was many months after Oscar had suffered a stroke and believed his playing days were over. In the course of the evening, I wandered over to where Oscar was seated in his wheelchair, to say hello and chat with him. In the course of our chat, I mentioned that we were planning the fundraising concert for Helen and he surprised me by saying "I'll be there."

"You mean it?" I asked.

"I'll do anything for Helen," he said.

(I felt like kicking myself then. If I had thought we could get Oscar on the program, I might have been tempted to book Massey Hall instead of the small Du Maurier Theatre.)

Oscar even took out an ad in our program (in association with Telarc and Verve records) saluting Helen McNamara.

Looking back on it, I find it hard to believe that Billy and I worked on planning that concert for six months. It was in May 1997 that I approached Oscar at *The Jazz Report*'s annual awards night—and we had already booked all the other musicians. But the concert itself was not held until the evening of September 24 of that year.

As long as I live, I won't forget the night of that Helen McNamara concert. Every seat in the house was filled. I was lucky enough to serve as master of ceremonies for the concert (Billy O'Connor didn't want to do it) and it was a great pleasure for me.

The program opened with Phil Nimmons. One of the reviews of the concert singled out Nimmons' playing, noting that, as usual, Nimmons was "way out in front" of everyone else as a jazz pioneer.

We had asked each group to play for about twenty minutes, but Phil's segment ran well over half an hour—but how beautifully they played! (On that night, all the groups played longer than their allotted twenty minutes, but nobody minded—least of all the enthralled audience.)

Then followed the other groups—Appleyard, Galloway, McConnell, Koffman and so on. Oscar would, of course, close the program. O'Connor and I had discussed that and agreed it made sense for one simple reason: "nobody was going to top Oscar, so nobody would want to follow him." Nobody argued.

I can remember introducing Oscar. To my surprise, he didn't come out in his wheelchair. He stood up in the wings and walked, slowly, carefully, out to the piano—to a deservedly tumultuous welcome.

After I introduced him, I retreated to the wings, and I can still remember watching him. His back was to me, and I could see him use his right hand to lift his left hand and set it down on the keyboard. The Peterson left hand struck an occasional complementary chord, but the right hand was so dazzlingly active—and so wonderfully inventive—that nobody worried much about the apparent lethargy of his left hand.

When Oscar agreed to play at the concert, he said he wanted

Dave Young as his bassist. Dave was then playing in Quebec City, but Oscar insisted he had to have Dave. In his mind, I'm sure, it was a kind of payback for Dave's singular role in persuading Oscar to play again after his stroke. So Dave managed to get time off from his Quebec gig and return to Toronto to play with Peterson. He just couldn't say "no" to Oscar.

Oscar also had a young drummer named Mark McLean, whose talent had already made an impression on Peterson.

After Oscar had held the audience spellbound with his playing (for a good half-hour) he brought out Peter Appleyard to join the group for an impromptu bluesy encore that was as big a hit as everything else on the program.

When it was over, between the ticket and CD sales and the advertising sold in the program, we were able to turn over to Barbara, Helen's youngest sister and (since Marion's death) her closest friend, something like $30,000 to help with the ongoing expenses of caring for Helen McNamara.

No, it wasn't exactly what you could call a windfall, but it was at least a tangible gesture to help this talented and much beloved woman.

Nothing I have ever been involved with, in more than half a century of working in newspapers, magazines, radio and television, has given me as much satisfaction, or feeling of accomplishment, as that night.

And it *was* a magical night. All the musicians were "up" for it. Their unanimous, profound respect, admiration and affection for this remarkable woman—truly a pioneer among women interested in and capable of writing intelligently and engagingly about jazz, as far back as the early 1940s—was evident in the enthusiasm with which they played.

24

OSCAR'S KEY

It's surprising the things you can learn by leafing through your old magazines.

For a decade, from 1991 to 2000, I wrote regularly for *The Jazz Report*, the quarterly magazine published by Bill King and Greg Sutherland. This was literally a labor of love, based on my life-long love of jazz. In the Winter 1992–93 issue, I wrote a piece about the abundance of jazz videos then available.

They ranged from Billie Holiday (the first one I bought) to Chet Baker, Stephane Grappelli, Miles Davis, Ray Anthony, Stan Kenton, Sarah Vaughan, Buddy Rich, Dizzy Gillespie, Nat King Cole and Stan Getz.

Some time earlier, I had interviewed Whitney Balliett, the highly respected jazz critic for *The New Yorker*, and he told me that he preferred to close his eyes while listening to a jazz musician or group in a club. The two senses, he claimed—seeing and hearing—worked against each other, and the only way to appreciate the full import of the music was by closing his eyes and listening, so that his focus would not be divided between the visual and the aural elements.

(I didn't agree with him, but we'll let that go. Not long before this, I had received as a gift my first jazz video. It was titled *Jazz Masters—Volume 1*, and was originally aired as a CBS television show in 1957. It featured musicians like Henry "Red" Allen, Vic Dickenson, Pee Wee Russell, Roy Eldridge, Lester Young and others. I loved it. Oh, and one other thing. While doing some research on that video, I discovered that the CBS program was produced by two famous jazz writers—Nat Hentoff and Whitney Balliett. And nowhere on the video is there any recommendation that we should close our eyes and just listen to the music.)

To further research my piece, I checked out a Music World shop in the suburbs of Toronto. It had no music section specifically labeled jazz. But in the "Easy Listening" section I found Harry Connick Jr. and Nat Cole—nestled in among Pavarotti and Kenny Rogers.

In writing my piece, I lamented the absence of Canadian jazz artists such as Oscar Peterson, Moe Koffman, Peter Appleyard, Rob McConnell and others who had done television programs, mostly for CBC.

Now, I have to take time out for a moment to blush at my own sloppiness. It wasn't until I was at work on the latter stages of this book about Oscar that I leafed through my old copies of *The Jazz Report*. I discovered that in the same issue that carried my piece about the plethora of jazz videos available—plus my complaint about the absence of any Canadian jazz musicians on these videos—was an interview Bill King had done with Sylvia Sweeney, Daisy Peterson's daughter, who had produced, along with Sara Levinson, a serious, skillfully made biographical documentary about Peterson, titled *In the Key of Oscar*. What a fine piece of work it is. There is, naturally, a good deal of archival footage in it—Peterson playing at the Alberta Lounge in Montreal with his first trio (which had bassist Austin Roberts and drummer Clarence Jones), the Bermuda Onion in Toronto and other venues and comments from various sidemen, including Ray Brown and Herb Ellis, and others.

A few samples:

Brown: "He [Oscar] wanted it perfect. Not good, but perfect. He demands the same of himself. What it's done for me is make a better musician of me."

Daisy, Oscar's sister: "I was overpowered by the freedom with which Oscar could play."

Herbie Hancock: "Oscar Peterson is the greatest living influence on jazz pianists today."

In my opinion, it can't be just coincidence that the linking scenes in this splendid video are of Oscar on a train trip from Toronto to Montreal, obviously traveling first class. I feel somehow that Oscar intended this metaphor—it's as if he's reminding us that he had succeeded in escaping his father's fate. He had fulfilled the dream of that very determined man, Daniel Peterson, his father, that, through music, Oscar could rise up from the level of a sleeping-car porter to become arguably the best jazz pianist in the world.

In that issue of *The Jazz Report*, I noticed an interview with Oscar conducted by Bill King, in which he discussed, among other things, his own collection of LPs.

"I've had people say to me they can't listen to their LPs, but I can listen to my albums. As long as someone's playing, I'll go through hell and high water to hear what they're doing. Be it Roy Eldridge, Coleman Hawkins, Dizzy, or whoever. There are certain solos or pieces that will not be reissued on CDs and I treasure these recordings and still want to hear them."

Later in the interview, King asked Oscar to name some of the great jazz personalities that he missed.

"First of all, I miss Basie," said Oscar. "Bill Basie and I were very, very close in his later years. It's funny, I was just saying to Ray Brown last night, I remember the phone ringing and I'd be in San Francisco, New York, or Europe, it didn't matter, and it would be Basie on the other end with a record playing. He'd ask, 'What do you think of this?' I really miss him. I miss Duke. I miss Roy Eldridge. I miss Prez. I miss them all."

25

"SOMETHING SCARY"

On May 13, 1993, *The Globe and Mail* carried a story headlined: "OSCAR PETERSON SUFFERS MILD STROKE." In the story under that heading, Sylvia Sweeney, Oscar's niece, was quoted as saying: "He's recovering right now. It was a mild stroke. He apparently had it when he was in New York. He was experiencing some type of heaviness in his arm and he performed with that."

Later in the interview, Sweeney said: "There's a history of stroke in his family so it's something that's scary for all of us."

Under a doctor's order Oscar was forced to cancel a European concert tour that had been scheduled for that summer.

But long before that awful stroke, Oscar had been suffering (since the early 1970s) from arthritis in his hands. "It almost always hurts when I play now," he said in one interview.

In a talk with André Previn in 1977, Oscar had said: "I could never think of giving up what I'm doing. I could never, for instance, settle down and become a studio musician. That kind of job was offered to me years ago, but it doesn't represent the way I want to live."

Just two years before his stroke, in an interview with *Now Magazine*, Oscar had said: "To me, it really doesn't matter where I play. I'm happy just playing. The first night that I stand in the wings and think 'I don't really want to do this,' I would go out there again. What's important is the incentive. If I ever lose the desire to play, I'll know it's time to stop. The way I look at it now, though, physical handicaps notwithstanding, I'm going to play until the day I die."

Nevertheless, it was to be almost two years before he played in public again. During that terrible time, Oscar truly believed he could never play again. It was, to say the least, a stressful and depressing period for him.

But that was when Dave Young re-entered Oscar Peterson's life. I talked with Dave in March 2001, at his Toronto home. Mostly, we talked about Oscar, whom Dave had first met in 1974, at a Banff School of Fine Arts summer school in jazz, where Oscar was teaching for several days.

"That's when we played together for the first time, and got to know each other," Dave told me. "We played a concert together the following November. He said, 'Would you like to go on a tour of Japan, would you like to join the group?'" The "group," the moment Dave agreed to join it, consisted of Oscar and Dave.

"I had just gotten a job with the Winnipeg Symphony, I had worked hard to get the job," said Young. "I was playing principal bass out there. So I quit the Winnipeg Symphony. But I never regretted it. That would be 1975, and I did about six months straight with him."

Young said he had spent some "great times with him, musically and socially. He's a great guy."

I asked Dave to talk about that *Jazz Report* awards evening in 1997, when Dave had been chosen as Musician of the Year by that publication. This was some time after Oscar's stroke.

"That was obviously a very difficult time for him," said Dave. "I guess I hadn't been in touch with him very much, but I heard about the event six or eight months later. I phoned him and said, 'How you doing?' And then I said, 'You know, I think we should play.' He said, 'No, no.' I said, 'I'm gonna bring my bass over and we'll see how it feels that day.' He said, 'Don't bother.' But, anyhow, I showed up with the bass, and Kelly [Oscar's wife] was there. She was kind of dubious. But we went downstairs and we played. It was the first time he had played in months, and it was tough. But when we got finished playing, I could see that he was disappointed, but he was still interested, like, you know, 'Maybe it'll work.' And we subsequently played a couple of other times after that, so I think it lit the fire again, because he wasn't very enthusiastic at all.

"Well, I only did it because I was a friend of his, and I think from then on he sort of gradually got back into it and he's been performing quite a bit, considering his condition."

Knowing Oscar's fondness for gags, I asked Dave Young if he had ever been the object of Peterson's sense of humor.

"He pulled a couple of things on me," Dave replied. It was on a plane trip, he explained, and "I had the bass in the seat next to me and he comes in and he's sitting right behind me, and he starts this commotion. He said, 'Stewardess, I won't have this in front of me. I won't fly on this plane if that thing is in front of me,' and I had to move the bass to another part of the plane. He said, 'I don't know who you are.'"

He also remembered Oscar's trio with himself and Joe Pass, at the Fairmont Hotel in San Francisco. "Joe would be presented nightly, doing a solo," Dave recalled. "Oscar would come on at the beginning of the second half and say, 'And now, we'd like to present this fantastic guitarist, Joe Pass.' Joe walked out and said, 'Oh, shit, where'd I put my guitar?' So he goes back to the room where all the tables are, with people around them, all in the dark. So Oscar stands up and says, 'That was Joe Pass.' Joe finally found his guitar, but all of us had to laugh. I don't know if Oscar was *that* amused, but he had to laugh."

Dave credited Oscar with "making me take the music more seriously, and really be exact about what to do when I go out to play. He made me work on the music. Once you learn that particular discipline, it affects everything that you do. I would have to credit him with making me be much more exact about what I do musically, which has affected my style of playing. I don't think I'm a sloppy player, and a lot of that I can attribute to him and his encouragement to really be precise about what I do.

And the other thing he taught me was, if we've had a rough day or we don't feel good, or for any reason we don't feel like playing this music, make sure when you walk out on that stage, make sure that you give one hundred percent. I don't want to hear about anything, your mother died or whatever; we have to go out there and perform. These people came out to hear us and the music that they've bought on record. We have to go out and give it to them. He taught me that. He practised what he preached. If he didn't feel good, you would never know it."

Dave also mentioned that Oscar always acknowledged good playing, giving his sidemen public credit for a good solo.

"Of all these guys I played with," said Young, "nobody could swing like Oscar. Even now, with just the right hand, nobody can touch him. I think that Oscar is one of the most copied pianists of all jazz history, because his style is very clear, and people can figure out what he's doing. There are guys who are coming close technically, but they miss out on the swing factor, and the experience and the personal connection of what he's doing. He's certainly been a role model for a lot of pianists."

He also remembered that Oscar used to write poetry. "He wrote poems to all the guys, you know, Lester Young, Coleman Hawkins, Charlie Parker," Dave remembered. "He wrote poems to all those guys. I remember being in L.A. and he said, 'Come back to the hotel' and he read them to me. He read me a couple of them and I was really knocked out. [The poems were about] Ella, all the ones that were close to him."

Dave didn't think Oscar had ever published any of his poems.

Young also remembered the one—and only—occasion when he and Oscar had "a bit of a falling out, a bit of a disagreement." This was at a jazz festival at Juan-les-Pins, on the French Riviera. Dave acknowledged that he had been "kind of upset" when he left to go home.

"Within several days," Dave continued, "he phoned me and said, 'Come on up to the lake, we'll spend a week together.' That was his way of saying, 'Come on, forget it.'

"We spent a week, the four of us [Dave's wife and Oscar's were there, too]. We went out on the boat, had a great time. He had a lovely cabin—cabin!—it was a lovely spot, and we spent a whole week up there."

Obviously, Dave Young still has the highest regard for Oscar Peterson, both as a musician and as a human being. And, with typical modesty, he downplays the importance of his role in the rehabilitation of Oscar Peterson. As he said, "I only did it because I was a friend of his."

But there had to be another underlying reason, it seems to me. He must have felt that this terrible stroke did not necessarily spell an end to Oscar's playing career.

After all, physical handicaps had been surmounted by other jazz musicians. A twisted spine didn't prevent Chick Webb from becoming one of the great drummers and bandleaders of the swing era. And blindness didn't stop Alec Templeton or Art Tatum or George Shearing from pursuing their careers as pianists.

26

TOWN HALL TRIBUTE

In March 1990, Oscar Peterson went on a recording frenzy. During that month, evidently in the space of a few days, he recorded four CDs on the Telarc label, all with Herb Ellis, Ray Brown and drummer Bobby Durham. The titles are *Live at the Blue Note, Saturday Night at the Blue Note, At the Blue Note: Last Call,* and *Encore at the Blue Note.*

The *Last Call* CD, recorded on March 18, 1990, includes such Peterson standards as "March Past" and "Wheatland," both from his famous *Canadiana Suite.*

For my taste, the highlight of the session is a two-tune medley: "It Never Entered My Mind," by Rodgers and Hart, and Johnny Green's complex but immortal melody "Body and Soul." It runs a shade over nine minutes, but there isn't a dull note to be found in it.

Even longer, just under ten minutes, is another medley, this one offering David Rose's "Our Waltz," which then blends into two Peterson originals, "Adagio" and "Bach's Blues." Oscar is in a relatively reflective mood during most of this, although he gets somewhat funkier as the medley progresses.

On the CD liner notes, Oscar pays typically gracious tribute to his two veteran sidemen, Ellis and Brown, as well as to drummer Durham. But his warmest praise went to Ray Brown, with whom he had made his spectacular New York debut at Carnegie Hall half a century earlier: "I don't think there will ever be a bassist like him," wrote Oscar of Brown. "All my bassists had something special, something I wanted at the time. . . . But Ray had it all—and nobody ever swung harder."

Three years after his series of sessions at The Blue Note, Oscar suffered his stroke. Not surprisingly, friends and colleagues rallied round to give him their support. It's a measure of Oscar Peterson's standing in the musical community of North America that a group of his colleagues should gather to pay tribute to him.

That's precisely what happened on the evening of October 1, 1996, at New York's Town Hall, in a concert co-sponsored by the Jackie Robinson Foundation and Telarc Records.

"Anyone in the full house might agree, after witnessing the strong musical and personal vibrations that passed between the honored guest and his fourteen old and new friends heard on this document of the evening, that there is no greater affection than that shared by creative artists," wrote Bob Blumenthal in his liner notes for the recording of that memorable evening.

The creative artists referred to included Milt Jackson, Stanley Turrentine, Clark Terry, Benny Green, Roy Hargrove, Lewis Nash, Niels-Henning Orsted Pedersen, The Manhattan Transfer, Shirley Horn and, of course, Ray Brown and Herb Ellis.

The night before the concert, all these musical artists gathered at the Town Hall, embraced Peterson and then proceeded to discuss and plan the upcoming event. "The joy of these encounters—Peterson resembled nothing so much as a kid on Christmas morning—" according to Blumenthal, "was as obvious as their ease. Some of the friends were venerable, some quite new, yet all spoke the pianist's language and felt comfortable in his presence."

Said bassist Pedersen: "What Oscar is doing, and what he's always done, is using people to do the best of what they can do. To me, Oscar is like Miles Davis in this way. He is totally and fully aware of who he has around him."

To some of the musicians, like Milt Jackson, Clark Terry and Brown and Ellis, playing with Oscar was like Old Home Week—they were reuniting with a friend and colleague for this quite special occasion.

For others—most notably Shirley Horn and Roy Hargrove—
it was a rare treat. Hargrove, at twenty-six the youngest musician
present, had made Peterson's acquaintance only a few months
earlier, when he took part in recording the Telarc CD *Oscar
Peterson Meets Roy Hargrove and Ralph Moore*. For Shirley
Horn it was a first.

"I was in New York," she recalled, "and my manager, John
Levy, asked me whether I wanted to hear the Basie band at Bird-
land or Oscar at the Vanguard. Oscar's been my number-one
pianist all my life, so the Vanguard it was. But this was my first
chance to sing with Oscar, which was something I've wanted to
do all of my life. When I heard him playing behind Billie Holiday, that was the best ever."

Horn's heartfelt rendition of "I Can't Face the Music" stands
out as one of the highlights of this musical tribute to Peterson.
She's also heard, both singing plaintively and accompanying
herself on the piano, on "Here's to Life."

Tenor saxophonist Stanley Turrentine joins the Peterson quartet on Duke Ellington's "In a Mellow Tone." Curiously, Peterson
had never met Turrentine until the evening before the concert, yet
he was eager to include Turrentine in the concert. Someone
described Turrentine's vibrato as being "as wide as his grin."

Roy Hargrove plays a majestically mellow flugelhorn solo on a
lovely old standard "My Foolish Heart," and displays exactly
the sort of sensitive approach to both the instrument and the
tune you would expect of a veteran player like Guido Basso.
Once again, Peterson and his sidemen are equal to the occasion,
giving him just the right kind of understated support the mood
called for.

Milt Jackson teams up with the Peterson quartet (with Lewis
Nash on drums) on "Bag's Groove," his own signature tune, and
an eloquent workout on "Willow Weep for Me," on which
Oscar's piano adds wondrous support of his own.

The inimitable Clark Terry adds yet another chapter to his
ongoing saga of the mysteriously comprehensible, wordless

woes of a man who knows how to express his emotions without the aid of a lyricist. This is surely one of the funniest jazz vocals ever conceived.

More vocal magic is applied by The Manhattan Transfer on "The Duke of Dubuque," which is sung a cappella, and then, backed by the Peterson quartet, the old Bobby Troup song "Route 66" (first recorded by Nat Cole, who was one of Peterson's early icons).

To close out this lively concert, Clark Terry joins the Oscar Peterson Quartet (with Pedersen on bass) in a rousing version of the Kurt Weill—Marc Blitzstein classic "Mack the Knife."

It's difficult to think of a jazz musician more deserving of this sort of tribute from his colleagues than is Oscar Peterson, not only because of his achievements as a musician, but because of the high esteem in which he is held by lovers of jazz throughout the world.

Wrote Bob Blumenthal: "This knack for getting the best out of others as well as himself is what makes playing with Oscar Peterson such a memorable experience, and ensures the musical quality of events like the Town Hall summit. There is a refreshing blend of ego-less camaraderie and serious creation that sets the perfect atmosphere—no attitudes, and no coasting, either. This is why Peterson found such a wide array of musicians eager to participate in this tribute."

And Blumenthal adds one final, but important, point about the audience at this tribute: "Some were no doubt doubly amazed [at Oscar's playing] given the knowledge of Peterson's 1993 stroke, but as Benny Green, who played piano that evening when Oscar was not at the keyboard, noted: 'No physical affliction can ever impede pure love.'"

There were, of course, many other awards, honors and tributes, and there would certainly be more, but it seems likely that this salute from his fellow jazz artists had a special meaning for Oscar Peterson.

Peterson, however, has never been one to rest on his laurels. He still faces new challenges with his customary gusto.

A good example was the concert he gave at Massey Hall on June 16, 2001. If there were still any doubters concerning his place in the pantheon of jazz greats, Oscar made it plain he was still capable of conquering an audience.

On that night, he led a stunning group—he referred to them as "my NATO group," because it included the Danish-born bass player Niels-Henning Ørsted Pedersen, the Swedish guitarist Ulf Wakenius and the British drummer Martin Drew. Oscar's entrance brought the evening's first standing ovation; there were to be several more during that magic night.

Musically, it was a decided improvement over the previous year's Roy Thomson Hall concert. Indeed, Massey Hall proved to be a far better venue than Roy Thomson Hall.

Oscar played with much more self-confidence than he had on the earlier occasion. He was clearly out to demonstrate that he was still The Man when it came to jazz piano.

Anyone in the audience could hardly miss the evidence of Oscar's affinity for blues, with a sprinkling of bop influence. Also noticeable was a more active left hand than had been the case at Roy Thomson Hall.

If there was one highlight—and there were actually several—it was his rollicking version of "Sweet Georgia Brown," which closed this exciting concert.

But, of course, the delighted crowd wanted more. And so Oscar came out once more, to play as an encore his deeply felt "Hymn to Freedom," a fitting end to a thrilling evening of peerless piano jazz.

27

OSCAR PAYS HOMAGE

Oscar Peterson has never had any trouble communicating with people, especially people he knows well. In some cases, he has coined nicknames for his musical associates. For instance, he often referred to Count Basie," whom he revered, as "Base." Ella Fitzgerald was often referred to as "Fitz" or "Miss Fitz." And Dizzy was sometimes called "Birks." (His full name was John Birks Gillespie.)

But he can also relate to things—pianos, of course, but also gadgets, from cameras to synthesizers. Given his proclivity for gadgetry, it should come as no surprise that he is on the internet, sending out sermons and paeans, tributes to some jazz musicians whom he admires or with whom he feels an affinity, or occasionally (but rarely) dressing down those for whom he has little or no respect.

On the occasion of his 75th birthday, August 15, 2000, Oscar was interviewed by Rosemarie Godina and Janusz J. Uiberall for *Digital Journal. com.*

"I am a Web addict," he said in the interview, "I love to surf the Web. Most of the instruments that I own were originally investigated on the Web. A couple of them were bought from the Internet."

Peterson also told the *Digital Journal* interviewers: "I am very excited about the Internet because I think it's going to free many, many artists from the captivity of money grabbers."

On his web site (*www.oscarpeterson.com*) there are several articles of interest. These pieces by Oscar come under the general heading, "My Favourite Musical Moments."

Not surprisingly, the first of these concerns Nat Cole, an early idol of Peterson's. He bases it on a Capitol album called *The Nat King Cole Trio*, and wrote that it served as an inspiration to him as a pianist. He was especially impressed by Nat's rendition of "Easy Listening Blues," which he regarded as a complete thesaurus for any aspiring jazz pianist . . . simple and direct; yet containing all of the components that were necessary to play the blues.

In a discussion of Nat's rendition of the Johnny Green classic, "Body and Soul," Oscar called it a performance that would live forever as a masterpiece of trio integration.

Next come tributes to the jazzmen Oscar admired and respected—all of them now gone. They are trumpeter Clifford Brown, tenor saxophonist Sonny Stitt and vibraphonist Milt Jackson.

Much of the Clifford Brown piece relates to a 1955 album the trumpeter made with Harold Land on tenor sax, Max Roach on drums and George Morrow on bass. He was particularly intrigued by the work of Brown and Land, commenting that these two soloists were so well attuned to each other's skills and thoughts that at one point it became almost a single line that one could imagine being performed by a single soloist.

On Sonny Stitt, Oscar wrote that Stitt always played well, but on this occasion (a JATP concert in Edinburgh) he had played so brilliantly, so spectacularly, that when he got on the bus as the last member of the troupe, to return to London, everyone to a person, including Ella, stood up on the bus and applauded him.

Peterson was equally lavish in his praise for Milt Jackson, particularly with regard to a recording date in 1981 for Norman

Granz's Pablo album. This one is titled *Ain't But a Few of Us Left* and involves, besides Jackson, bassist Ray Brown, drummer Grady Tate and, of course, Oscar.

"I was particularly pleased," wrote Oscar, "with the rhythmic carpet we supplied for Bags [Jackson] to walk on, and this he did magnificently."

But it was in 1999 that Oscar's eloquence reached a new peak. In September of that year, he received a telephone call from Norman Granz, in Geneva, Switzerland, the purpose of which was to inform Oscar that Granz had been voted the *Lifetime Achievement Award* from Jazz at the Lincoln Center, but because of ill health was unable to attend. He asked if Oscar could go in his place to accept the award for him. Peterson told Granz he would be "more than happy" to accept on Granz's behalf, because, he said, "it seemed to me, he had become somewhat disillusioned about whether or not his efforts in the recording field were truly appreciated and recognized."

The text of Oscar's speech that night speaks for itself:

> Good evening ladies and gentlemen. I can't tell you what a great pleasure it is for me to be standing here before you tonight to receive this honour on behalf of a man that I not only love dearly, but also on behalf of the jazz world, which has flourished and grown through his tireless dedication and devotion to it. I am referring of course to the gentleman that this trophy now belongs to, and rightfully so.
>
> I agreed to represent him tonight due to the fact that he is unable to be here, and so I am standing here proudly in the realization that the world of music, and certainly Lincoln Center, have finally decided to pay him a long overdue and certainly well-earned tribute. There is another side to my acceptance of this award on his behalf that I feel I should make you aware of. Norman Granz is most certainly proud of the voluminous and important musical legacy that he created during his years as a record

producer and an impresario in the jazz concert world. Nevertheless, I know for certain that his initial pride is rooted in his accomplishments in the field of civil rights. Having been a member of his Jazz At The Philharmonic concert packages, I was able to experience his unflagging will and dedication to change the bigoted and hurtful segregationist attitude of the people that he had to deal with below the Mason-Dixon line. His unflagging devotion and dedication to this purpose is remembered by those of us that followed him through his various performances in the South in that era. I can recall as a Canadian alien, sitting various nights in various hotel and motel rooms nervously wondering if our troupe would end up being some of the "strange fruit" that Billie Holiday sang about. I can also recall him standing his ground at the Houston airport when the sheriff pulled his gun from his holster and jammed it into Norman's stomach while telling him how he hated him more than he hated blacks because he was creating this situation by insisting that Ella Fitzgerald be allowed to ride in a "white" taxi cab. I can also recall his insistence throughout the whole southern tour that the seating for both races be equal, thereby destroying the heretofore of the group playing one concert at eight o'clock for whites, and another at midnight for blacks. I can also remember his insistence in what then were the pure "white" upper-class hotels catering to our inter-racial entourage. None of this attitude fazed Norman in any sense because his dedication was resolute and unshakable, not unlike his belief in the music that he was presenting. This, ladies and gentlemen, is the part of his career in the music field that I honestly feel that he is most proud of, and with due purpose for the single reason that throughout all of these reprehensible vignettes and instances, he won his battles. His unflagging dedication in the record business to presenting a legacy of the music of

America of his period is vividly reflected in the incredible log of timeless recordings, such as the Art Tatum collection, the Ella Fitzgerald songbooks, the works of Ellington, Basie, Dizzy Gillespie, Coleman Hawkins, and on and on. I have no words for this voluminous work that he has created for generations to enjoy, and I am more than proud and honoured to accept this trophy on his behalf. Would you please stand and applaud this musical and humane giant that we know as Norman Granz.

Not long afterwards, Oscar received a letter from pioneer jazz impresario George Wein, telling him he had tears in his eyes during Oscar's speech, and his secretary informed him that several newspapers had called for copies of his speech. I treasure the copy I received, for it speaks so well to Oscar's admiration for Norman Granz.

"Apparently," said Oscar, "my talk had generated some form of emotional response."

(Sad to say, Norman Granz died in November, 2001 at the age of 83.)

*   *   *

Being something of an old dog to whom new tricks don't come easily, I am not on the internet. However, my daughter Kate is, and I turned to her to find some extra details of Oscar's remarkable career.

Among other things, she found an item listed as "Awards" which Oscar had won, and honourary degrees conferred on him, so I asked her to get me a copy of it. It was stunned by the results of her search. It ran to six pages—some 88 awards or honours. Eighty-eight—how appropriate for a pianist.

And what a list! They range from assorted Grammy and Gemini Awards to having the concert hall at Concordia University (Montreal) renamed the Oscar Peterson Concert Hall to a UNESCO International Prize, from a citation from President

Bill Clinton to an Oscar Peterson Day proclaimed in Baltimore, Maryland, and another one in Dade County, Florida; from an Oscar Peterson Scholarship founded by the Berklee College of Music in Boston to a Genie for the best film score for the film, *The Silent Partner*; from being appointed Officer in the Arts and Letters, in France, to being appointed Chevalier de l'Ordre du Quebec; from a Certificate of Merit and Appreciation from the Los Angeles Cultural Affairs Commission, to the Order of Arts and Letters in France; from the Glenn Gould Prize to the Mexico City Award of Thanks, to a Juno Award for Best Jazz Album in 1992; plus two awards (1993 and 1996) from *The Jazz Report*.

In September, 2000, *Maclean's* magazine ran a piece saluting 25 historically important Canadians. They included James Naismith, the Almonte, Ontario-born physical education teacher who, in 1891, invented the game of basketball; Lester B. Pearson, one of Canada's most distinguished political leaders; the renowned Ottawa-born novelist Margaret Atwood; and Oscar Peterson. The magazine's salute to Oscar listed his considerable achievements and honours—the Grammy count was up to eight by then—and informed its readers: "In Oscar's case, the right hand not only knows what the left is doing, but approves and co-operates."

And the above list of honours couldn't include the impressive Peterson display at the National Archives in Ottawa, or his being inducted into the Canadian Jazz Hall of Fame the following year, or the special tribute paid to him by the Royal Conservatory of Music in Toronto, in May 2001.

It would seem highly unlikely that any other musician in the 100-year history of jazz has been so frequently honoured—which, after all, seems only fair.

Nor is Oscar one to rest on previous laurels. In June 2001, he was set to perform yet another concert at Massey Hall, heading a quartet that would include bassist Niels-Henning Orsted Pedersen, guitarist Ulf Wakenius and drummer Martin Drew.

28

OSCAR'S NIGHT

Great artists—be they painters, sculptors, playwrights, novelists, dancers, choreographers, actors or musicians—are sometimes accorded the designation "genius." And, often, rightfully so.

But some things just naturally go together—like ham and eggs, Dunn and Bradstreet, gin and tonic, Wayne and Shuster, to and fro, up and down—and genius and ego.

One of the ways my *Oxford Dictionary* defines genius is an "extraordinary capacity for imaginative creation, original thought, invention or discovery." *Webster's New Collegiate Dictionary* defines "ego" as "the self, especially as contrasted with another self or the world."

Nobody would deny that Mozart was a genius. He was a child prodigy, and he was certainly full of self-confidence, at least in his earlier years. But few would suggest seriously that Wolfgang Amadeus Mozart was a wonderful, lovable, warm-hearted human being. He was certainly not devoid of ego.

But the burden of genius—and the ego that inevitably goes with it—is an inability to understand that other mortals are not quite capable of meeting the sometimes impossibly high standards of the "genius." To the genius/egotist, anyone who can't reach the lofty high of the genius's abilities is simply a slacker.

Jump ahead a couple of centuries and consider the case of Benny Goodman, the renowned "king of swing" in the era of the big bands. Goodman, too, was a child prodigy and, as he grew up and became justly famous, he truly believed not only in his own genius but also, unfortunately, in the simplistic notion that every other professional musician should be capable of meeting his lofty musical standards. If they couldn't, Goodman had no patience with them.

(Goodman was also famous for his absent-mindedness. Once, when he was dissatisfied with the playing of a young tenor saxophonist in his band, he had to ask another of his sidemen for "the kid's name"—so he could fire him. The "kid's" name was Wardell Gray. On another occasion, he was trying to study while his two little daughters, Rachel and Benji, were nearby, playing and distracting the genius. He looked up irritably and said, "You, what's-your-name, be quiet.")

To some degree, Oscar Peterson fits the same mold. As bassist Ray Brown famously said of Oscar: "He doesn't want it good—he wants it perfect."

In fairness, there's little evidence that Peterson's ego was ever on a level with Goodman's. But some of the ego that goes along with genius is present. For instance, despite Oscar's flashes of temper, his mercurial mood swings and his capacity for sometimes "being difficult," Phil Nimmons remains a friend. He was aware of a rumor I had picked up about a "falling out" between Peterson and "a well-known arranger," evidently Nimmons. But while Phil does not deny the incident, he is inclined to dismiss it; his friendship with Peterson is easily strong enough to overcome such minor clashes of creative direction.

But there is evidence that at least some of those partings between Oscar and other musicians were not altogether amicable. And although the reasons have long been shrouded in mystery, it is true that Oscar Peterson and trombonist Butch Watanabe have not so much as spoken to each other in many years.

Inevitably, Oscar's perfectionism—like Goodman's—has something to do with this. Again like Goodman, Peterson drives himself as relentlessly as he does the musicians who accompany him, and it is also true that he expects from his sidemen the same sort of genius that he has been endowed with.

Of course, there is more to Peterson than the genius he was born with. He has worked hard, studied hard, first classically and then in jazz, pushed himself to become better. But he is guilty (if that's the right word) of expecting everyone else he works with to have done the same, with the same degree of intensity, dedication and application that Oscar himself has displayed again and again, over the years. Not even his stroke of 1993 has diminished his determination to play at his greatest level of capability.

Perhaps this is part of the secret of his enduring success—his sheer invincibility.

That's not a bad quality to have, for a musician who was determined to push the boundaries beyond those established by the great Art Tatum.

Once, when Oscar and Norman Granz were discussing the question of who was the greatest jazz pianist ever, Oscar kept saying it was Tatum. But Granz insisted it was Peterson.

After years of virtually worshipping Tatum, of living in his mentor's shadow, he experienced a sudden awakening to the fact that he himself was capable of getting out from under that self-imposed slavery and achieving a level of musical mastery at least equal to (some would say beyond) Tatum's artistry.

Oscar Peterson is not one to hold grudges—another fine quality. Personality conflicts between artists are hardly rare, not only in jazz, of course, and, indeed, not only among musicians. No doubt, his sense of humor and love of practical jokes have helped him to keep his ego in check.

And yet, his run-in with Jorn Winther (see the chapter "Oscar and the Viking"), even though Oscar was mostly in the right, suggests that the Peterson ego came into play during this confrontation.

On the other hand, Peterson's loyalty to musicians with whom he has had generally good relations—or to whom he feels somehow indebted—is far more impressive than his disaffection regarding those musicians with whom he has had any sort of falling out. The case of Dave Young is a good example. (See the chapter "Something Scary.")

In brief, Oscar Peterson is usually too busy and too involved in playing and/or composing music to bother with such relatively insignificant bumps on the roads of life.

In October 1999, Concordia University in Montreal renamed its Concordia Concert Hall, officially calling it the Oscar Peterson Concert Hall. It was the idea of Neil Schwartzman, director of the hall, who said of Peterson:

"He certainly has a generous understanding of who he is and where he stands in the world, and he is very definite in what he wants, but I don't think that is ego. You would think that after receiving as many accolades as he has over the years, he would be unimpressed by a small concert hall, but he reacted extremely emotionally, so much so that everybody else became equally as emotional. I think he can't be as great an artist as he is without having the ability to tap that side of his personality, of being in touch with those things, and obviously he was not afraid to show them."

In accepting the honor, Oscar paid tribute to his sister and first piano teacher, Daisy Sweeney, "the lady who meant an awful lot to my life; without her I would not be sitting here tonight."

It is also a measure of the high esteem in which he is held by his fellow musicians that when Peterson was honored by the Royal Conservatory of Music on May 29, 2001, some of Canada's leading jazz musicians turned out to pay him not only verbal but musical tribute. Among those who performed were Phil Nimmons, Joe Sealy, Carol Welsman, Bill King, Dave Young and Renee Rosnes.

(I enjoyed most the inventive playing of the Dave Young group and the dynamic piano work of Joe Sealy. But I must confess that I nurtured a wish, admittedly an unreasonable one in the circumstances, that Oscar would also play that night.)

The entire evening was what used to be called a "love-in."

In attendance were former Ontario premier Bob Rae, who is chairman of the Royal Conservatory of Music, former Ontario premier Bill Davis and federal Liberal deputy leader Herb Gray. Ross Porter, host of CBC's "After Hours," was the emcee. (It isn't every day that you see a large photograph of a jazz pianist on the front page of *The Toronto Star*, but that's where Oscar was on May 29, 2001, receiving a congratulatory kiss on the cheek from Bob Rae.)

This "Royal Occasion," as it was billed, was a resounding success from every aspect. It was the Conservatory's fifth annual Royal Occasion and was held at the Concert Hall of the Royal York Hotel in Toronto. Monies raised at the event were slated to go to a new Oscar Peterson Scholarship for the Royal Conservatory's innovative Learning Through the Arts program.

At a press conference earlier on that evening, Oscar fielded many questions. One of them was about what pianists had influenced him when he was starting out on what was to become a legendary career in jazz. He mentioned three pianists who had influenced him: Art Tatum, Teddy Wilson and Nat Cole. Then he elaborated: "Tatum out of a sense of fear; Wilson out of a sense of hope; and Cole out of a sense of love."

Oscar spent another part of the day being interviewed by CTV's Sandy Rinaldo, and he spoke about his music and his life: "The music is my opinion about certain tunes. That's what I always say about jazz—when I play a Gershwin tune I'm not playing the way he would play it. I'm playing it the way it affects me. That's the way I feel about it."

He said the "competitive spirit" that existed in the jazz scene was "good" for him. When he decided to take his music outside of Canada, to the United States and Europe and Asia, he reflected, "there was a funny kind of prejudice. You know, 'He's from Canada. What does he know about jazz?' That's what made me persevere."

On the subject of his stroke, he didn't recall any "down time, when I sat and sulked about it." Then, he added: "I'm a reasonably devout man and I prayed that the good Lord would let me play again."

Also on that same day, Oscar was feeling feisty enough to let loose a broadside about the state of the jazz music world today. He told *The Toronto Star*'s Geoff Chapman that one problem was that jazz impresarios tend to flock to large venues where "you lose contact with the audience in such spaces and that's why I seldom play jazz festivals."

Then he added this comment: "Another factor is festivals tend to bring in rock and Kenny G. types, and I don't want any part of that. There's too many weird people in the lineups who don't play jazz—I'd give anything to see a Duke Ellington or a Count Basie band on a festival stage. There's too much big business involved. Today anyone can make a CD. When I came in, only talented people could make their way in this music—now all you have to do is dress in weird clothes."

* * *

The evening of Sunday, February 24 was a big one for jazz in Canada, and especially for Oscar Peterson. On this night, at the Randolph Academy of the Performing Arts in Toronto, the inaugural presentation of the National Jazz Awards took place under the stewardship of Bill King and Thom Hirtz. (King, as publisher of *The Jazz Report* established that magazine's annual awards decade ago, but branching our Canada-wide was a significant step forward.) The Awards were carried live by CBC Radio.

There were numerous presentations to deserving musicians and supporters of Canadian jazz—from musicians like Jane Bunnett and Phil Nimmons to broadcaster Ross Porter and jazz historian Mark Miller.

But to begin the evening, an official from the makers of the famed Bosendorfer piano—considered the Rolls Royce of pianos—extended to Oscar Peterson the "Musician of the Century Award," the first of its kind. Now, the Bosendorfer company some time ago had wanted Oscar to endorse their product. Oscar indicated that the price of such a piano was well beyond his reach—so they gave him one. Oscar was invited to go to the factory in Austria and 27 pianos were there, awaiting him. He loved the seventh instrument he played, but the company insisted he try every one. That seventh piano is in his home in Mississauga.

For the Jazz Awards, a huge Imperial Bosendorfer graced the stage, and after receiving the award Oscar played "Wheatland" from his *Canadiana Suite*. He was appropriately and ably accompanied by bassist Dave Young. It was Dave who persuaded Oscar to play again after he suffered a stroke. It was both musically and emotionally a magic moment for Oscar Peterson, not only Canada's but the world's king of the jazz keyboard, champion of champions.

DISCOGRAPHY

This Is Oscar Peterson – 1945 – Victor

I Got Rhythm – 1945 – RCA

Tenderly – 1950 – Verve

Oscar Peterson Collates No. 1 – 1950 – Mercury

Oscar Peterson Collates No. 2 – 1950 – Clef

Oscar Peterson Plays Pretty – 1950 – Clef

Keyboard Music by Oscar Peterson – 1950 – Verve

An Evening with the Oscar Peterson Duo/Quartet – 1950 – Clef

An Evening with Oscar Peterson – 1950 – Verve

Oscar Peterson at Carnegie Hall [live] – 1950 – Mercury

Oscar Peterson Piano Solos – 1950 – Mercury

Nostalgic Memories by Oscar Peterson – 1951 – Clef

Just a Memory – 1951 – CBC Radio

Oscar Peterson Plays Cole Porter – 1951 – Verve

Pastel Moods by Oscar Peterson – 1952 – Verve

Romance (The Vocal Styling of Oscar Peterson) – 1952 – Verve

Oscar Peterson Quartet – 1952 – Clef

Oscar Peterson, Vol. 2 – 1952 – Clef

The Oscar Peterson Quartet, No. 1 – 1952 – Verve

Oscar Peterson Trio at JATP [live] – 1952 – Verve

Stage Right – 1952 – Clef

The Trio Set – 1952 – Verve

Jazz at the Philharmonic [live] – 1952 – Verve

Oscar Peterson Plays the Jerome Kern Songbook – 1952 – Clef

Oscar Peterson Plays Duke Ellington – 1952 – Verve

Oscar Peterson Plays George Gershwin – 1952 – Verve

Oscar Peterson Plays Irving Berlin – 1952 – Mercury

Oscar Peterson Plays Richard Rodgers – 1952 – Clef

Recital by Oscar Peterson – 1952 – Verve

Oscar Peterson Sings – 1953 – Clef

Jazz at the Philharmonic (Hartford 1953) [live] – 1953 – Pablo

Oscar Peterson Plays Vincent Youmans – 1953 – Clef

Oscar's (Oscar Peterson Plays the Academy Awards) [live] – 1953 – Verve

Oscar Peterson Plays Harry Warren – 1954 – Clef

Oscar Peterson Plays Harold Arlen – 1954 – Clef

At Zardi's [live] –1955 – Pablo

Night Train, Vol. 2 – 1955 – Verve

Peterson Plays the Count Basie Songbook – 1955 – Clef

In a Romantic Mood – 1955 – Verve

Oscar Peterson Plays Count Basie – 1956 – Verve

Oscar Peterson Trio at the Stratford Shakesperian Festival [live] – 1956 – Verve

The Oscar Peterson Trio – 1956 – Clef

Soft Sands – 1957 – Verve

The Oscar Peterson Trio and ... – 1957 – Verve

Louis Armstrong Meets Oscar Peterson – 1957 – Verve

The Oscar Peterson Trio with the Modern Jazz Quartet – 1957 – Verve

Newport Jazz Festival – 1957 – Verve

The Oscar Peterson Trio at the Concertgebouw [live] – 1958 – Verve

Thoroughly Modern Twenties – 1958 – Verve

A Night on the Town with Oscar Peterson – 1958 – Verve

Oscar Peterson Plays "My Fair Lady" – 1958 – Verve

Oscar Peterson Trio with David Rose – 1958 – Verve

Songs for a Swinging Affair: A Jazz Portrait – 1959 – Verve

Jazz Portrait of Sinatra – 1959 – Verve

Jazz Soul of Oscar Peterson – 1959 – Verve

Oscar Peterson Plays the George Gershwin Songbook – 1959 – Verve

Oscar Peterson Plays the Irving Berlin Songbook – 1959 – Verve

Oscar Peterson Plays the Richard Rodgers Songbook– 1959 – Verve

Oscar Peterson Plays the Jimmy McHugh Songbook – 1959 – Verve

Oscar Peterson Plays the Vincent Youmans Songbook – 1959 – Verve

Oscar Peterson Plays the Harry Warren Songbook – 1959 – Verve

Oscar Peterson Plays the Harold Arlen Songbook – 1959 – Verve

Oscar Peterson Plays the Duke Ellington Songbook – 1959 – Verve

Oscar Peterson Plays the Cole Porter Songbook – 1959 – Verve

Swinging Brass with the Oscar Peterson Trio – 1959 – Verve

Jazz Soul – 1959 – Verve

Fiorello – 1959 – Verve

Porgy and Bess – 1959 – Verve

Carnival – 1960 – Verve

London House Sessions – 1961 – Polygram

The Sound of the Trio – 1961 – Verve

Trio [live] – 1961 – Verve

Very Tall – 1961 – Verve

West Side Story – 1962 – Verve

Put on a Happy Face – 1962 – Verve

Live at the London House – 1962 – Verve

Night Train, Vol. 1 – 1962 – Verve

Something Warm – 1962 – Verve

Bursting Out – 1962 – Verve

Affinity – 1962 – Verve

The Oscar Peterson Trio and Nelson Riddle – 1963 – Verve

The Oscar Peterson Trio Plays – 1964 – Verve

Oscar Peterson Trio Plus One – 1964 – Mercury

Canadiana Suite – 1964 – Limelight

We Get Requests – 1964 – Verve

Easy Walker – 1964 – Prestige

Eloquence – 1965 – Limelight

Oscar Peterson Plays for Lovers – 1965 – Prestige

Exclusively for My Friends – 1965 – Polygram

The Canadian Concert of Oscar Peterson – 1965 – Can-Am

With Respect to Nat – 1965 – Verve

Blues Etude – 1965 – Verve

Soul Espagnol – 1966 – Universal

On a Clear Day (You Can See Forever) – 1967 – Prestige

The Greatest Jazz Concert in the World – 1967 – Pablo

Girl Talk – 1967 – MPS

My Favorite Instrument – 1967 – MPS

The Way I Really Play – 1968 – MPS

Soul-O! – 1968 – Prestige

Great Oscar Peterson on Prestige – 1968 – Prestige

Mellow Mood – 1968 – MPS

Travelin' On – 1968 – MPS

Motions and Emotions – 1969 – Verve
Hello Herbie – 1969 – MPS
Tristeza on Piano – 1970 – Verve
Another Day – 1970 – Verve
Walking the Line – 1970 – MPS
Tracks – 1970 – MPS
In Tune – 1971 – Verve
Reunion Blues – 1971 – Verve
Great Connection – 1971 – MPS
History of an Artist –
 1972–1973–1974 – Pablo
Oscar Peterson Featuring Stephane
 Grappelli – 1973 – Prestige
The Good Life – 1973 – Original Jazz
The Trio – 1973 – Pablo
In a Mellow Mood – 1973 – MPS
Canadiana Suite (with Phil
 Nimmons) – 1973 – CBC
Oscar Peterson in Russia [live] – 1974 –
 Pablo
Oscar Peterson and Dizzy Gillespie –
 1974 – Pablo
Peterson/Gilles – 1974 – Pablo
Satch and Josh (with Count Basie) –
 1974 – Pablo
The Giants – 1974 – Pablo
Oscar Peterson and Harry Edison –
 1974 – Pablo
Oscar Peterson and Roy Eldridge –
 1974 – Pablo
Jousts (Oscar Peterson and the Trum-
 pet Kings) – 1974–75 – Pablo
Oscar Peterson et Joe Pass à la Salle
 Pleyel [live]– 1975 – Pablo
Oscar Peterson and John Faddis –
 1975 – Pablo
Oscar Peterson and Clark Terry –
 1975 – Pablo
The Oscar Peterson Big Six at
 Montreux – 1975 – Pablo
Ella and Oscar – 1976 – Pablo
Porgy and Bess – 1976 – Pablo
Oscar Peterson Jam Montreux [live] –
 1977 – Pablo
Trio in Transition – 1977 – EmArcy
Satch and Josh Again – 1977 – Pablo
Oscar Peterson and the Bassists –
 1977 – Pablo

Time Keepers – 1977 – Pablo
The London Concert [live] – 1978 –
 Pablo
The Paris Concert [live] – 1978 – Pablo
Night Rider – 1978 – Pablo
Yessir That's My Baby – 1978 – Pablo
The Silent Partner – 1979 – Pablo
Night Child – 1979 – Pablo
Skol in Scandinavia [live] – 1979 –
 Original Jazz
The Personal Touch – 1980 – Pablo
The Trumpet Summit Meets the Oscar
 Peterson Big 4 – 1980 – Pablo
Live at the Northsea Jazz Festival –
 1980 – Pablo
The Alternate Blues – 1980 – Pablo
Let the World Sing (A Royal Wedding
 Suite) – 1981 – Pablo
Nigerian Marketplace – 1981 – Pablo
Freedom Song – 1982 – Pablo
The Oscar Peterson Big 4 in Japan '82
 [live] – Pablo – 1982
Face to Face – 1982 – Pablo
Two of the Few – 1983 – Pablo/OJC
If You Could See Me Now – 1983 –
 Pablo
A Tribute to My Friends – 1983 – Pablo

Oscar Peterson also played on many
LPs as a member of JATP or as part of
Pablo's concert parties and jam
sessions. He can also be heard playing
accompaniments or guest solos with
Lester Young, Buddy DeFranco, Stan
Getz, the Modern Jazz Quartet, Louis
Armstrong, Ella Fitzgerald and Gerry
Mulligan, among others. These are all
on the Verve label.

Oscar Peterson with Harry Edison and
 Eddie "Cleanhead" Vinson – 1986 –
 Pablo
Benny Carter Meets Oscar Peterson –
 1986 – Pablo
Time After Time – 1986 – Pablo
Oscar Peterson Live – 1986 – Pablo
The MJQ Plus (Oscar Peterson played
 on two cuts) – 1987 – Verve

Very Tall Band [live] – 1988 – Telarc

The Legendary Oscar Peterson Trio Live at the Blue Note – 1990 – Telarc

Saturday Night at the Blue Note – 1991 – Telarc

Last Call At the Blue Note – 1992

Extraordinary Jazz Pianist – 1992 – Polygram

In Concert [live] – 1992 – Sound

1953 Live – 1992 – Jazz Band

Jazz 'Round Midnight: Oscar Peterson – 1992 – Verve

Live and at Its Best – 1992 – SND

Encore at the Blue Note – 1993 – Telarc

Vienna Concert [live] – 1993 – Philology

Hallelujah Time – 1993 – Moon

Three Originals – 1993 – Polygram

All of Me – 1994 – Jazz World

Love for Sale – 1994 – Jazz World

Side by Side – 1994 – Telarc

Fallin' in Love with Oscar – 1994 – Jazz Door

In Europe 1961–63–66–69 – 1995 – RTE

The More I See You – 1995 – Telarc

An Oscar Peterson Christmas – 1995 – Telarc

The Lamp Is Low – 1995 – Four Stars

Oscar Peterson and Stephane Grappelli Quartet – 1995 – Accord

The Max Roach 4 Plays Charlie Parker – 1995 – Verve

Oscar Peterson Meets Roy Hargrove and Ralph Moor – 1996 – Telarc

Oscar in Paris [live] – 1996 –Telarc

Like Someone in Love – 1996 – Jazz Hour

Trio + One – 1997 – PSM

Live at CBC Studios 1960 – 1997 – Just a Memory

Oscar Peterson Tribute Live at Town Hall – 1997 – Telarc (Among those saluting Oscar were Shirley Horn, Milt Jackson, Clark Terry, Stanley Turrentine, Roy Hargrove, Lewis Nash, Benny Green and, of course, Ray Brown and Herb Ellis, who reunited with Oscar.)

Oscar in Paris: Live at the Salle Pleyel – 1997 – Telarc

Oscar and Benny – 1998 – Telarc

Triple Play – 1998 – Telarc

1959–1998 – Giants of Jazz

Oscar's Boogie – 1999 – Jazz Hour

A Summer Night in Munich – 1999 – Telarc

The Very Tall Band – 1999 – Telarc

Les Incontournables – 2000 – WEA

Oscar Peterson Trio Live at the Barbican – 2000 – BBC

Oscar Peterson Trio Live in Tokyo – 1964 – Pablo

The Ljubliana Conert, July 24, 1964 [live] – 2000 – Jazz Life

Quiet Now: Time and Again – 2000 – Polygram

Trail of Dreams: A Canadian Suite – 2000 – Telarc

The Composer – 2001 – Pablo

LIST OF PERMISSIONS

Excerpts from Shari Steiner's articles, published in the *Toronto Star*. Excerpts from Greg Quill, "Real Jazz Is Still Alive at Oscar Peterson's Fingertips" in the *Toronto Star* (June 19, 1988) reprinted with permission from The Toronto Star Syndicate. Excerpts from Mark Miller, "Peterson the Jazz Composer Grabs the Spotlight" in *The Globe and Mail* (April 13, 2002) reprinted courtesy of the author. Excerpts from Mark Miller, "Oscar Peterson Falls Short of Standard He Set Himself" in *The Globe and Mail* (June 20, 1988) reprinted courtesy of the author. Excerpts from Mark Miller, "His Boogie-Woogie Still Has That Zing" in *The Globe and Mail* (February 17, 1986) reprinted courtesy of the author. *Down Beat Magazine.* Excerpts from pp. 126, 165–66 from *The Great Jazz Pianists* by Len Lyons, copyright © 1983 by Len Lyons, reprinted by permission of Harper-Collins Publishers Inc. Excerpts from Geoffrey C. Ward, *Jazz: A History of America's Music*, published by Knopf in 2000 reprinted courtesy of the publisher. Excerpts from John Gilmore, *Swinging in Paradise: The Story of Jazz in Montreal*, published by Véhicule Press, copyright ©1988, 1989 by John Gilmore, reprinted courtesy of the author. Excerpts from Reuel V. Lubag's liner notes to *The Oscar Peterson Trio: Live at the Concertgebouw* (Verve Records). Excerpts from Bill Crow, *Jazz Anecdotes*, published by Oxford University Press. Excerpts from Gene Lees' liner notes to *My Favourite Instrument* (Polygram/Universal) reprinted courtesy of the author.

Every effort has been made to ensure copyright protected text is used by permission and credited. Please advise us of any omission by writing to the Editorial Department care of the address listed on the copyright page.

INDEX OF NAMES